SO...
THIS
IS
WHY I'M
BROKE

SO... THIS IS WHY I'M BROKE

MONEY LESSONS ON FINANCIAL LITERACY, PASSIVE INCOME, AND GENERATIONAL WEALTH

MELISSA JEAN-BAPTISTE

CORAL GABLES

For permission requests, please contact the publisher at:
Mango Publishing Group
2850 S Douglas Road, 2nd Floor
Coral Gables, FL 33134 USA
info@mango.bz

For special orders, quantity sales, course adoptions and corporate sales, please email the publisher at sales@mango.bz. For trade and wholesale sales, please contact Ingram Publisher Services at customer.service@ingramcontent.com or +1.800.509.4887.

So...This is Why I'm Broke: Money Lessons on Financial Literacy, Passive Income, and Generational Wealth

Library of Congress Cataloging-in-Publication number: 2022952084
ISBN: (pb) 978-1-68481-183-0 (hc) 978-1-68481-276-9 (e) 978-1-68481-184-7
BISAC category code: BUS050030, BUSINESS & ECONOMICS / Personal Finance / Money Management

Printed in the United States of America

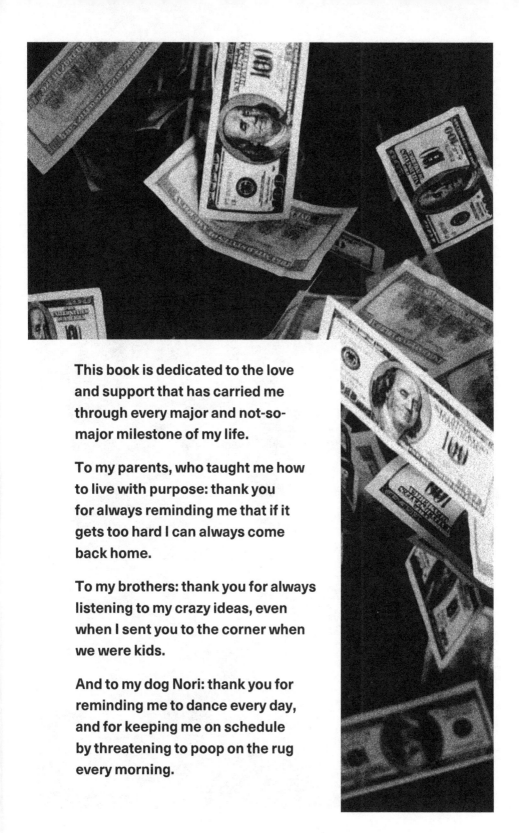

This book is dedicated to the love and support that has carried me through every major and not-so-major milestone of my life.

To my parents, who taught me how to live with purpose: thank you for always reminding me that if it gets too hard I can always come back home.

To my brothers: thank you for always listening to my crazy ideas, even when I sent you to the corner when we were kids.

And to my dog Nori: thank you for reminding me to dance every day, and for keeping me on schedule by threatening to poop on the rug every morning.

TABLE OF CONTENTS

INTRODUCTION   8

PART I: FINANCIAL FUNDAMENTALS   13
EATING COSTCO SAMPLES FOR DINNER SO YOU DON'T HAVE TO

CHAPTER 1—MY BUDGET GOT LEFT OFF BAD AND BOUGIE   14

CHAPTER 2—SAVE LIKE I'VE GOT SOME CENTS   31

CHAPTER 3—TO ALL THE CREDIT CARDS I'VE SWIPED BEFORE   49

CHAPTER 4—MY DEBT IS UP, AND I'M STUCK   68

PART II: I MAKE MONEY MOVES   91
THE ROAD TO FINANCIAL INDEPENDENCE

CHAPTER 5—GET RICH OR INVEST TRYING   92

CHAPTER 6—THIS GIRL IS ON FIRE   114

CHAPTER 7—SIDE HUSTLE & CHILL   131

CHAPTER 8—JUST HOLD ON...WE'RE BUYING HOMES   148

PART III: 173
STARTED FROM THE BOTTOM...NOW WE'RE WEALTHY-*ISH*

CHAPTER 9—TAKE CARE: ESTATE PLANNING 101   174

CHAPTER 10—DON'T MESS WITH THE IRS   192

CHAPTER 11—RECLAIMING MY TIME: RETIRING AS A MILLIONAIRE   209

CHAPTER 12—FIRST COMES LOVE, THEN COMES THE PRENUP   229

CONCLUSION   241

MILLENNIAL IN DEBT'S FAVE FINANCIAL RESOURCES   242

ACKNOWLEDGMENTS   243

ABOUT THE AUTHOR   245

INVESTING GLOSSARY   246

INTRODUCTION

At twenty-one years old I was a first-generation college graduate with not
one but two degrees, yet everything I knew about money could fit on an
index card. Four years later, when I attempted to buy a house, I quickly
learned everything I actually knew about money could be summed up on a
single Post-it.

As a Haitian American woman, former New York City high school teacher,
and self-proclaimed wanderlust I can 100 percent say I have *lived* and have
the stories to prove it. Taking public transportation in New York City alone has
provided me with an ample supply of "you won't believe what I just saw" moments
for a lifetime. I jumped out of a plane, wrote an award-winning web series, visited
sixteen countries, traveled to twenty-five states, bought a house, and paid off
$100,000 in student loan debt, all before thirty-five years old.

Of all the unique things about me, my lack of financial literacy was not one
of them. According to the 2014 S&P Global Financial Literacy Survey, only 57
percent of US adults are financially literate. For a long time, I was a part of the 43
percent of people navigating my finances without an understanding of the four
basic financial concepts assessed in the survey: risk diversification, numeracy,
inflation, and compound interest.

In 2013 I tried to buy a house with zero dollars in emergency savings, and no
idea how to calculate my net worth. The realtor—who lives rent-free in my mind,
might I add—deflated that fairytale rather quickly. "Your debt-to-income ratio is
too high; you won't be pre-approved for more." Did I know what "debt-to-income
ratio" meant? No! Was I furious that he wouldn't help me get pre-approved for a
million dollars to buy the house of my dreams...*yes*! Talk about being *completely*
out of touch with my financial reality.

Unfortunately, I am not alone in this. You've probably heard some version of
the widespread Jim Rohn quote, "We are the average of the five people we spend
the most time with." My Biggie vs. 2pac, Mr. Belding vs. Mr. Feeny, stoop kids
afraid to leave the stoop, Myspace Top 8, Harry Potter–obsessed ass fell right into
the law of averages as expected. While I like to think I have a diverse collection of

dope-ass people in my inner and extended circle, the fact remains that none of my friends knew anything substantial about money either.

My two brothers and I grew up in a Black household, and not just any Black household, a Caribbean household. This came with its own set of rules and ideologies that superseded common law in traditional Black households. If you got a 99 on a test, the first question was always, "What happened to the other point?" The second question, "Who got the highest grade in the class?" You're at a large gathering? Every elder in the room must be greeted with the standard kiss on the cheek because in some way, shape, or form they are related to you, even if they are not. Sleepovers...out of the question.

Even with rules that were stricter than necessary and utterly ridiculous justifications, my brothers and I had a great childhood. We were blessed with two hard-working immigrant parents who focused on providing their children with as many experiences and opportunities they never had. They gave us all the comforts they could afford and enjoyed watching us pursue whatever we dreamed of. And I seriously mean whatever we dreamed of. My twenty-six-year-old brother has been deejaying since he was nine years old, and my father bought him his first turntables from a discount aftermarket electronic store on Jamaica Ave.

All they asked for in return was for us to be good people and do well in school. My parents created an environment that allowed for academic success and encouraged open dialogue. We were always told to use our heads to make calculated, smart decisions. So, you can imagine how embarrassed I was during my first week in college after over-drafting my account buying Coach sneakers at the mall.

You would think I had more sense. Despite what my mom may humorously tell you, I was a parent's teenage dream. I'm the girl who convinced my first boss to hire five of my friends and me as camp counselors, even after I wasn't initially offered the job. I lived off Pringles and water my entire senior year so I could save to buy an iPod Touch and pay for my prom dress. I balanced extracurricular activities and a strenuous course load and graduated with a 5.0 GPA. There was no way I should be over-drafting my account to buy sneakers because I simply had to know better. So I tucked my tail between my legs, asked my dad to borrow seventy dollars to bring my account out of the red, and vowed to make better money decisions.

That vow lasted all of six months. After securing my first campus job in the spring, I ended up on academic probation. This meant my $7,500 merit scholarship—the one I earned with a stellar high school academic record—was about to be snatched away. I was mortified. Not only did my GPA drop below 3.0, but I also now had to figure out what I was going to do to come up with another $7,500 to cover more of the tuition I already couldn't afford.

I come from a supportive and loving family. What I don't come from is a family rolling in dough. For all intents and purposes, I would never classify my family as poor. For most of my childhood and adolescence we were a two-middle-income family. We were "too wealthy" to receive government assistance but just broke enough to live paycheck to paycheck. This is no anomaly. As of January 2022, 64 percent of middle-income earners making between $50,000 and $100,000 a year are living paycheck to paycheck. It doesn't stop there; the 50-to-90 percentile of Americans also carry about $7.3 trillion in debt as of December 2021.

America runs on Dunkin' and debt, and so did we. It's a precarious act to balance, so it is no surprise that we were always one big emergency away from financial ruin. Adding another $7,500 to the subtraction column of the budget wasn't an option my parents could take on. And at $7.15 per hour, neither could I.

The average eighteen-year-old today could come up with five different side hustles to help supplement some extra cash. The average eighteen-year-old in 2007 was drafting a dramatic away message on their T-Mobile sidekick. Me...I was that eighteen-year-old. I was scared, confused, and mostly embarrassed yet again.

Thankfully, I got my shit together just enough to keep my scholarship. In true dramatic Leo fashion, I overcompensated for my initial failures and took eighteen credits a semester, went to school year-round, and bodied a twenty-two-credit summer. All of this to complete my bachelor's and master's programs at the same time. Honestly, I just wanted to give my parents extra bragging points at the family gatherings. I loved hearing them speak about me to their friends because they did it with their whole chest. They were proud parents, and you couldn't tell them anything.

On paper I was a West Indian success story. I earned two degrees, secured a full-time teaching job right out of college, and paid my bills on time. All that was left to accomplish was to buy a house, get married, and have 2.5 kids. That would truly be the definitive moment where I could say I finally achieved the American Dream. And I wanted it all by twenty-five.

Why? Because when you turn twenty-five, you realize you're five years from thirty. And if you're that close to thirty, you're damn near fifty. And there was no way I could justify sneaking out of my parents' house at night to go have sex in my car at fifty. My joints just weren't up for the job anymore.

In all seriousness, when my mom was twenty-five she was already a wife and a mother. By the time she was thirty, she was a mother of three. Though she never explicitly pressured me to follow in her footsteps, the silent societal pressures were just enough to make me feel like I was ten steps behind everyone else.

So I put on my big girl pants, called a real estate agent, and learned a crucial lesson that day. I didn't know *shit* about money. I like to call that chapter in my life "delusions of grandeur" because I didn't know the first, second, or third thing about buying a house. When the agent asked me how much I saved for a down payment versus how much I saved for closing costs, my silence spoke loudly. The immediate answer was shame. The follow-up was not enough. If I told you my checking account had more than two thousand dollars in it at the time, I'd be lying to you and myself. I was in no position to buy anything substantial, especially not a huge financial responsibility like a house.

As someone who is rarely ever stubborn, I pressed on anyway. The preapproval process was even more embarrassing. I was approved for a $100,000 mortgage. Similar to the housing market today, NYC in 2013 was experiencing a severely overpriced sellers' market. The median sale price increased 5.6 percent and hovered around $227,000. That $100,000 preapproval wasn't going to get me very far. My immediate thought was, "Am I supposed to get a Barbie house with this?" but my actual response went more like this: "Why so low? I pay all of my bills." If he could respectfully laugh at that moment, I'm sure he would have. I would have too. "Your debt-to-income ratio is too high; you have a lot of student loans." Of course I do! Who doesn't? What I didn't see was what he was seeing. He encouraged me to reach out to my loan provider and discuss options with them to help decrease my debt to have a better chance of getting approved for more money. The American way. Pay off some debt so you can have space to take on more debt. It makes sense, doesn't it?

Was I disappointed? Absolutely. But that moment changed my life and financial trajectory. It's a big part of why I'm here writing this book for you. That moment forced me to start asking questions. Those questions led to answers that led to even more questions. If it weren't for that hard no, I would have never known that while I was out here frolicking, my student loan debt was ballooning. I learned about fancy terms, systems, accounts, and processes from people who were tone-deaf to the realities of the world.

The nice, polished version of my story goes a little something like this: I paid off $102,000 in student loans on a teacher's salary. Over nine years, I have gone from a negative net worth to a net worth of nearly $500,000. A picture-perfect, started-from-the-bottom-now-we're-here storyline. No Ivy League education, no trust funds, no high-paying job. Just a first-generation Black girl figuring it out on her own.

And I don't want that for you. Oh, don't get me wrong, I want you to be filthy stinking rich. Beyond rich, I want you and your entire bloodline to be wealthy AF. I want you to check in on your six-figure portfolio from a tropical island of your choosing. But I don't want you to figure it out yourself. I don't want you to do it like me; I want you to do it ten times better. That is what this book aims to do: give you the tools, foundation, and support you need to manage your money better than the people writing books about money.

You're getting the cheat code. This book is written by me to you to remind you that you don't have to feel ashamed or embarrassed by your financial mistakes. And as you've read so far, I've made quite a few. They do not define you or your financial outcome.

This book is deeply rooted in supporting your financial journey. My mission is to create a safe space for you to navigate through the financial concepts that are often purposely made difficult to understand. There's plenty of gatekeeping in finance, and there will be none of that here. From sinking funds to investing strategies, I've laid it all out for you in a manageable and approachable way, wherever you are in your financial journey.

Although I have learned a lot about money, it was rarely if ever from anyone who looked or sounded like me. It never felt like my intersectionality was acknowledged in big conversations or addressed in financial policies. Most discourse centered on having money or not having money. You were either financially literate or weren't. I sure as hell never felt like I would ever have a seat at the fancy finance table. So future millionaires, hear me when I say this book *is* for the culture. The fact that you have a copy in your hands right now means it *is* on the table. So, pull up and grab a seat.

PART I: FINANCIAL FUNDAMENTALS

EATING COSTCO SAMPLES FOR DINNER SO YOU DON'T HAVE TO

CHAPTER 1

MY BUDGET GOT LEFT OFF BAD AND BOUGIE

You know those people who wake up on a Tuesday and decide to just quit their job, pack a duffle bag, and move to Australia? Those free-spirited, everything-works-out-for-a-reason people whose lives are filled with romance and adventure? You know the type of people I'm talking about. Even if you don't know them personally (which, surprisingly, I do), you've probably seen some version of that person in a movie. Uh, *Eat Pray Love*, anyone?

I find myself asking the same question every time. "How did they budget for all of this adventure?" And while that ever-so-sexy question may not be at the forefront of the film director's mind, it is a question I want to bring to the forefront of your mind.

Let's not mince words here: the price of everything, *especially* rent, is too damn high. Inflation is a hot financial topic that's top of mind for many people right now. Rightfully so, with wage growth currently averaging 5.1 percent, abysmally trailing behind inflation, that has hovered between 6.0–9.1 percent over the last 14 months. Simply put, it is becoming more and more difficult to make ends meet. Therefore, it only makes sense for us to start Chapter 1 discussing budgeting strategies to meet your everyday needs. It is an imperative financial routine that is crucial to your financial success. And since it is the foundation, we must make sure it's strong so you don't have to have dinner made up of free samples from Costco. Speaking from experience, trust me...it's not lit.

What does every great and not-so-great romantic comedy have in common? That awkward first encounter between the two romantic leads where they stumble through the entire experience. Sometimes they'll quite literally bump into each other on a random street. Other times their best friends fix them up on a blind date. No matter how they meet, they meet and the rom-com formula proceeds to wind through the cat-and-mouse, "will they or won't they get together at the end" process. Sometimes they don't, and most times they do. I have something surprising to tell you: the rom-com formula we all deeply love or hate is the exact same formula used to budget. *Say what?* In fact, rom-com writers stole the entire budgeting flow, word for word, bar for bar.

Okay, I wouldn't take it that far, but budgeting can be as simple as a basic romantic comedy plotline.

So where do you begin? You begin with the first date.

You are going to take yourself on a money date. The best part about this date is you can order whatever you want; it can be any day of the week, at any time of day. You can choose to be as swaggy as you'd like or show up in sweats. The most important part is that you show up. You cannot cancel this date. This is going to be your first money date with yourself, so let me show you exactly what you need to do to ensure this date successfully leads to a second date.

MONEY DATES 101

Your first money date is going to be a little nerve-racking. There is a level of financial vulnerability you're about to subject yourself to that you may have never experienced before. A little stress and anxiety about the numbers are completely normal. You are learning to navigate a new relationship with your money, and you are allowed to do so in a shame-free, comfortable environment.

STEP ONE: MAKE SPACE FOR YOURSELF TO BE FINANCIALLY VULNERABLE

This means one of two things:

1. Choose a physical space that brings you comfort and minimal distraction. That can be your bedroom, office, living room, park, library, etc. Wherever you choose, make sure you're 100 percent

comfortable unpacking your finances in that space. Personally, I love having money dates in my house with my dog curled up at my feet and a pizza slice in my hand.

2. Money dates can be uncomfortable, so it is important to remember to be honest. Whether it is your first or fiftieth it can be difficult grappling with your financial status no matter how good you get at it. I teach people about personal finance all the time. I talk about money every single day and I still have those "WTF happened?" moments during my money dates from time to time. The discomfort is normal; perseverance is key.

STEP TWO: GRAB YOUR FINANCIAL DOCUMENTS & MAKE THEM EASILY ACCESSIBLE

What do I mean by *financial documents*? Every institution that gives you money or takes money from you is going to provide a record of that exchange. So that means things like your monthly bank statements, credit card bills, and student loan documents.

Pull up a copy of each and keep them in one organized space that you can quickly and easily access. If you receive hard copies, I suggest getting an accordion folder to house all your papers. If you are using digital statements, download the PDFs into a folder on your desktop as we prepare to move into step three.

STEP THREE: GRAB A WRITING UTENSIL AND LET'S DO SOME MATH

I am not a fan of math in the slightest bit, so I promise we won't be doing too many complex math problems during our time together. So once we've got tackled this arithmetic we'll move on to bigger and better things. It is time to calculate your net worth.

Yes, I know it is 2023, so there are tons of apps that can do the math for you. In fact, I've shared all my favorite personal finance apps in the resources at the end of this book so you can use them as a quick reference. But what kind of teacher would I be if I didn't teach you the factors that impact the number you're about to see? A terrible one. And I refuse to be a terrible teacher on your money journey.

Shall we begin? I like to get the bad news out of the way before hearing the good news, and that's the same practice I put in place when calculating my net worth. Always start with your debts. Take full stock of your liabilities by adding up any money you owe. Even if it's a hundred dollars you owe to granny, if she is expecting repayment, add it to the total sum. As a millennial riding until the wheels fall off, a few common liabilities that often impact net worth are consumer credit card debt, payday loans, auto loans, mortgages, medical debt, and good ol' student loan debt.

Make sure you include only liabilities and not your monthly bills while looking through your financial documents. Your cell phone bill is not considered a liability; it is an expense.

What is a liability? While the term itself is not as fancy-sounding as let's say the word *fiduciary* may sound, a liability is simply a fancy word for debt. To increase your exposure with money talk, I'll always provide the laymen's term first. But I also want to give you opportunities to put the fancy terms into practice too. So for those purposes, let's refer to debt as a liability for the remainder of this chapter.

Liabilities often reveal many things about your relationship with money. The more liabilities you have the harder it is to budget, build assets, and pursue financial freedom. Then you add in a sprinkle of immense out-of-pocket inflation...*fuggedaboutit*! Inflation often causes liabilities to cost more in the long run than they traditionally would during times of economic prosperity.

At this point you are probably fed up with this money date, and you have every right to be. But the financial breakthrough you're preparing for comes on the other side of that frustration. We started with the bad news first for that exact reason. No one likes to add up their liabilities, but you cannot calculate your net worth without it.

I sat down with Mykail James, affectionately referred to as the "The Boujie Budgeter," to discuss one of her largest financial milestones: growing her net worth from negative to positive. As the founder of BoujieBudgets. com, an online platform dedicated to teaching young professionals how to finance their best lives, I asked her about the key turning point in her personal finance journey that helped her grow her net worth. She stated, "A lot of us are starting with a financial net worth that is lower than zero. You should always remember that no matter where you are starting from it is not where you are ending. When making the decision to change your financial net worth you have two choices, pay down debt or increase your investments. Think about what strategy will give you flexibility. Paying down debt can feel rewarding but increasing investments was the way that provided me with more options for growth."

So, what's next?

You're going back into your financial documents to add up the value of all the things you own. We are going to call these items your assets. Common assets that traditionally impact net worth are real estate, vehicles, investment portfolios, checking, savings, and retirement accounts.

You now have two numbers in front of you. Your assets = all your things that hold monetary value. Your liabilities = your debt. There's just one more mathematical step to take. Subtract your liabilities from your assets. That final number that you're left with is your net worth.

I'm not a betting woman, but if I had to take an educated guess, I'd say you're feeling one of two things right now. You're either pleasantly surprised or unbelievably mortified. Personally, the first time I calculated my net worth I felt the latter. Why? Because my shit was hella negative. When I sat down to calculate my net worth, I don't know why it never crossed my mind that the number could be negative. After adding up my assets (my 2009 Nissan Altima, the $2,000 in my checking account, and my 403B) and subtracting my student loans, I had a net worth of negative $56,000.

The all-too-familiar shame and embarrassment crept in immediately, as the tears flowed freely. There it was, right in front of me in bold-ass black and white. I was literally worthless. Needless to say, I was ready to call that money date a wrap and relinquish myself to the idea that I permanently messed up my life and could never do anything to fix it. I was too far behind, so the only option was to keep putting on the same façade of success in front of my friends and family.

As trash as I felt that potential reality was far worse than admitting I didn't know what I was doing or how I got here. So, I chose (after many, many days of tearfully feeling sorry for myself) to continue the money date. It took me a while to internalize the actual truth of that matter, which was, "Yeah, this is where I am, but this is *not* where I'm staying."

So let me share that with you again. Repeat after me, "Yeah, this is where I am, but this is *not* where I'm staying." Honestly, if you want to repeat it one more time for good measure in your best British accent that will probably help it stick a little stronger. The first money date *must* continue even when you don't think it's going well.

Ready? Let's go get 'em.

STEP FOUR: GET TO KNOW YOUR NUMBERS

Calculating your net worth is the appetizer on your money date. Now, we must transition to the main course. This step can be done in a multitude of different ways, but the process will always lead to the same outcome. The primary goal of step four on your money date is to obtain a dynamic understanding of your full financial landscape.

You're going to need your financial documents again for this step. If you like writing with pen and paper, you can use the free expense tracker provided on sothisiswhyimbroke.com.

When I started taking myself on money dates, old-school pen and paper helped me focus in on what I was spending versus what I was saving. As I started going on money dates more often, I shifted into digital spreadsheets I filled out and stored on my tablet. So even if you start tracking your expenses one way, it doesn't mean you have to stick with that one way forever.

The four main buckets you will initially focus on are:

1. Income
2. Saving/investing
3. Housing
4. Food

These four expense categories are the big key players in your budget, followed by expenses regarding healthcare, transportation, personal and family care, and debt. Whatever expense tracker you choose to use, make sure it gives you the opportunity to fill in all the aspects of your finances.

Use your most recent documents to focus on the four main expense buckets before branching into the ancillary expenses. Your documentation should reflect your spending and income from the last thirty to sixty days to get the most accurate reflection of your financial landscape. The numbers you're about to write down on your tracker are the numbers you want to be fairly cognizant of at all times. Knowing your numbers is half the battle when it comes to budgeting.

It is a lot easier to blow through a budget when you have no idea what your actual monthly take-home pay is. When you think about the money you bring in, the trick is to always operate under your net income instead of your gross income. What's the difference? Well, your gross income will have you spending a gross amount of money that you aren't actually bringing home.

Gross income and net income are often thrown around conversations with little context, so it can be hard to know which is which. Your gross income or gross pay is the larger number on your paycheck. It's the amount you've earned before any taxes or deductions have been taken out. Your gross income is the total sum of all sources of income you have. This could consist of things like rental property income, dividends, or interest earned from a savings account or CD.

Your net income is the amount of money on your paycheck that you get to spend. This is the income deposited into your account that you use to cover your day-to-day living expenses. Your net income will be the smaller number.

According to my 2022 W2, I made $120,000 from my 9-to-5, but in reality, I operated as though I made $72,800. That was how much I took home after taxes and deductions. So, if I spent like I brought in $120,000, I would have been operating at a $47,000 deficit. To avoid this, use your net pay.

Once you've calculated your monthly net pay, this number will be your North Star as you continue into steps five and six of your money date.

Continue to fill out your expenses as honestly and openly as you can. If there are expenses that vary from month to month, make a note of that and implement an estimated average amount. In this instance, it is better to overestimate than underestimate the numbers. Remember, we don't want to work from a financial deficit, so be as accurate as you can.

STEP FIVE: SET GOALS YOU CAN TRACK AND MONITOR

This by far is my favorite part of my money dates, and I hope it is enjoyable for you as well. At this point, you have calculated your net worth and have identified your numbers. You now have a pretty good idea of what you're earning, what you're spending, how much you're saving, and how many times you've ordered Uber Eats in the last four weeks.

I never promised you a pretty picture, but it is a clear picture, and that is what's most important. And since this is a shame-free space, don't be embarrassed by what you've uncovered about your spending patterns. Steps five and six of your money date are all about plugging those spending leaks you weren't aware of and creating a functional budget for your lifestyle needs. You're doing the work, and there's no shame in that!

As a former teacher, I can't begin to tell you how difficult it was to teach students how to create SMART goals. That's because on the surface it seems like an extremely simple process until you realize it isn't. Thankfully after being in the classroom for eleven years, you pick up a skill or two to turn the most difficult concept into the most approachable. That's what we're going to do right now with your numbers.

The concept of SMART goals was created to make those large scary life-changing goals achievable. They are time-bound and rooted in practicality to increase your likelihood of success. The more successful you are in achieving your goals the more likely you are to continue the behavior patterns associated with those exact goals.

Your SMART goals must adhere to the following parameters:

- Specific
- Measurable
- Achievable
- Relevant
- Time-bound

These parameters will help you define the criteria you use to determine what success looks like to you. Your SMART goals won't look like anyone else's because they will be specific to the numbers you have documented in step four. This means that you are also the only one who can determine what a win looks like. Don't compare your goals or your success to anyone you see on the internet or in person. And trust me, it's easy to fall into the comparison game when people are only posting their highlight reels on the 'gram. We all have our unique "why." So even if you discover similarities between you and someone else on your money date, how you address them will unfold differently.

For example, my initial money date revealed many hard truths that were difficult to accept as reality. One of those realities was I lacked a personal spending allowance in my budget. This meant if I was ever in the mood for anything besides the Haitian food in my parents' house, I would be having Costco samples for dinner or heading to Applebee's with somebody's unfunny son. I had to make a SMART goal that would put an end to both of those scenarios as quickly as possible.

You may be tempted to start big and create a long list of goals you want to achieve this month. Money dates take you through a range of emotions, and when I get to the goal-setting step, I'm always invigorated and excited to tackle my money goals in order to get one step closer to reaching my full financial potential. If that's how you're feeling, I couldn't be happier to hear that. I'm going to strongly warn against overextending yourself to reach any and every goal that comes to mind. In fact, for this first money date, I want you to focus on creating three SMART goals maximum. Here's why.

First, quality over quantity is key. Having one strong SMART goal that you can focus on achieving is better than having ten goals that become overwhelming by week two. Secondly, money management is an immensely emotional process, as are many other aspects of life. You still have so many other things in life to handle and worry about. Giving yourself the best possible opportunity to achieve success with your money goals is the type of financial self-care that needs to be always put into practice.

HERE ARE SOME QUICK TIPS TO USE AS A GUIDE TO CRAFT YOUR FIRST THREE FINANCIAL SMART GOALS

Tip One: Look back at your expense tracking in step four. Identify one thing you want to do, improve, or change about your current financial landscape. This is going to help you solidify the specificity needed to build a strong SMART goal. Write it down as an "I want" statement.

Example: I want to build a six-month emergency savings with a total of $6,000.

Tip Two: Identify where you are in your journey in comparison to where you want to be.

Example: I currently have $500 saved and need to save $5,500 more to reach my goal.

Tip Three: Set up a realistic timeline and actionable steps. How long will it take you to achieve your goal and what actions will you take to make the goal a reality?

Example: With my current income, I can set aside $500 a month toward my savings. At this pace I will have a fully funded emergency fund in eleven months.

By following these three tips, you have identified a goal, created a timeline, and set up an action step that allows you to track and monitor progress. *Boom*, a SMART goal without any complexities. This process also leaves room for you to change your action steps or alter your timeline as life changes.

Once you've written out at least one SMART goal, you are one step closer to the end of your first money date. A date simply isn't complete without dessert. You've got one more decision to make: what budget are you going to follow to not only stay on track but also grow your wealth?

As a certified financial literacy instructor with an MBA in accounting, Mykail firmly believes it is important to make positive money moves because you can only live your best life when it is properly financed. With Mykail's support of young professionals, I asked her to share more about how she believed budgeting could have a tremendous impact on the younger generations' ability to build wealth. Mykail stated, "Your budget is your guide to achieving your goals. Having a dependable budget creates organization within your finances. Getting organized with your money relieves stress and anxiety as well as providing a clear path to success. The earlier you start the better. When you establish your financial foundation sooner rather than later, it's like a cheat code to build wealth faster."

STEP SIX: CHOOSE A BUDGET TO FOLLOW FOR THIRTY DAYS

Adulting is not for the faint of heart, so you don't need to use a budget that will overcomplicate your already complicated adult existence. If you've ever said or thought you hate budgeting, budgeting doesn't work for you, or you can't stick to a budget, chances are you're doing it wrong. You're likely trying to use your fave influencer's budgeting routine or a budgeting technique your great-uncle Franklin suggested. Maybe you saw a YouTube video that said something like, "Five budget hacks that can work for anyone." The problem is none of those people are you, and there are few things that can work for anyone. Your budget needs to be For U By U (yes, that was my attempt at making a parallel comparison to FUBU).

Mykail admitted during our chat, "Creating a budget that worked for me took over six months. I tried different iterations of zero-based budgeting, cash envelope method, and other methods. Nothing felt good and nothing stuck. Ultimately, I created a flexible budgeting method using multiple bank accounts to create a budget that I could actually stick to. Most methods felt too restrictive, almost like looking at a bad report card every month. Creating a flexible budget that worked with my habits made the most positive impact on my finances."

You want your budget to be an experience that allows for a healthy balance between doing the things you want to do and doing the things you have to do. If your budget isn't supporting your SMART goals or helping you reach your vision of financial independence, choose a different one. If that one doesn't work either, try another. No one will fight you about it. I promise.

There are five main budgeting techniques with a slew of budget subsets. For the sake of simplicity, we're going to stick to the main five.

These budget techniques are meant to be adapted to your lifestyle. If you choose one and don't like it, you are under no obligation to continue to use that budget the following month. I do ask that you give it thirty days to marinate, so to speak, before you are on to the next one. The point of using a budget is to make sure it is simple enough that it doesn't overcomplicate your daily routine or cause you to anxiously overthink every time you spend money.

ONE: TRADITIONAL BUDGETING

As the name suggests, traditional budgeting is typically the OG when it comes to budgeting your money. If you've followed the steps of the money date accurately, you've already done 90 percent of the traditional budgeting method.

To traditionally budget, you calculate your total monthly net income (which you've already done), calculate your total expenses, and find the difference. The main point of this practice is to ensure that you are spending less than you are bringing home. Once you've confirmed that is the case, you set categorical goals for the following month.

So if you spent three hundred dollars on groceries this month, a potential goal you could make for the grocery category of your budget could be to spend fifty dollars less next month.

This budget takes a bit of time and energy to initially set up because you are going line by line into what you've spent and determining what you will spend next month. The longer you follow the traditional method, the easier it becomes, especially if you are a detail-oriented person. If you are usually low on time, this method may be more of a hassle for you.

TWO: 50/30/20

The 50/30/20 budget was my go-to budget when I started focusing on improving my financial health. Why? Because I hate math and numbers, the simplicity of setting up this budget was hella appealing. The 50/30/20 budget focuses on three main categories: needs, wants, and savings. At twenty-five years old, that's all I had the capacity to truly conceptualize.

Fifty percent of your net pay (I told you this number would be your North Star) goes directly to your needs, thirty percent goes toward your wants, and 20 percent goes toward saving. Beyond simplicity, I gravitated toward this budgeting technique because it also aligned with the initial SMART goals I created for myself on my first money date.

I wanted to save more money because I did not have nearly enough in my emergency savings fund. Okay...I didn't even have an emergency savings fund. Once I started using this technique, I automated a specific amount of my checks directly into my savings account. This was a game-changer for me. It opened my eyes to what I could do with money if I had the right organizations in place.

Besides saving, I wanted to improve my relationship with money in terms of self-care. This was extremely hard for me since I was also trying to focus on paying down my student loans. So instead of using the complete 30 percent for my wants, I used it to build a sinking fund for my student loans because I wanted out of debt. This is why I stress flexibility when budgeting. Nothing is as rigid as it seems, and for me the 30 percent toward debt was a choice I made even though the technique said otherwise. If you want to make changes, do it. The remaining 50 percent goes toward life's necessities like monthly bills, housing, food, utilities, etc.

At the precipice of my money journey, I was all about the 50/30/20 budget with flexible modifications to fit my financial needs. However, once I started becoming more hands-on with my financial journey, the 50/30/20 budget no longer worked for me for two specific reasons.

Though the 50/30/20 budget is a great baseline for those starting out who want a simple, straightforward method to follow. If you are looking to start or expand your investing journey, you'll notice there is no distinction for investing within the 50/30/20 buckets. Investing is crucial to building generational wealth, and I needed a budget that prioritized that. There is no specific bucket for those who are on a debt-repayment journey either.

Secondly, with the 50 percent going toward needs, it can become a bit blurry classifying what is a need vs. what is a want. Food is obviously a need, but is pizza a need or a want? Making those decisions gets a little harder during more emotionally stressful times.

I suggest using the 50/30/20 method as a starting point for those looking to get their feet wet with budgeting. The simple straight forward nature of the 50/30/20 will provide a stable foundation to build a more a robust budget as you advance through your personal finance journey.

THREE: 70/20/10

Yes, I know I promised you minimal arithmetic, and here I am giving you more percentages to calculate. I don't make the rules; I simply report them!

The 70/20/10 budget shares similarities with the aforementioned 50/30/20 rule, so the outline will be familiar. These percentage breakdowns, however, are set up to address some of the things the 50/30/20 does not. Seventy percent of your take-home pay goes toward your spending. The 70 percent is a culmination of your fixed costs and your disposable income. Twenty percent continues to go toward your savings goals, and the remaining 10 percent of your take home is set aside for debt repayment or charitable donations.

While I do appreciate that this budgeting technique addresses the people on their debt repayment journey, this structure can be a little too unstructured for those who are just getting started budgeting or struggle with overspending.

Lumping disposable income and fixed costs together into one bucket will make distinguishing between the two difficult to track. If overspending is not an issue for you, and you want a little more freedom in your budget, this technique is worth a shot.

FOUR: ZERO-BASED BUDGETING

Ahh, we have reached the zero-based budget. I have been using a modified version of this budgeting technique since I bought my home in 2019. It is a bit more hands-on than the 50/30/20 or 70/20/10 budget, which was an immediate turn-off when I was just starting out on my finance journey in 2013. At this moment, however, this budgeting method is the appropriate technique I need to meet my current lifestyle needs. I can't stress this point enough: choose and modify the techniques that work best for who you are and where you are. Twenty-five-year-old me would not last more than a month on a zero-based budget. Thirty-four-year-old me loves it! And here's why!

Every single one of my dollars is put to work with this technique. It also allows me to cover my fixed expenses, save, and most importantly, pay myself first.

To excel with zero-based budgeting, you'll need to do two things (one of them you already partially have done). The first thing is you'll look at the last three months of expenses. If you traditionally have the same amount of expenses month after month, the month of expenses you calculated in step four will suffice. If you know that your monthly expenses greatly vary, you're going to pull out your financial documents from the last ninety days and repeat step four for each month.

You now have a wider view of your financial landscape and will use that to determine your budget for next month. On a digital or hard copy spreadsheet, you're going to balance your budget so that your income minus your expenses equals zero. This is what I meant when I stated that every dollar would have a job. If that sounds like a whole lot of confusing work, let's take a quick look at a visual zero-based budget below to help clarify the process.

Total monthly take home: $5,000

FINANCIAL CATEGORY	EXPENSE	REMAINING DOLLARS
Housing	$1,100	$3,900
Utilities	$75	$3,825
Saving (emergency)	$1,000	$2,825
Investing	$500	$2,325
Debt repayment	$700	$1,625
Cell phone	$85	$1,540
Subscriptions	$125	$1,415
Groceries	$400	$1,015
Self-care	$400	$615
Sinking fund (holidays, vacation, travel)	$615	$0

Zero-based budgeting allows for quick monthly adjustments when life comes at you fast, which if you've been adulting for more than five minutes, you know it comes quicker than ever anticipated. Just like with the traditional budgeting method, zero-based budgeting works well if you have a predictable income and are detail-oriented. This budgeting technique can be overwhelming if you're just starting out. To save on time, this method is one that best operates digitally in an app that automatically calculates what you've spent and which category that spending falls into.

If you find this is still too much to keep mental tabs on, even with the use of a budgeting app, I've got one more option for you.

FIVE: CASH ENVELOPE BUDGET

Cue the almighty cash envelope budgeting system. I call this the old-school zero-based budget because you're following similar steps but in a tangible manner. Just like with the zero-based budget you're going to backtrack and look at what you've spent in the last three months. Then you're going to grab envelopes and label them with your monthly expense categories.

With the cash envelope budget, you can get as granular as you'd like (similar to the zero-based budget), or you can make your categories a little more generalized (similar to the 70/20/10 or 50/30/20 budget). If you are currently trying to navigate out of an overspending habit, it is wise to get as specific as possible with your discretionary income categories. For example, instead of labeling your envelope as "self-care money," you could break that down to "nails," "eating out," and "clothes." The more specific you get with this budget, the more you'll be able to track where you may be overspending and what adjustments you need to make for the following month.

As with every budget I've mentioned, there are definite pros and clear-cut cons. The cash envelope budget is great for those just getting started budgeting who want to control their spending and avoid using credit cards. Once the cash runs out, that's it. It is a way to force yourself to budget and stick to the budget as long as you don't reach for the credit card if the funds get low.

I like to think of the cash envelope budget as a strong intro to budgeting. A starter budgeting system that helps you practice spending behaviors that align with the financial goals you have in place. Long term, it may become too restrictive during moments when you need to make larger purchases that you have responsibly planned to pay off in the future. Thankfully, we're all about adjusting and adaptation around here. You can always pivot as life demands.

STEP SEVEN: PLAN THE SECOND DATE

You did it. You worked your way through the discomfort and got vulnerable with your finances. Your first money date is complete. The only thing left to do on this date is to schedule the next one. When I started taking myself on money dates, I scheduled them biweekly to align with my paychecks. As I became more comfortable with my finances, I could set long-term money goals that I could check on monthly instead of every two weeks.

This monthly money date has been scheduled on my iCal for the last three years. Oh yes, I absolutely set reminders because I don't like breaking promises or dates with myself. Always make time for yourself on your calendar, and that goes beyond your money dates.

———

You've set the goals, familiarized yourself with your numbers, and mapped out a plan to meet your needs. You're shifting your narrative, and you are already ten steps ahead of where you were when you picked up this book. You can do hard things; you can learn all about money, so take the time to applaud yourself because you're just getting started!

CHAPTER 2

SAVE LIKE I'VE GOT SOME CENTS

If you think you're bad at saving money because you've got three dollars sitting in your saving account right now, remember I over-drafted my account to buy a pair of sneakers. I'm also the one who tried to buy a house with no emergency savings in sight. We've all had our moments, but saving money is 40 percent planning and 50 percent execution. That remaining 10 percent is all about the bounce back—the steps you take after your saving doesn't go as planned.

WHAT'S THE 411?

You're not bad at saving. You think you are because of past mistakes you have made with your money. You think you are because your money may be looking a little funny in that bank account right now. You think you are because everyone on Instagram is in Dubai, and you're simply hoping your savings can cover an unforeseen emergency expense. You're not alone in that. A 2022 Bankrate survey uncovered 56 percent of Americans cannot cover a thousand-dollar emergency expense. Even more alarming, about a quarter of people would have to go into debt to cover that same thousand-dollar emergency.

There are quite a few variables that can impact people's ability to save money. To minimize socioeconomic disparities as "people are just bad at saving" is not only corny AF it is also not true.

We are living through a global pandemic. As if that itself wasn't bad enough, women and BIPOC have been disproportionally impacted financially by said pandemic. When we read headlines and stats that report one in five Americans didn't save any money in 2021, it is critical to interpret this data through a macro lens. To approach the data from a micro level would reveal a much darker truth.

Prior to COVID-19, the gender pay gap persisted at a steady pace. Over the last fifteen years, women have earned 84 percent of what men earned. This stat of course does not speak for women of color. The numerous equal pay days scattered throughout the calendar year stress this not-so-fun fact clearly. Black, Latina, and Native American women have a much steeper hill to climb at fifty-eight cents, forty-nine cents, and fifty cents earned for every white man's dollar. Over the course of a forty-year full-time career, this traditionally translates to a loss of one million dollars over their working lives. Seems difficult to just keep up, doesn't it? The racial wealth gap has joined the chat.

Just as you're trying to catch your breath, let me introduce you to yet another social barrier that greatly heightens economic inequality. The racial wealth gap, a subset of the general wealth gap, makes it incredibly evident that the perceived progress of Black Americans has not led to true economic equality or financial mobility. A 2018 analysis of US incomes published by the Federal Reserve Bank of Minneapolis tracked household data surrounding income and wealth since 1949. Economists Moritz Kuhn, Ulrike I. Steins, and Moritz Schularick concluded, "The historical data also reveals that no progress has been made in reducing income and wealth inequalities between black and white households over the past seventy years."

Due to historical discrimination and systemic inequalities, the racial wealth gap continues to widen at frightening rates. As of 2021, the Federal Reserve reports, the average Black and Hispanic households earn about half as much as the average white household and own only about 15–20 percent as much net wealth. The median family wealth of a white family in 2019 was $188,200 compared to the median family wealth of a Black family, which was $24,100. The same inequitable pattern of wealth distribution holds true for other diverse family groups, including Asian and Native American households.

My intersectionality is gasping for air right now. It can't get any worse, right? LOL, cue COVID-19. The gender pay gap and racial wealth gap made a new friend in 2020 and have been bonding ever since. The Coronavirus will undoubtedly contribute to the widening of gender poverty gaps, which means more women will be pushed into extreme poverty than men. Antra Bhatt, statistics specialist, states the reasoning for this is because "women typically earn less and hold less secure jobs than men. With plummeting economic activity, women are particularly vulnerable to layoffs and loss of livelihoods."

The pandemic exacerbated the preexisting challenges women, especially women of color, face in the US workforce. Many lower-paying positions in the service industry are held by women, which unfortunately was one of the industries hit the hardest.

Between February and December 2020 job losses for women exceeded job losses for men by one million. According to the National Women's Law Center, in December 2020 alone, women accounted for 86 percent of the 227,000 job losses. Women of color bore the brunt of pandemic-related job loss in 2020, with Latina women carrying 8.8 percent unemployment, Black women carrying 8.5 percent, and Asian women at 7.9 percent.

Those not-so-pleasant racial wealth gap numbers I shared a few moments ago—yeah, COVID-19 made them frighteningly worse. The initial economic challenges Black Americans were already facing in the country became fundamentally more difficult. Black families on average found it more difficult to absorb the sudden economic downturn caused by the pandemic due to minimal financial buffers. Pre-COVID economic disparities that contributed to the racial wealth gap, similar to the gender pay gap, were only amplified by sharp increases in wage loss and food insecurity within Black and Hispanic households.

And now in 2022, the year of our renaissance queen Beyoncé, we are staring down the barrel of another recession while facing unprecedented rates of inflation. I don't know about you, but I am sick and tired of living through unprecedented times. I need some precedent back and I need it now. 2020 was hard, painstakingly so. Just as you were starting to feel like your feet were on solid ground, *boom*, another unprecedented time.

No wonder it has been impossible to save; the game has clearly been rigged. To think you're simply bad at saving money is more likely than not an inaccuracy. Given the multitude of factors that impact your economic well-being, you're doing the best you can with the cards you've been dealt. So now it's time to reshuffle the deck.

IDENTIFYING YOUR FINANCIAL HABITS

Outside of circumstantial disparities, our behaviors are also factors that impact our ability to save money. There's a long-withstanding popular ideology floating around that it takes twenty-one days to form or break a habit. My therapist and the entire first page of Google beg to differ. Though there is no hard and fast rule, scientific research suggests it takes anywhere between eighteen to 254 days to form or break a habit, with most people typically experiencing success closer to sixty-six days. That means that you usually need to actively build a new behavior into your day to day for about two months before you shift into comfortable autopilot.

You may not believe me, but your biggest and smallest life decisions impact your financial habits. Your financial habits will strengthen or weaken your financial health. If your financial health is at risk, this impacts other aspects of your physical, mental, and emotional health. The most frustrating part of all this? If you're physically, mentally, and emotionally tapped out, the last thing you want to do is sit down with a spreadsheet looking at numbers that don't make you feel any better. It's a vicious cycle that can be difficult to assess, let alone bring to an end.

The thing is, you're the only one that can stop it. No one else can save you; you have to save yourself. That goes for pretty much anything in life: you are your own superhero. I'm just here to help you unlock your dormant superpowers and identify your kryptonite. This means we're going back to those financial documents you probably tucked away after your money date in Chapter 1. Pull those back out along with your favorite writing utensil and a blank sheet of paper. If you choose to be a little more technologically advanced a phone or tablet will work just fine for this as well.

Thanks to your money date, you already understand your numbers and have an overall picture of your financial health. Now we're going to take it a step further. By examining your financial habits and triggers, you'll have a clearer picture of your discretionary spending habits and any spending leaks you may not be aware of.

We'll be using your last three bank statements to identify your financial habits. You want to make sure you have your savings and checking account documents ready to look through for this exercise. The easiest way to proceed through this next step is to annotate directly on the statement whenever you run into a discretionary expense. A discretionary expense is any spending that is not essential, like hobbies or travel, whereas non-discretionary expenses are essentials like food and housing.

When looking through your bank statements, what patterns do you notice in your discretionary spending? How many Amazon charges were on your statement this month? Are you ordering Uber Eats a couple of times a week? How many days did you run into Target to grab one thing and ended up leaving with everything except that one thing? Do you have any monthly subscriptions you aren't even using let alone enjoying anymore? These tiny little life moments are all important financial habits you may not pay close attention to because they seem so insignificant.

Grabbing a coffee? No big deal. Picking up lunch? Sounds divine. Splurging on yourself occasionally is highly encouraged around here! Spending four hundred dollars a month on coffee and lunch without realizing it—that's a significant spending leak. You may probably be thinking, *How can anyone spend four hundred dollars without realizing it?* On average we have twenty workdays a month, give or take a holiday or two. Spending twenty dollars absentmindedly in New York every day on coffee and lunch is not as farfetched as it sounds. In fact, thanks to inflation and food service delivery fees, some may even consider twenty dollars a day to be a deal. The point is not to focus on the bigger picture, which would be the total four hundred dollars spent. The point is, we've all had a moment or ten where we thought, *Oh, it's just __ dollars. Swipe!* Those are the small moments we need to watch out for.

Dyana King, founder of *Money. Boss. Mama* and single mother of two, openly discusses the detriment that emotional spending can have on financial routines and financial independence as she teaches other single women to maximize their nine-to-five income to get out of debt and build their savings. During our conversation, I asked what would be one of the first steps she suggested to anyone who struggles to stop emotional spending on a consistent basis. Dyana replied, "I recommend discovering what's triggering the emotional spending. Is it your stressful job or a limiting belief that's menacing you? It's not until you understand why you spend the way you do that you will be able to establish methods to keep yourself in check."

To do this Dyana recommends asking yourself a series of questions she calls the "WTF method." Dyana's method consists of the following:

List out your last two emotional purchases and ask yourself:

- **Where** was I when I made this purchase? Certain places can trigger emotions and thoughts that influence the desire to spend.

- **Who** was I with? Those we surround ourselves with often have an impact on our financial decisions, whether positive or negative.

- What **thoughts** was I having? All purchases start with a thought that influences the action we take.

- How did I **feel**? When we're sad, overwhelmed, and anxious we tend to want to self-soothe to experience relief from those unwanted feelings. Happiness plays a role too. If it's sunny outside and you're having an amazing day you may see purchasing something as a way to amplify those emotions you want to feel on a grander scale. Really explore why that is.

Those are the moments that create spending leaks. In addition to Dyana's methods I also suggest you look at your bank statements. Where do you notice you're spending a larger amount of money than expected? On your sheet of paper (or likely your digital device), make a T-chart. Very old-school, I know, but once a teacher, always a teacher. On one side, write down what you recall feeling or thinking when you made these discretionary purchases. Were these purchases pre-planned or impulsive buys? Especially the purchases that carry a larger price tag or any repeat offenders. Were you upset when you swiped your card? Were you sad, anxious, tired?

These are important feelings to pinpoint because when left unaddressed they can often lead to that continuous cycle that feels impossible to break. Recognizing your money difficulties and the associated feelings they create is uncomfortable, without a doubt. You can do uncomfortable things; you already have. Take the space you need to acknowledge what you felt and write it down for as visual confirmation.

On the other side of your T-chart write down how you felt after making the purchase. Were you excited about what you ordered? Were you feeling buyer's remorse or guilt? I regret 83 percent of what I impulsively buy, and I refuse to keep what does not bring me joy and functionality. Returns are a form of self-care!

This exercise may feel trivial in theory, but a huge part of getting your finances together is tapping into the emotional and mental triggers that lead to certain financial habits. The quicker you can pinpoint how you financially react to stressors in your life, the quicker you can start practicing habits that help you manage and navigate those feelings. If you become cognizant that stress causes you to impulse shop online, you can now start to implement steps that make it harder to act on those habits. For me, that meant removing any credit cards stored on my electronic devices. It doesn't mean I never stress-shopped again. Taking this step, however, helped decrease the frequency of impulsive moments as I worked on curtailing that habit with my therapist. If this was never a trigger I identified, I would have remained stuck in that same frustrating loop and one step further away from my savings goals.

You have your budget and SMART goals from Chapter 1, and you've just taken stock of your emotional triggers. Now what? It is time for us to intentionally develop financial habits that will be the foundational blocks we build into our daily routines. They may feel weird or forced at first, but remember, you're going to gracefully give yourself at least two months of practice before you give up. Some days will be easier to maintain your new habits than others but that's okay. Every day will be different, but the intentionality behind your financial habits will help make those hard days a little easier.

So what do healthy financial habits look and sound like? If you don't know where to start, or can't think of some new habits you'd like to implement into your daily routine, here are ten ideas to get you started:

1. Making and following a budget (someone is already ahead of the game here, aren't they?)

2. Planning and saving for big purchases

3. Tracking your spending

4. Paying yourself first every check

5. Checking your credit report annually

6. Paying off credit card balance in full every month

7. Saving money regularly

8. Review and update your financial plan as needed

9. Set meaningful financial goals (*coughs* someone is getting this done already too, huh?)

10. Build an emergency savings fund to cover three to six months of expenses

Now it's your turn. Write down the financial habits you'd like to adopt into your daily routine, and don't worry about trying to have a long list. You can start off by writing down one habit you'd like to try and reinforce. Once you've made your list, it's time to start integrating the habit into your routines.

BUILDING FINANCIAL ROUTINES

I am one of those annoying people who love to exercise and go to the gym. *Gross*, I know. Even worse...I also actually *enjoy* cardio and going on runs. Eww...un-freaking believable. *But*, this wasn't always the case. I was relatively thin in high school through no real effort of my doing until I gained the Freshman Forty in college. After a dramatic break up junior year, I decided I wanted a revenge body and went to the gym sporadically. That decision lasted all of two months. I lost a good amount of weight and stopped going to the gym because it felt like a chore.

Little did I know that *six* years later, my lungs would be fighting for their life after climbing one flight of subway stairs on my first day commuting by train. *Nah, I can't go out like this.* I immediately walked my ass to the gym down the block from my job. And I haven't stopped working out since (the subway stairs still take me out a little, though).

Saving money is a skill that requires practice and steady financial habits. If you want results you've never had, you have to actively make moves you've never made before. Every night when I went through my routine to prepare for the next day, I made sure to add a step that would make it easier for me to go to the gym the next day. This was because I knew that any slight inconvenience would sway me from working out the next day. After a while, that additional preparation step became a fully formed habit that no longer felt extraneous. It was now routine.

The financial habit(s) you've written down need that same preparation step to become a part of your routine. The preparation step doesn't have to be complex. In fact, the easier it is, the more likely it'll stick and become second nature. Let's use the financial habits mentioned previously and examples of what that preparation step could look like.

FINANCIAL HABIT	PREPARATION STEP (*TURNING HABIT INTO ROUTINE*)
1. Making and following a budget	1. Having a monthly money date to check in with your budget.
2. Planning and saving for big purchases	2. An item you want costs five hundred dollars. Adding a byline to your budget to save a specific amount a month for this purchase.
3. Tracking your spending	3. Download a budget app and connect it to your accounts. Check the app weekly to see what you've spent money on.
4. Paying yourself first every check	4. Set up an automated transfer from your checking to your savings every time you get paid.
5. Checking your credit report annually	5. Set up an annual reminder on your smartphone to check your credit report.

6. Paying off credit card balance in full every month	6. Only charge items to your card that are in your budget. Use the budgeted money to cover the charges.
7. Saving money regularly	7. See the fourth tip.
8. Reviewing and updating your financial plan as needed	8. During your money dates look back at your previous data. Decide what routines you want to keep and which routines you'd like to adjust to match any pending major life changes.
9. Setting meaningful financial goals	9. Create at least one SMART goal during each money date based on your previous data and future financial needs.
10. Building an emergency savings fund to cover three to six months of expenses	10. Calculate your expenses for three to six months. Decide on an amount you can comfortably put into a savings account and on what cadence (e.g., my expenses are six thousand dollars for three months. I can put away five hundred a month). Divide your total number needed by the amount of money you can set aside. This will tell you how long it will take (e.g., to fully fund my emergency savings at five hundred dollars a month would take me twelve months).

You've set up the budget, you've set your goals, the triggers are identified, and the routines are automated...*whew.* WTF happens next? Exactly.

WTF: WATCH THE FUNDS

Did I just make the cringiest millennial dad joke? Perhaps I did; either way, WTF is your next move when it comes to saving?

I have seven bank accounts, one for each savings bucket in my budget. You may be asking one of two things:

1. Am I doing too much?

or

2. Do I also need seven bank accounts?

The answer to both is *no*. I'm not doing too much; I'm doing what works well for my financial habits and routines. Therefore, you don't need seven bank accounts. What you need is exactly what supports the routines and habits you created to support your financial goals.

That's the beauty in personal finance; it's hella personal! I opened seven bank accounts to help me watch the funds. This was how I monitored and tracked how much money was going in and out of each category in my budget. Having just one account with all my savings in one place didn't work for me. It felt confusing and I was overwhelmed trying to track different expenses in one space.

This wasn't always the case. I started slowly, one additional account at a time until I felt mentally capable of managing another. I did the same when it came to managing credit cards as well, but we'll get to more about that in Chapter 3. If you're just getting started saving, or you're reconditioning your routines and financial habits, I don't recommend juggling seven bank accounts. A good place to start: three. A checking account for your day-to-day expenses and bills, emergency savings to house three to six months of expenses, and discretionary savings for anything you may be planning on purchasing in the near or distant future. Simple to set up, easy to manage.

Thankfully for you I've made just about every money mistake one can make, all the way from simple to ridiculously absurd. Because of this, I've crafted a list of savings problems and solutions to help you avoid these mistakes by any means necessary. *Or* if you've already made similar mistakes this list will help you create a strategic plan to get you back to your healthy financial habits.

THE PROBLEM: YOU WANT SOMETHING YOU DON'T HAVE MONEY FOR RIGHT NOW

The first thing I remember ever truly saving for was a Sanyo 8100 flip phone in 2004. My father was still paying my cell phone bill at the time, a luxury I would have loved to keep well into adulthood. *But* he wasn't keen on updating to a newer phone when your current one was still operational. I, on the other hand, a teenager living in a false sense of reality, could not fathom walking into sophomore year with the same cell phone from my freshman year. So, my dad and I made a deal.

Back in the day, before the cost of phones was rolled into the monthly bill, mobile companies used to offer you a discounted price if you signed a two-year contract. My dad agreed to renew the contract so we could get the discounted price, but I would foot the $199 bill. I saved every dollar that came my way and didn't spend them on anything. Just before school started, I excitedly walked into the Sprint store with excitement in my eyes and $200 in my hands.

The minute the customer service rep brought over the box I immediately imagined how cool I would look walking in slow motion down the hallway of my Catholic all-girl high school, snapping pictures in 140p on my 1.8-inch screen. The woman scanned the box; *beep, $216.41*. My ass did not account for sales tax. As my father leaned over to pull out his wallet, he looked at me, said, "You owe me money," and handed the sales rep a twenty-dollar bill.

I walked out of the Sprint store with the phone of my dreams and a stern reminder that my father would later turn into his favorite mantra: "*You have to save your money.*" A few weeks later he marched me straight into Astoria Savings Bank to open my first checking and savings account. The "bank of daddy" was drying up and I was sick about it.

Money. Boss. Mama founder Dyana King became debt-free on a moderate income and is adamant about discussing strategies that support a healthy financial lifestyle without operating in a scarcity mindset. While she has spoken about delayed gratification as one strategy, I wanted to learn more about the steps she took that she would have changed during the process of saving to become debt-free. Dyana stated, "I would have allowed myself to buy more things that weren't a necessity. In the thick of my journey I went through more 'extreme' measures to save money such as sewing up tattered clothes instead of just getting new clothing. Thinking back, I had allowed my scarcity mindset to convince me that if I spent money then it wasn't ever going to come back. It was a very miserable time and to this day I still struggle with allowing myself to spend outside of necessities. Controlling your spending is important, but so is remembering that you are still living during the journey and rewarding yourself (within your budget) is necessary to keep up the momentum."

THE SOLUTION: WORK BACKWARD AND MAKE A SINKING FUND

Sinking funds have been a game-changer in my financial life. A sinking fund is another one of those fancy finance terms that you'll want to familiarize yourself with. Why? Because if you're serious about getting your money right, you'll be using them quite often.

A sinking fund is, *drumroll please*, money you put aside for a specific upcoming expense. Yep, that's it! If you know you have a big-ticket purchase coming up or a routine expense, setting up a sinking fund is an optimal financial decision. I used sinking funds for the entire five years I focused on paying off my student loan debt, and I couldn't have gotten it done without implementing them into my financial strategy.

Setting sinking funds up is super simple and requires little of that math I hate so much. You start with the end in mind first. How much money will you need to cover this expense? After you've figured out the total cost, calculate how much time you have from today until the day you need the money.

I prefer for my sinking funds to be in separate accounts, and I like to set them up for every expense on the horizon, no matter how big or small. If you're going to be a bridesmaid, set up a fund! Planning a trip to Costa Rica, set up that fund. Trying to buy a new washer/dryer...you know the vibes. Open that sinking fund.

I have a sinking fund set up for my annual homeowner's insurance and Amazon Prime renewals, my bi-annual car registration fees, and expected birthday or holiday spending. There are two things you'll need to know when setting up a sinking fund. First you need to know the specific dollar amount you will need to save. For things like trips or gifts that have a variable cost you can set a dollar amount you're comfortable with spending. The second thing:

how much time you have to save that amount. The less time you have, the more you'll have to put away at a quicker pace, so it is best to try and give yourself as much lead time as possible.

Once you know the amount of money you'll be saving and the amount of time you have to get it done, the last piece is to figure out your sinking fund routine. Will you be saving a certain dollar amount daily? Weekly? Monthly? Choose the cadence and automate it. This way you don't have to think about it, and when you need to use the funds for their purpose, they will be there waiting for your use. Budget protected and expense covered!

THE PROBLEM: YOU'RE OVERSPENDING

By the end of my junior year, I secured my first job as a camp counselor and my parents couldn't have been happier. They were more than ready to stop funding some of my expenses. I worked from nine to six, Monday through Friday, and brought home a whopping eight hundred dollars a month for 180 hours of work. Though minimum wage was $6.00 in 2005, the camp that shall remain nameless was paying my friends and me $4.44 an hour to keep children alive. It's safe to say, a few child labor laws were broken that summer.

Out of the $1,600 I earned, I spent approximately 80 percent of it at the mall and Applebee's. This was before the two-for-one appetizers were a thing...so honestly, I was *ballin'*! But when senior year rolled around I had less than $300 in my checking account and zero dollars in savings. I knew I had senior dues and other senior activities I wanted to partake in. What I didn't know was how much they were going to cost. The Melissa of today would have a spreadsheet pulled up on my tablet with the numbers mapped out over the next twelve months. The Melissa of yesteryear didn't have that much forethought about money so there was no savings plan to execute.

To avoid hearing my parents talk shit even though they had every reason to do so, I went off and got another job I could work after school to pay for my senior activities.

I wish I could stop right here and say I went on to save so much money during my senior year. I went on to pay for all my dues, prom life, and all the vibes in between. I wish I could say that, but I'd be lying.

THE SOLUTION: TRACK YOUR SPENDING

The traditional old-school finance books I used to read always used to say: to stop overspending you need to spend less than you make. Well...*duh!* But that's not a solution that leads to action.

There can be many reasons why someone is overspending, but telling them to stop isn't going to magically solve the problem. If you've completed the financial habit activity, you may now have why you're spending more than you should.

Tracking your spending helps you see the "what" after you've uncovered the "why." What are you overspending on? Is it makeup? Eating out? Plants? I know how wild my green thumb people can get at a nursery.

After tracking your spending and identifying what is eating up the bulk of your discretionary income, the next traditional piece of financial advice would usually be to cut out the extra expenses. Instead of telling you to stop spending, I want you to keep spending. I want you to keep spending within your budget.

Are the items you're overspending on bringing you joy? Are they experiences that help alleviate stress or genuinely make you feel good? Add a byline for those expenses to your budget so that you are prepared to spend money on them as you see fit. These are the types of expenses that should be covered in the self-care bucket of your budget. Don't have one of those? Go back and add it in. Your self-care budget can roll over from month to month, or you can empty out that bucket every month. But the fact remains you are still spending money on experiences or items that you value. *Surprise,* you've just reframed your spending narrative. You're no longer blowing your budget or overspending because you have planned and saved for these expenses. This is how you treat yourself on a budget!

However, if there are things you are spending money on that are extraneous expenses and do not bring much value to your life—*cut that shit out!* This is one of those moments where you will have to look at your budget, look at your spending habits, and get honest with yourself. Everything we buy is not of value. Ask yourself, "What do I truly value?" Follow up that question with, "What am I spending on that doesn't align with what I value?" The honest answers to both of those questions will help you identify the things you're spending on that you can and should cut out.

This solution comes with a bonus solution. So yes, it's a twofer. If you know that you have trouble overspending, the cash envelope budget method is a strong budgeting technique to build into your financial routine. Sometimes when we're swiping, the bigger picture is often blurred. When you separate your expenses using cash, you can visibly see when you're out of money. No more cash in the envelope, no more spending. Though it may seem overly stringent, it's a temporary practice to help you build a healthier habit. If you're like me and *hate* carrying around cash, you can create separate bank accounts that operate the same as the cash envelopes. Once the account hits zero, there's no way to overspend, because there's no money left.

THE PROBLEM: YOU'VE GOT NO MONEY LEFT TO SAVE AFTER YOU'VE PAID YOUR BILLS

Adulthood is the most ghetto hood I've ever experienced. You have to feed yourself, make your doctor's appointments, remind yourself to eat, maintain friendships, and sleep the right way to avoid neck pains, all while working and paying bills. I don't know how people with kids handle managing themselves and another human because it is a full-time hard-ass job raising myself.

From 2010 to 2013, I made between $45,530 and $55,278 as a high school English teacher. At that time I was bringing home between $1,100 and $1,300 biweekly. Thankfully I did not have to pay for housing when I lived with my parents, so I could cover all of my bills. On average I would have about $400–$500 remaining.

I don't tend to "shoulda, woulda, coulda" but I will do so for you, just this once. With that remaining $500 a month, I should have opened a Roth IRA back in 2010. The potential earnings on those contributions from 2010–2013 would have been worth about $47,000 even if I never contributed again after 2013. I could have made extra payments on my car note or student loan payments to save myself on interest. That would also have freed up more money to invest with in the near future. But I didn't do that. Instead, I spent it on clothes and jewelry I don't own or wear anymore from Forever 21 and Aldo shoes. I took domestic trips (which I don't regret) and went to group birthday dinners often.

Frequently I'd spend more than the $500 remaining from my checks, which meant next month I was automatically operating from a deficit. None of this bothered me because my bills were *paid*. In my mind that's what adulting was all about.

When the real estate agent asked me about savings and then told me to speak to my loan provider, I was annoyed. I'm a teacher! I don't make a lot of money! I can't save a large sum of money! I'm living paycheck to paycheck! *Now sis*...that was a lie. I could save money; I could pay more toward my debt. These are all things I could do and should do, but it would take time and effort to reframe not only my thinking but my process.

THE SOLUTION: AUTOMATICALLY PAY YOURSELF FIRST

You need to be the priority in your budget. Point blank, period. When I prioritize myself, I like to do it with the least possible resistance and the least amount of work possible. I want you to keep that same energy as well. This solution should be an easy lift because you've already done all the other leg work: automate your savings.

You know how much money you need to pay for all your mandatory expenses and how much you have left over. That leftover is your glorious gap, a.k.a. your discretionary income. What you do with your discretionary income makes a huge impact on your financial independence and ability to build generational wealth. If you always have three hundred dollars remaining at the end of the month, don't leave that money sitting in your checking account. That often leads to the temptation to spend it because it's sitting there. Give the leftover money a job and automate it so you don't have to lift a finger. Well... after setting up the automation, of course.

My first check of the month covers my major bills; my second check covers my minor bills. That second check is also the check I use to save and invest. That check contains my glorious gap. So once the check hits my account, a certain amount is pulled into my savings and another into my investment account. All while I sleep. I don't have to think about it or worry that I didn't save this month. Move the money into their accounts so you don't miscalculate or overspend by accident.

Set up the automation in a way that works for your needs and budget. Now you've got a financial habit that you don't even have to think about. You've created a routine, and that routine revolves around putting more bank into your pocket before anyone else's. A round of applause for that!

CHAPTER 3

TO ALL THE CREDIT CARDS I'VE SWIPED BEFORE

Do you remember how old you were when you received your first piece of life-changing memorable advice? I was seven. Do you remember what that advice was? If I had to guess I'd bet it was something along the lines of don't do drugs, don't talk to strangers, don't you dare bring home a baby to this house. You know...the typical everyday stuff. Mine was don't ever apply for a credit card with a man. Sincerely, mom.

My mother handled the back-to-school shopping until my dad took over when I reached high school. Even though I wore a uniform my entire K–12 existence, I needed new school shoes to start off second grade in style. We were next in line waiting to pay and my kid brother was driving both of us nuts. After countless hours of strutting her stuff on Jamaica Ave with a toddler and seven-year-old she walked up to the counter, handed the sales lady the shoes, and proceeded to dig her American Express out of her purse. The next few moments were not pretty.

My meticulously flawed memory recalls this moment clearly. 1, 2, 3, *swipe!* seconds later...*decline!* She was furious and knew instantly that my father had made a purchase. This was a purchase that he not only didn't run by her but also a purchase that maxed out the card. She did not wait for the sales lady to ask her to try another card, and she did not let her swipe the AmEx again. She grabbed my brother's hand, signaled for me to follow, and made a beeline for the exit. As we walked out of the store and started walking toward the bus stop, she looked at me and said, "Don't ever apply for a credit card with a man; they will ruin your credit."

It's hard to know for sure which credit-ruining factor my mom was referencing specifically when she said "they." Was it the men that would be doing the ruining of the credit or the credit cards themselves? As you can imagine, at seven years old I wasn't quite equipped to ask for clarification on the matter, so I decided to heed the warning and stay away from both. At least until thirteen, when I started making out with my eighth-grade boyfriend in front of the 99-cent store.

Though I got a little braver in the boy department, I stayed away from credit cards until I got to college. Anytime my best friend used her credit card at the mall or Applebee's, I held my breath and thought, *Okay, this is the moment she ruins her credit*. Two things are true here:

1. I spent way too much of my teenage years fine dining at Applebee's.

2. I had no idea how credit or credit cards really worked.

The bulk of what I knew was solely based on the fragmented comments I'd overhear from my mother as she argued with my father about a purchase on the joint credit card that he had no business making.

I didn't know my best friend was an authorized user on her mother's card. I didn't understand how she was building her credit even before she could legally apply for a credit card on her own. Credit scores and credit history were words I heard in my house quite often, but the context was never clear enough to gain a critical understanding. If someone told me their credit score was 1500, I would believe them. If they then said credit scores have only existed since 1989, I would say they were liars. Only one of those statements is false, and it isn't the latter.

THE HISTORY OF THE CREDIT SCORE

The credit score as we know it today was created in 1989. I was born in 1988. For the rest of time, I will have to live with the fact that I am older than credit scores, and that fact will never sit right with me. Your credit score is a number that falls between 300 and 850 and is a depiction of your creditworthiness. In layman's terms, your credit score tells lenders whether you can handle debt and credit responsibly or if you're a liability. With a higher number you represent financially healthy habits and will receive more favorable offers in comparison to someone with a lower credit score.

Credit bureaus generate your credit score based on your credit report. Your report is made up of your existing credit accounts with any loans you may have taken out, open lines of credit you have, and active credit card accounts. The report will also contain information about your identity, public records, and any inquiries requested by individuals or companies. Basically, your credit report is dry snitching on you, so you want to work as hard as possible to ensure there's minimal to no bad intel to report.

The three largest credit bureaus that maintain and track your credit report are Equifax, Experian, and TransUnion. The data pulled from your credit report paints a clear picture of who you are based on your ability to manage your debt obligations.

How did we get here and why are there so many moving pieces? This process and credit score model was developed for consumer use by the Fair Isaac Corp, presently known as FICO. The why is both complex and simple at the same time, as most things in life are.

The FICO score was created to help remove bias from consumer lending. As department stores and large retailers gained more popularity in the 1960s, consumer lending became more chaotic. With no centralized credit bureau established, there were over two thousand credit bureaus across the US. Take a moment to picture what two thousand bureaus look like with hundreds and thousands of people applying for loans with no type of computerization. The physical chaos of the lending process doesn't even begin to compare to the mental gymnastics that occurred during the actual loan approval or denial phase.

Prior to the modernization of the credit system, consumer lending was extremely subjective and would often be determined by marital status, ethnic background, gender, and moral character. The birth of the FICO score in 1989 essentially changed the lending landscape by focusing on mathematical calculations instead of character assessments and vibes. Your social status was no longer a factor in whether you would be approved for a loan. All that mattered was whether you could pay back the loan.

By the mid-1990s the FICO score became a generalized mainstay in financial decision-making that evaluated consumers equitably. The intention was there; the initial execution lacked social nuance. While the FICO score was widely accepted as the great equalizer in the lending space, it unfortunately added another systemic barrier for Black and Hispanic Americans. Jay Moon, the general manager of credit at Credit Sesame, said it best, "While the credit system was created to be blind, this data shows that Black and Hispanic Americans are being unfairly shut out of the system."

Navigating creditworthiness prior to the modern FICO score was a social nightmare, and the aftermath, though better than before, still managed to keep Black and Hispanic people from widespread equitable access to credit. Many argue that this is simply due to poor financial practices or a lack of financial literacy, but there is nothing simple about it. A Credit Sesame survey revealed the startling results that Black Americans report having the lowest overall credit scores. The survey states, "More than half (54 percent) of Black Americans report having poor or fair credit (a credit score below 640) or no credit at all, while 41 percent of Hispanic Americans, 37 percent of white Americans and 18 percent of Asian Americans fall into this category."

The public and private disadvantages that Black people have struggled to overcome since the country's inception has played a large hand in the barriers that present themselves today. The establishment of the Freedman's Bank Act in 1865 authorized the organization of a national bank for recently emancipated Black Americans. Success. By 1871 mortgages and loans were largely provided to white borrowers, even though the bank's savings and income came from Black depositors. We see the irony here clear as day, right? White borrowers were successfully advancing economically, while Black people were excluded from doing the same. By 1900 when the bank was shut down due to mismanagement and corruption, Black depositors lost most if not all of their savings (deposits worth about $22 million in today's economy).

This is one of many racially motivated systemic barriers that has impacted the advancement of Black wealth. The constant inequitable mishandling supports a consistent financial pattern that traditionally leads to one progressive step forward and ten steps back. The ripple effect of previous mistreatment appears tenfold. Case in point: FICO score calculation, which we'll cover in just a moment, doesn't take into consideration that Black Americans carry the highest median debt-to-asset ratio, while also having the least amount of housing debt. What does that mean? Black families have fewer resources and assets to pay off debt, especially if their income is insufficient. This means constantly playing catch up, living paycheck to paycheck, and the mental/emotional stress that comes right along with it.

So while the modern credit score's main intention was to be a bias-free calculated metric, the measures of creditworthiness have negatively affected specific populations more than others.

However, all is not lost. Credit-reporting services have started to make adjustments that help level the playing field by including payment history in more accessible financial routines. This includes things like your monthly payments toward your rent, utilities, cell phone, and landline bills. The first major step forward outside of reporting adjustments required visibility and awareness. By providing free annual credit reports, credit score tracking, adjusting payment history outlines, and specific intel into how your credit score is calculated, we can take two steps forward! As you hang out with me here and learn about these practices, go ahead and take one more step forward toward financial freedom!

HOW IS YOUR FICO SCORE CALCULATED?

Back in my day (yes, I'm aware I sound like a boomer right now), your FICO was an elusive number that you would only ever get to see if you were denied credit. That's when you'd get that letter in the mail telling you that you were eligible for a free credit report since you were not approved. You now get to see the details on your report that are:

1. Preventing you from getting approved.

2. Keeping your credit score lower than you want it to be.

By law, even if you were not denied credit, you were eligible for a free credit report every twelve months. When the pandemic hit the three bureaus announced they would temporarily make credit reports readily available for free every week on annualcreditreport.com through the end of 2022.

But what exactly does your credit score have to do with your credit report? Your credit report does not include your credit score; however, it will detail the ins and outs of how your credit score was calculated. Your credit report is regularly updated with the latest financial information that can potentially cause your credit score to increase or decrease. It is imperative that you check your credit report consistently to make sure that the information collected is accurate. When information is documented incorrectly this tends to mean your report is mixed up with someone else's or you've been a victim of identity theft.

When you consistently check your report, you can catch errors way earlier that may negatively impact your credit score. The last thing you want is to learn of credit reporting errors when you're trying to open a new line of credit. Your credit report should be indicative of your financial habits and accounts. Those financial habits and accounts are key players in how your credit score is calculated.

The easiest way to think about your credit score is to think of it as a pie. Whether you go mathematical and think pie graph or go straight foodie and think pumpkin pie, your credit score will be calculated into the same five slices: payment history, amount of debt owed, length of credit history, new credit, and credit mix. Each piece is weighed differently and will require varying levels of time and effort.

CREDIT SCORE COMPONENTS

PAYMENT HISTORY (35 PERCENT)

The payment history component of your credit score is weighted the heaviest out of all five categories. Thirty-five percent of your credit score is based on how often you pay your debts on time. You want to do your best to pay your debts on time because even missing one payment can have a large impact on your overall score.

AMOUNT OF DEBT OWED (30 PERCENT)

Thirty percent of your credit score is based on the total amount of credit and loans you're using compared to the total credit limit you have. You will often hear people refer to this as your credit utilization. The rule of thumb is to keep your credit utilization below 30 percent, but the lower your utilization is, the better.

Simply put, keeping your utilization low lets creditors know you are using the credit you already have responsibly, therefore giving you better leverage for approval when you apply for more credit. You can determine your credit utilization by using the following ratio: your credit card balances/your credit card limits x 100 (e.g.: $5,000 balance/$10,000 limit x 100 = 50 percent utilization).

Your utilization information is usually updated every thirty to forty-five days on your credit report, so besides paying off your credit card balances to avoid interest, it will also prevent you from taking a negative ding to your credit score.

LENGTH OF CREDIT HISTORY (15 PERCENT)

This can be a tricky and annoying category for several reasons. First, if you are young, it is difficult to score well here because you simply don't have time on your side yet. Throughout my twenties this was always the weakest component of my credit score because there was no way for me to have over twenty years of credit history at twenty-three.

Another annoying factor that impacts this category is closing any accounts. I know people scream out, "Don't close any accounts," but sometimes, you don't have a choice. If you pay off your car or your student loans, those accounts automatically close. If those are your oldest line of credit (mine was my student loans) then you'll likely see a dip in your score, even if you're doing everything right.

Don't be discouraged, and don't think about keeping debt to appease this category. Remember: 65 percent of your score is made up of paying your debts on time and utilizing minimal amounts of credit in general. Remember I said each category requires different levels of your effort; this is one of them. As time progresses, your length of credit history will grow.

NEW CREDIT (10 PERCENT)

Have you heard that you shouldn't open too many accounts at one time? This is why. Ten percent of your credit score is impacted by how often you open new accounts. If you apply for credit and you're approved, you will likely have experienced a hard inquiry. This is not to be confused with when you check your credit score or credit report. Those are soft inquiries.

A hard inquiry stays on your report and affects your overall credit score for two years. The worst part is that you can have a hard inquiry on your report even when you are not approved or choose not to accept the line of credit. When creditors see too many hard inquiries in a short time, it makes them cautious of offering you a new line of credit.

Be mindful of how many hard inquiries you have on your report, especially if you are hoping to take out major lines of credit for a car or a home.

CREDIT MIX (10 PERCENT)

The last piece of the credit score pie is your credit mix. This category identifies the variety of credit products you have. The more variation you have, the better it will be on your score. This includes credit products such as mortgage loans, credit cards, installment loans, auto loans, and student loans.

Though these five components are straightforward, still, twenty-six million Americans are considered credit invisible because they do not have a credit history. This credit invisibility often marginalizes low-income Black and Hispanic people more than any other population in the country. Experian and FICO have attempted to help rectify this by creating reporting systems that take alternative data into consideration (rent and utility payments).

———

Before we dive into credit cards, because you can't have a chapter on credit without talking about credit cards, let's tackle some of the most common frequently asked questions about credit scores. Bookmark this page as your ultimate quick-hit credit score resource.

CREDIT SCORE FAQS

Q: I closed an account and my credit score dropped; why did this happen?

A: You've paid off an account, closed it, *boom*! You did the responsible adult thing you're expected to do. Then why did your credit score drop? This has happened for two reasons:

1. You closed an account that was one of your oldest existing accounts. This impacts the "length of credit history" category that weighs in on 15 percent of your overall score.

2. The second factor that may have caused your credit score to drop is you have decreased your total amount of available credit. For example, if you closed a credit card that had a $10,000 limit, you now have $10,000 less in available credit. This impacts your credit utilization, which factors into 30 percent of your overall credit score.

Instead of thinking you've done something wrong, continue to make the payments on your remaining bills/debt on time. Keep your utilization as low as you can (remember utilization is calculated every thirty to forty-five days). Your score will continue to benefit positively from these two large factors, and you will move the needle back toward the higher score you're aiming for.

Q: What is the highest and lowest credit score I can get?

A: The typical range for your FICO and Vantage score is 300 to 850. The ratings that you see go to 900 and up include older credit score models or alternative scores. It is unlikely that you'll run into these scores often, and it is even more unlikely that these models will be used to determine whether you are approved for a new line of credit. For most of your credit needs, you'll stick to the FICO range of 300–850.

Q: What is considered a good or bad credit score?

A: The credit score range is often broken down even further to help lenders determine what types of rates to offer consumers. Typically, anything about a 670 is considered "good credit." FICO identifies this determination like this:

- **Poor:** 300–579
- **Fair:** 580–669

- **Good:** 670–739
- **Very Good:** 740–799
- **Excellent:** 800+

Q: Can I pay someone to fix my credit for me?

A: You absolutely do *not* need to pay anyone to fix your credit. In fact, I strongly recommend you don't. Many "credit repair" businesses are scammers looking to make a quick buck off people in a vulnerable state. No one can remove negative information from your credit report. There are also many credit repair companies that suggest many illegal practices like using an EIN instead of your social security number.

Don't do it! Not only is it illegal, but it is not actually fixing anything on your credit report.

Q: How many times can I check my credit report, and will it bring down my score?

A: You can request a copy of your credit report from each major credit reporting bureau (Equifax, Experian, and TransUnion) for free once a year by heading to AnnualCreditReport.com or calling 1-877-322-8228. Checking your credit report does not cause an inquiry so it will not affect your credit score.

Q: How do I dispute errors on my credit report?

A: If you get a copy of your credit report and notice errors, here's what you should do:

1. **First:** You need to start your dispute by contacting the bureau that the error reported came from. You can contact via phone, email, or snail mail. All three bureaus now accept digital disputes, so that is the fastest route to take. No matter the method of communication you choose you're going to need to explain what is specifically wrong and include copies of documentation that support your claim.

2. **Second:** You'll also want to contact the organization that has reported your information incorrectly to the bureaus. They must also update and correct the inaccurate information under the Fair Credit Reporting Act.

You can expect updates to your report to usually take thirty to forty-five days after the investigation has been completed.

Q: How long does negative information stay on my credit report?

A: On average, negative reports like delinquencies, foreclosures, late payments, and past-due accounts take about seven years to "fall off" or be removed. It can be longer or shorter, depending on the circumstance, but most will last for at least seven years. An important tip to remember: The older the negative information is, the less of an impact it'll have on your score. So, you may see that the negative info is still popping up on your report, but after years pass it will not impact your score as much as it did when it first happened.

Besides typical judgments, lawsuits and some bankruptcies can stay on your report for up to a decade.

Q: What happens to my credit score if I file for bankruptcy?

A: Whew, this one is loaded! Bankruptcy has a significant impact on your credit score—no ifs, ands, or buts about it. There is no one-step formula to calculate the impact of bankruptcy on your score because of all the potential variables. For instance, if you have a 700 credit score, you stand to lose more points (usually 200) than if you have a credit score of 500 (usually 130–150). No matter what, you will lose a substantial amount of points and will typically end up with poor credit upon filing. Different types of bankruptcies will also have different impacts.

Chapter 13 bankruptcy remains on your credit report for seven years and has less of an impact than other forms of bankruptcy. Chapters 7, 11, and 12 remain on your report for ten years because you don't usually have to make any repayments; therefore you are viewed as a bigger credit risk to lenders.

Q: Whoa…what other things can negatively impact my credit score?

A: Late payments, too many hard inquiries on your credit report, high credit utilization, poor credit history, and even divorcing your partner can impact your score. Just think of it this way—most financial decisions you make can either positively or negatively impact your credit score.

Q: What is the difference between a hard inquiry and a soft inquiry?

A: When applying for a new line of credit, the potential creditor will make an inquiry to request a copy of your credit report. You can think of these inquiries as a financial background check. There are two types:

1. **Hard inquiries** will include checking in on your credit to open a new line of credit. For example, you would receive a hard inquiry if you were looking to obtain a mortgage, car loan, or personal loan. Each time a creditor makes an inquiry (also called a hard pull), that will show up on your credit report as well. Hard inquiries will stay listed on your credit report for two years, and each inquiry will impact your credit score. The only exception to this is if you are "credit shopping" and looking for the best rate before accepting an offer. So, if you're looking for a new car and visit multiple dealers or looking to buy a home and visit multiple banks, these will all show up as a single inquiry if they occur within a similar time frame.

2. **Soft inquiries** are moreso a quick inquiry into your credit history usually used for pre-approval purposes. Inquiries from your employer, lenders you already have an account with, or inquiries made by you are considered soft inquiries and will not impact your credit score.

Q: Is my FICO score different from my credit score?

A: Not all credit scores are FICO scores. Usually, the score most people are referring to when they talk about credit is the FICO score. In fact, 90 percent of lenders use the FICO score to make their credit approval decisions. That means most of the time, when you're applying for credit, they are looking at your FICO score.

Q: Should I open multiple credit cards to improve my credit score?

A: This is what we call a one-step-forward, one-step-back kind of situation. Having multiple credit cards gives you a larger total credit line. If you keep your overall utilization low, this will have a positive impact on your score. Opening multiple credit cards, especially in a short period of time, will lead to hard inquiries that will negatively impact your score.

If you are already thinking about opening a new line of credit because you need it or to capitalize on points and other benefits, go for it. The two *biggest* things to remember and focus on when you are trying to move the needle toward the 800+ club are to pay your bills/debts on time every month (remember that counts for 35 percent) and to keep your utilization low on your current lines of credit.

Q: How can I build credit if I don't have any credit history?

A: Ahh...tale as old as time. You're expected to have something without ever actually having it! If you've ever been in the market for a job, you know this paradox all too well. Thankfully, if you're just getting started with credit, or you're rebuilding your score, there are a few things you can do.

Here are three action steps you can take to help get you started.

1. **Get a secured credit card:** A secured credit card is different from a traditional credit card and is usually easier to qualify for if you have poor credit or no credit history at all. A traditional credit card offers you a line of credit with a limit and you can make purchases up to that limit. With a secured credit card, you put down a deposit and that deposit becomes your spending limit. There are many pros to obtaining a secured credit card on your credit-building journey.

   One major pro is most financial services won't do a credit check if you are opening a secured credit card, so you get the chance to build your credit without starting with a hard inquiry. With every purchase and payment, you are building credit simply by replenishing your initial deposit. Many credit card companies have now started transitioning their users from secured to unsecured credit cards after they exhibit responsible behaviors for a certain period of time.

   The main complaint that secured credit cards get is the minimum deposit. However, as the times evolve, so do benefits, rewards, and minimum requirements. Secured credit cards offer many similar perks (and cons, a.k.a. interest) to traditional credit cards such as cash back, sign-on rewards, and low deposit minimums. You can now find companies requiring minimums between $49 and $500. Just keep in mind that your initial deposit will become your credit limit.

2. **Earn credit history credit for paying your bills:** As mentioned earlier in this chapter, FICO and Experian offer two similar services that allow you to build your credit simply by paying your utilities, cell phone, rent, and streaming services. You would sign up for these services and connect the bank account you use to make these payments. *Voila!* You're building credit.

3. **Become an authorized user:** This is what my best friend in high school was, and I had no idea! I thought she was simply running up her mom's card and would be facing the *chancleta* when she got home. Because she was an active authorized user, she was building credit history on her mother's coattails.

   Ask a friend or family member that you trust to add you as an authorized user. It's important that whoever you ask also has good credit and responsible credit practices. The last thing you want is for your credit score to tank before you've gotten a steady footing on this whole credit-score thing in the first place. Both parties involved in this must exhibit good healthy credit practices for the arrangement to work best.

MANAGING CREDIT CARDS LIKE A PRO

If you are trying to improve your credit score, credit cards can be a great tool—not the *only* tool, but a great tool to do so. This is only the case if you know how to manage them properly. Here are three tips to help you manage your credit card like a pro and maximize your reward benefits.

I now have four credit cards and use them to pay for just about everything I can. Two of those cards I opened in 2022, one in 2015, and my ride-or-die first credit card has been active since 2008. Besides the student loans, which I paid off in 2018, my first credit card is my oldest line of credit. And for a long while it was the only active line of credit I had that didn't have a direct debt attached to it.

Throughout my twenties, I gained a severe allergy to adulting and everything that came along with it...including bills. I juggled my monthly bills and one revolving credit card. Anything I charged to the card, no matter how big or small, I made sure to pay it off in full to avoid receiving a bill. I didn't want another company asking me for a monthly payment. At the time I didn't know this was considered a healthy financial habit; I knew it prevented me from getting a bill or charged interest.

TIP ONE: PAY OFF YOUR CREDIT CARD BILL EVERY CYCLE

I know I know this is not a groundbreaking tip, but it is a crucial one for two major reasons. The first reason of course is to avoid paying interest on your purchases. One of my biggest pet peeves with myself is charging an item, paying "X" amount of interest on said item, and hating that item in four weeks. The real pain in the situation isn't that I hate what I bought; buyer's remorse happens all the time. The real pain is paying more than the item cost.

Besides avoiding interest, by paying off your credit card bill every cycle, your payment history data will flourish while your credit utilization remains low. FICO has released that "high score achievers (people with credit scores between 800–850) only utilize 4 percent to 5 percent of their credit card limits."

But What If I'm Struggling to Pay Off These Credit Cards?

I thought you'd never ask! If you currently have credit card debt, the next chapter about debt is written for you. But I've got a few quick hits for you here:

1. Pay more than the minimum, even if it is just a few extra dollars. I mean it! Start slow and increase the amounts as you can. If your minimum credit card bill is twenty-five dollars, even adding an extra five dollars makes a difference. Create wiggle room in your budget to pay a little more so you decrease the amount of time it will take you to pay it off completely.

2. Choose to debt snowball or debt avalanche. You know yourself best! Decide whether you want to tackle your smallest debts first (debt snowball) or your debts with the highest interest rates (debt avalanche). Each method has its pros and cons, which we'll dive further into in Chapter 4.

3. Last tip: automate as much as you can! Remember when we spoke about financial habits and routines in Chapter 2? You want to automate your debt payments so:

   a. You don't have to think about it.

   b. You won't miss any deadlines.

   c. It makes life easier!

What If I Don't Have Credit Card Debt and Need to Make a Really Big Purchase?

Is it weird that I'm typing out your present thoughts from the past? Is that meta? Are we in the matrix? Either way that leads us to tip two.

TIP TWO: PLAN ACCORDINGLY FOR LARGE PURCHASES

I love making big purchases on credit cards because I love collecting rewards points. I am the credit card rewards master. I leave no benefit and membership perk unturned, especially if the card has an annual fee. You got to earn your keep, AmEx! But, the magic behind maximizing credit card points and making large purchases without paying interest all lies within *the plan*.

There are two ways you can plan to put a large purchase on your credit card. The first way is to use that almighty powerful sinking fund I love talking about so much. If you know you've got your eyes on a shiny new big-ticket item, start mapping out your savings plan now. How much is the item going to cost? Include that tax and any other fees associated with the purchase as well. Don't be like me with my Sanyo 8100.

Once you know the cost, decide how long it's going to take you to save that amount of money over time. Last decision is to decide where you're going to store that money. Are you going to open a separate savings account (an HYSA would be a great option) or stuff the money in an envelope and hide it under your mattress (0/10 do not recommend)?

Umm...but I Needed to Make This Purchase Like Yesterday.

If you need the big-ticket item a lot sooner and you can't go the sinking fund route, there is another viable option for you, but it comes with caveats. You can apply for a card with a 0 percent APR promotional period that will allow you to make your big purchase and pay over time without paying interest. It is important to note that if you choose to go that route, you're going to have a hard inquiry that dings your credit score. You also want to be cognizant of the credit limit they offer you with this card. Yes, you will have more available credit, which looks great through the credit utilization lens. However, if you're offered a card with a $5,000 limit, and your item costs $4,999, that will negatively impact your utilization.

I Actually Didn't Even Wait to Read This Chapter; I Already Made the Purchase on My Credit Card and I'm Kind of Drowning Right Now. Help!

No problem; another option (we're all about options here) is to still follow through using the advice in the aforementioned paragraph. This time you wouldn't be looking for a credit card with a 0 percent APR; instead you'd be looking for financial institutions that offer 0 percent APR and a $0 balance transfer fee. Even better if that comes with no annual fee at all. This way you can transfer the big-ticket item purchase to your new account and pay as you go without paying any interest.

I Can't Qualify for Any New Lines of Credit!

If you've exhausted the other options, I still got you! See Tip One and head to Chapter 4 for more details on credit card debt and repayment strategies.

TIP THREE: SPEND WITH PURPOSE

At the top of 2015, I was in the market for a new laptop and started toying around with the idea of traveling a little more. Which, of course, wouldn't be too hard since I wasn't traveling at all. When you're taking vacations to your parents' sidewalk, there's no place to go but up.

I spent time researching which credit cards met my three stipulations:

1. No annual fee.

2. Focused on leveraging points for travel.

3. Had 0 percent intro APR for twelve months.

I did not have the money to pay for the laptop upfront and my 2009 MacBook Pro was on its last leg. I needed a laptop quickly, so the sinking fund route was also out.

The twelve-month 0 percent APR sign-on bonus gave me the ability to buy the laptop with ample time to update my budget to incorporate monthly payments over the next six months. This way I gave myself wiggle room if I needed to extend beyond six months and wouldn't have to pay interest. Besides the 0 percent APR, I would also earn 50,000 bonus points if I spent $3,000 in the first three months. A task that would prove to be easy AF since my new laptop cost me about $1,500. I was already halfway through the goal on my first swipe.

Over the next few months, I charged all my purchases to that credit card and paid my monthly budgeted laptop payment as well as any new charges.

By June 2015 I paid off the laptop and booked my first flight to California using the points I earned from the card. Since then I have used the points I've earned on the same card to book flights to Phoenix, Toronto, Cuba, Mexico, and most recently, Colombia.

Here's the tea on how I did it: I spent intentionally. There was a purpose behind every swipe, and the purpose was never about going out of my way to earn points. Chasing after credit card rewards points often leads to overspending, which is exactly what credit card companies want you to do. A 2018 NerdWallet study shows that one-third of cardholders surveyed said they often overspend to earn rewards.

Spending with purpose not only helps prevent overspending but will also help minimize negative impacts on your credit score and decrease the amount of interest you pay in the long run. Think of it this way: earning 50,000 points (about a $500 flight) after spending $3,000 in three months that you were already going to spend is a win. That flight is going to feel amazing because it's the cherry on top of all your hard work. Spending an extra $3,000 you did not intend to or budget for to earn the equivalent of a $500 flight doesn't feel as magical. Especially if it causes you financial stress.

So I leave you here armed with the tools you need for success and a few motivating words: may your skin glow, may your credit score grow, and don't ever apply for a credit card with a man. Sincerely, my mom.

CHAPTER 4

MY DEBT IS UP, AND I'M STUCK

In 2020, *Good Morning America* ran a feature story about my student-loan-debt-payoff journey. This was my first major publication, so I was beyond excited. The feature went live on their website and all connected social platforms. My friends and family were so proud and gushed about me on the interwebs the entire day. As a "words of affirmation" love language girlie, I was on cloud nine. For twelve or so hours I was in a whirlwind of nonstop calls, emails, texts, and, yes...teaching. I was still a full-time teacher in the middle of an argumentative essay unit with my ninth graders.

I did not get a chance to bask in the reality that *my* debt story was featured in one of the largest media publications in the country until later that night. After adulting the entire day away, I turned on my laptop with a celebratory slice of pizza in hand and read the article about me. It was *perfect* except for one spot where they stated I was making $96,000 a year. At the time of the interview in December 2019, I was making $96,000. That wasn't what I was making while paying off my student loans. No big deal; people will obviously know that since the article talks about my career as an educator. Educators don't usually make $96,000 at the start of their careers. This common sense won't be an issue...right? *Wrong!*

I made the *one* mistake all content creators tell you not to make: I read the comments. Not only did I read them, I read them on Twitter, the platform you use when you want to talk as much reckless shit as you see fit with no filter and no chill whatsoever. That is when I decided to indulge in masochistic behavior.

"This is a perfect example of someone working hard and getting it done. F—k student loan forgiveness. If she can do it anyone can #MAGA"

Whoa...okay...maybe that's just a one-off. Let me continue to scroll.

"Too bad if the libs get their way, she'll have to pay everyone's loans off too. #VOTERED"

Um…WTF is going on in these comments? Let me keep scrolling; maybe these are just outliers.

"Yeah of course she paid off her loans. She lived at home and made almost $100,000 a year. Show me this with someone living a realistic life."

Wait…*what?* The very part of the article I feared would be misconstrued played the ultimate role in a slew of misinterpretations. The response to my story shocked me, and for the first and *only* time, though I had no real reason to be, I was embarrassed by my accomplishment. That same *Good Morning America* feature was publicly reshared again in August 2022 after the Joe Biden administration announced the student loan forgiveness plan. I didn't bother to tell my friends or family when I found out the post was reshared. In fact, I cringed at the dinner table when the link to the Facebook post popped up in my text box. My curiosity got the better of me. I clicked the link even though I knew I would regret it. *Surprise!* I did.

This time around the comment section was worse, which is not surprising, given it had two years of frustrated pandemic-induced vitriol serving as fuel. I was called everything but a child of God in those comments, and it was disheartening AF. However, this time around I didn't feel ashamed or embarrassed. You want to know why?

You. During the 2.5 years between the initial publication and the most recent release, *Millennial in Debt* grew drastically. You and I found each other. You and 200,000 other future millionaires (you know that's what I call y'all) found your way into my little corner of the internet and it's been the pleasure of my life supporting your personal finance journey. I tell you and the rest of the fam constantly: your personal finance journey is not linear, and your financial circumstances are nothing to be ashamed of. To feel ashamed of my debt story because some trolls on Facebook or Twitter have misconstrued assumptions about me would be doing myself and my platform a huge disservice.

So here's a reminder for both of us: your personal finance journey is *yours*. It does not have to look, sound, or feel like anyone else's. You are doing the best you can and there is nothing to be ashamed of.

I paid off $102,000 in student loan debt on a teacher's salary. I am a part of the 24 percent of the population that has achieved this accomplishment. Some parts of this story you're already familiar with, so I'll speed through those. We'll spend more time diving further into the other juicy parts just like the plotline of a good telenovela.

As a first-generation Haitian American, it was crucial to get all the adulting steps right on the first try. Instead of focusing on the affordability that CUNY and SUNY schools would offer, I focused on the prestige that a four-year private school would ensure. I wish anyone, literally *anyone,* had told me none of that would matter in the greater scheme of things. It's easy to get wrapped up in the look of it all, so if you ever find yourself trying to decide between affordability and appearance, here's your friendly gentle reminder: choose affordability every damn time.

With a slightly more developed brain than I had at seventeen, my current thirty-four-year-old self often thinks about the criteria I used to choose the college I attended. Honestly and truly, I couldn't tell you what type of prestige I thought I was going to get from a school in Long Island, New York. Though I loved my time there, Adelphi University wasn't exactly turning any heads. But, at $800 a credit (currently now $1,275 a credit) it surely cost me $50,000 in student loan debt to graduate.

When I graduated in 2010, I already unknowingly possessed more than $50,000 in student loan debt. Being financially illiterate is not only dangerous but also costly. The government felt I was responsible enough to sign up for $50,000 in student loans but not responsible enough to buy alcohol. At that time, all I was concerned with was paying tuition on time so I could register for classes. Another first-generation trauma bonding moment: you must be solution-oriented because you never want to embarrass the parentals. This was 100 percent self-imposed pressure, but my first gen people will tell you the pressure is *real*!

I couldn't make any mistakes that could potentially curtail my graduation. I didn't want to be locked out of the classes I needed to take because graduating was and always had been the imperative goal. For me, and for many, those student loans were a means to an end, so I signed those promissory notes without ever reading a single word. Aht aht...before you judge, think about all the terms and conditions you have agreed to without ever reading. We're all guilty...except for Erica on TikTok who reads all the terms and conditions for us, so we don't have to! Okay...now you can judge me.

It didn't matter what the promissory notes said because I knew no matter what I'd still need to take the loan to continue my education. There was no other way. This is often the reality for many people of color, especially Black people. In fact, a 2020 Student Loan Hero study found that Black families borrow student loans at higher rates than other races. Thirty percent of Black families hold student loan debt compared to 20.4 percent of white families and 14.3 percent of Hispanic families. Black families are not only borrowing at higher rates, but they also are borrowing larger amounts, with a median of $30,000, compared with $23,000 and $17,600 among their white and Hispanic counterparts.

The loans were a means to an end, and nothing in the promissory note would change that simple fact. However, it still would have been wise to read it, you know, for educational purposes I didn't realize I truly needed. I didn't know the difference between federal and private loans, had no idea what variable interest was, and couldn't tell you what subsidized or unsubsidized loans were if my life depended on it. You, however, don't have to worry about that. The personal finance glossary at the back of this book has got you covered for all of your student loan terminology needs.

Reading the promissory note, I would have known that my federal unsubsidized loans were gaining interest the minute the funds were released to the university. I also would have known that my private student loans could be sold at a moment's notice and operated at a variable interest rate. This is how I wound up with student loans that started at 7 percent interest with Citibank and ended up at 16 percent interest with Navient. Imagine my surprise when I realized my student loan debt was gaining more interest than my credit cards that hovered around 9 to 14 percent APR.

For three years after graduation, I blindly paid the smallest amount toward my student loan debt because the alternative was unfathomable. It never occurred to me to check my balances because I never missed a single payment. That's how math works, right? You pay for something consistently and over time the balance decreases to zero. Every year I filed taxes and saw I paid around $6,000 in interest. I was content because I thought that meant I'd be looking at a balance that was $18,000 less than where I started. Right?

By now you know my thinking was flawed and I was hella *wrong*! By 2013, after three years of payments my balance had grown immensely. This realization was the catalyst. My financial awakening, so to speak. Did I do everything right after that moment? *No!* First, I'm a firm believer that the concept of "right" and "wrong" is not as cut and dry as people think it is. Is murder wrong? Yes, duh! Is buying Starbucks or eating out when you have debt wrong? *Some* people think it is; I aggressively disagree. Secondly, no one does everything "right" with their money all the time. The birthday dinner where I spent $110 on a Caesar salad makes that more evident.

So, what did I do when I saw my debt ballooning? My typical go-to response, of course: I cried. Through the many, many, *many* tears shed, I also started to map out my game plan. Though the plan went through several iterations and adjustments, the original roadmap's directives held solid through the next five years of my debt-payoff journey. Listen closely because I'm about to drop the gems in 3, 2, 1...leggo.

STUDENT LOANS SUCK

...I NEED TO PAY THEM OFF

Duh! What else would I title this section of the book? As of 2022, the US student loan debt totals $1.75 trillion. That's trillion with a big fat capital *T*. A student loan at its very core is intended to represent a significant financial lifeline that provides access to higher education. This access in turn idyllically creates opportunities for greater career growth and financial independence. That is the ideal outcome.

However, the rising costs of higher education coupled with the predatory nature of student loan practices have burdened generations with consistent financial strain. Research analyst Melanie Hanson reports the average student loan debt has increased for all generations by 18 percent. With the median salary hovering around $54,000 a year, it is no surprise that ballooning average student loan debt makes most basic adult rites of passage, like home ownership, feel unattainable.

It is hard to consistently remember that your current debt situation is not your permanent financial situation. The best way to start your journey forward: call up good ol' Sallie Mae.

STEP ONE: CALL YOUR LOAN PROVIDER AND ASK AS MANY QUESTIONS AS YOU NEED TO

Our first instinct when it comes to communicating with our creditors is to run. Let me stop you right there, road runner: do *not* run! When you avoid your loan providers you are basically giving them the green light to do whatever they want. You are backing yourself into a corner and stripping yourself of your choices.

Lean into your power by making that first call.

After blowing my snot-filled face dry, my next step was to contact my loan providers so they could explain my options. Do not be ashamed to have them explain terms and conditions to you like you are five years old. The verbiage is intentionally confusing, so consumers don't know where to begin when it comes to asking clarifying questions. If there's something that isn't making sense, tell them to *make* it make sense!

My first question: how could someone pay their bill on time every month for three years and have a higher balance? I was informed that I was on an interest-only repayment plan and my monthly payments did not cover the additional monthly interest. None of my payments in the last three years were directed toward the principal. I was distraught. This felt like it should be illegal, and I high key feel still feel this way today.

That first phone call gave me all the information I needed to make an informed practical decision about my student debt repayment journey. I opted for a graduated repayment plan since I did not qualify for any income-driven repayment options. If I did not make that first call that interest-only repayment plan would have cost me well over $200,000 throughout the life of my loans. Make the call.

STEP TWO: CREATE A THREE-STEP PRACTICAL PLAN

By this point you know I'm a fan of simple yet effective game plans. Use the information your lender has provided as the stepping stone for your three-step plan. You don't need to over-complicate the structure because chances are you will have to adapt this plan as your life circumstances evolve.

Here's a look at how I set up mine:

THREE-STEP ACTION PLAN	HOW/WHY AM I TAKING THIS STEP?
1. Switch to a graduated repayment plan	**Why:** My loan payments will increase every two years so I have time to prepare to manage a larger payment. More of my monthly payments will be directed toward the principal. **How:** Call my loan provider to switch from an interest-only repayment plan to a graduated repayment plan.
2. Choose one loan to pay off + create a sinking fund	**Why:** As explained by the loan provider, the graduated repayment plan is set to a thirty-year repayment schedule. I don't want to take thirty years to pay my loans. So, I will tackle one loan per year to save on interest and pay them off sooner. **How:** I will choose the loan to pay off based on the interest rate (debt avalanche method). Whatever that amount is I will add more to the total to cover the interest. Then I'll work backward by creating a sinking fund specifically to use in December. I will add a specific amount to my sinking fund monthly. Side hustling extra income to meet my saving goal is key! This way I'll continue making my normal monthly payments and pay my other bills on time with my teacher income.

3. Pay off the loan at the end of each year and repeat	**Why:** By paying off a loan in its entirety at the end of the year I am closing the account, bringing down my total loan balance, and motivating myself to keep going. The finish line is in sight.
	How: I will use the money I put into the sinking fund to make one lump sum payment. This is a cause for celebration! Be sure to pay the "payoff amount" so you don't have any remaining balances.

Yes, that is how I write to myself, and yes, this is how simple your plan can be. The plan does not need bells and whistles. The plan just needs to be planned to prepare for execution.

STEP THREE: FOLLOW THROUGH. EASIER SAID THAN DONE FOR SURE, BUT THIS IS YOUR PERSONAL FINANCE JOURNEY

It can and will go through several iterations but at the end of the day, you're in charge of the process and procedure. Your step one will undoubtedly look different from someone else's, but the common denominator in all of this is that you must take action. Hoping, wishing, and dreaming about debt freedom isn't going to get the job done. Your ability to follow through on your plan will. Take step one.

...BUT I NEED THEM. WHAT SHOULD I KNOW?

PRIVATE VS. FEDERAL STUDENT LOANS

Many people who were unclear whether they had private or federal student loans found out pretty quickly when Miss Rona hit the scene. Federal student loan repayments were paused in March 2020, and will likely remain paused through August 2023. People who held private student loans did not benefit from this forty-one-month payment pause. They also were not eligible for the pause on interest accrual, which is often the silent but deadly culprit that leads to predatory extended repayment schedules.

It's important to understand that federal student loans follow guidelines laid out by the federal government, while private student loans follow a much different set of rules. Often when you hear politicians discuss student loan forgiveness policies, they are usually only referring to federal student loans. This is because private student loan companies aren't funded or controlled by the government, outside of the basic stipulations aligned with financial institutions. Think of it this way: taking a student loan from a private company is similar (with a few regulatory differences) to taking out a personal or automobile loan.

Elizabeth Warren was one of the few politicians during the 2020 electoral race that focused on the full scope of a borrower's circumstance, which often encompasses both federal and private student loans. This is why when good old Joey B popped up in the third quarter with his rendition of loan forgiveness (*better late than never, I suppose*), lawsuits were quickly drawn, triggering a massive reversal that went on to exclude 700,000 previously eligible people from receiving loan forgiveness.

If you are one of those people, I am truly so sorry. You very much have every right to scream out *why me!* And as you do...I'll explain why.

What's the Difference?

The first quick, simple clarifier you need to know about federal versus private student loans is how they are funded. This is where all the stickiness around loan forgiveness starts, but certainly not where it ends. Federal student loans are funded by the federal government, whereas private student loans are funded by a lender such as a school, credit union, or bank.

Federal loans are often referenced in one of four ways:

1. **Direct Subsidized Loans:** no interest is added while you're in school

2. **Direct Unsubsidized Loans:** interest is added once the loan is dispersed

3. **Direct PLUS Loans:** for graduate and professional students

4. Direct Parent PLUS Loans: loans taken out by a parent

Anything else you see on your list of loans is a **private student loan.**

If we had to choose between the lesser of two evils, a federal student loan is the better option for funding your education. That is because the terms and conditions are set by law and include benefits such as income-driven repayment plans, fixed interest rates, and student loan forgiveness. My federal student loans were capped below 7 percent interest while my private student loans were hitting double digits consistently. After working as a teacher in a Title I school for five years, I was eligible for five thousand dollars in loan forgiveness. That money was automatically deducted from a federal student loan balance, even though my main priority was paying down my higher-interest debt. For my educators and anybody else working in the public sector, the PSLF (public service loan forgiveness) program—yep, you guessed correctly—is only for federal loans.

My private loans were not eligible for any sort of forgiveness. There is no doubt in my mind that taking private loans was the more expensive route to fund my education.

Besides several repayment options, interest rate regulation, and loan forgiveness, which are three major factors in your student loan repayment process, private loans also do not offer the same protections or regulations when it comes to consolidation, postponement, and prepayment penalties. You cannot consolidate your private loans into a direct consolidation loan.

As the name would suggest, a direct consolidation loan allows you to consolidate multiple federal student loans into one loan. Long story short, they help the chaotic nature of student loan payments become just a little less chaotic.

Private loans also do not offer the same level of consistency across the board. Since each company makes its own rules, it is comparable to the Wild West. If you're having trouble paying back your student loans, you would have to check with your lender(s) to see what your options *could* be. If you have more than one provider, which does happen occasionally, you could be faced with two different outcomes addressing your singular overarching issue. As for-profit companies, private loan lenders do not have your best interests at heart; they have their profits in mind.

And this is what caused the student loan forgiveness reversal heard around the world. Okay…maybe not around the world since the lack of affordable higher education is very much a United States vibe. But the student loan forgiveness reversal that went on to exclude 770,000 previously eligible candidates fell through a skeevy federal loan loophole.

Borrowers with FFEL loans (Federal Family Education Loans) or Perkins loans were originally eligible for student loan forgiveness under the student loan forgiveness plan's initial release. A few weeks later, that was no longer the case. This is because although FFEL and Perkins loans were guaranteed by the government, they were issued and managed by private lenders. Those private lenders were not about to give up the profit they were set to gain off the backs of 770,000 people, and so…they filed a lawsuit. Both the FFEL and Perkins loans are no longer administered by the federal government, and it is a shame that those that have them fell through the cracks.

I know at this point you're probably thinking, *Okay, Melissa, I get it; private student loans are the worst. Enough already!* Trust me, I'm getting frustrated all over again simply informing you of the super sneaky snake shit (how's that for alliteration?) that is rooted in private student loan lending practices. Just take the many, many lawsuits that have been filed against big box lenders like Navient as exhibit A if you will.

So if private student loans are so bad, why did I take them? Why subject myself to lackluster financial benefits in the long run? Why would anyone choose to do this? Besides the obvious I-didn't-know-better, so-I-couldn't-do-better response, there was no alternative.

Federal student loans have limitations that can often leave students with a gap between what they need and what they are offered in their financial aid package. The annual academic loan limits depend on your year in school and your dependency status. Because of these factors the loan amount you're eligible to receive each academic year could potentially be less than the federally regulated annual loan limit. You do not get to choose how much you receive in federal aid, whereas with private student loans you can borrow the exact amount that you need. As per the Department of Education, the 2022 loan limits are as follows:

- If you're an undergraduate, the maximum combined amount of Direct Subsidized and Direct Unsubsidized Loans you can borrow each academic year is between $5,500 and $12,500, depending on your year in school and your dependency status.

- If you're a graduate/professional student, you can borrow up to $20,500 in Direct Unsubsidized Loans each academic year.

At about $1.620 trillion, federal student loans account for 92.7 percent of outstanding student loan debt. Private student loans constitute 8.4 percent of the nation's outstanding student loan debt, with 13 percent of students using them to fill their financial aid gap. What does that 8.4 percent equate to in dollars? One hundred forty billion and growing. That's $140 billion borrowed from financial institutions that not only continued to collect payments but also did so while charging variable interest during the pandemic.

OKAY, SO HOW DO I MANAGE MY STUDENT LOANS ONCE I'VE TAKEN THEM?

I used my student loan "refund check" to go shopping. Don't do that. Award-winning debt expert Nika Booth, speaker, personal finance content creator, and founder of *Debt Free Gonnabe* seconds that sentiment. Student loans are often vital for students to gain access to higher education. That's a fact we know; however, they oftentimes lie somewhere between predatory and confusing to most. Not for you though, because you've got me. Well, me and Nika, who specializes in teaching women how to better manage their money and pay off debt. During her stint in school, she made the same mistake I made and so many do. The all-too-alluring "refund check"...it ain't free money, y'all. Nika states, "One of my biggest mistakes with my student loans was taking on more student loan debt than I needed. I would accept the max amount of aid every single semester, year after year for more than I actually needed. I mismanaged those extra funds."

Instead, the better alternative to try out, "Take out only what you need to go to school and make sure to exhaust searching for grants and scholarships to minimize the amount of loans you take. There are a lot of scholarship and grant opportunities out there and unfortunately millions of dollars of these funds go unclaimed every year."

WHAT'S THE BOTTOM LINE HERE—WHY TALK ABOUT STUDENT LOANS SO MUCH?

I'm glad you asked. Discussing the true nature and impact of student loans is necessary, despite the unpleasantness of it. Why? That is because discussion leads to action, and my intention here with you today is to expand the student loan conversation into areas that are often overlooked or ignored. The conversation around student loan debt often does not touch upon the unethical, predatory practices and how they impact marginalized populations.

When you discuss student loans with anyone who has them, it will come as no surprise that most will describe them as immense burdens that lead to an overwhelming amount of lifestyle barriers. The skyrocketing costs of a college education have fueled the growth of student loans over the last two decades. With the average student debt sitting around $30,000 per borrower, the racial dynamics buried deep within these figures should always be a key talking point.

The 2019 Institute on Assets and Social Policy study goes on to reveal the immediate social disparities that predatory student loan practices and policies have caused for people of color. The economic trajectories of Black people are significantly impacted the most, thus further perpetuating the incessant growth of the racial wealth gap.

The mere existence of student loans highlights the inequitable access the cost of higher education creates while student loan repayment shines an even brighter spotlight on the systemic inequities engrained into the parasitical structure itself. With fewer familial resources, employer discrimination, and the all-too-familiar Black tax, people of color, particularly Black people's economic mobility, is often stunted post-graduation. The consequence of these circumstances has led to 33 percent of Hispanic students and 49 percent of Black students defaulting on their student loans. The Heller School for Social Policy and Management reports that 32 percent of first-generation students default within two decades of starting college. Are we starting to connect the dots from our previous credit score chapter? Good! Because I'm not done yet.

Often, we hear that blanket student loan forgiveness would only support the wealthy when the reality of that sentiment is simply false. Who does student loan forgiveness have the likelihood of impacting the most? Black women.

Let's take an in-depth look at the numbers, shall we? At $14.8 million, millennials quantitatively have the most student loans out of any other generation. If that isn't the most "we're all in this together," *High School Musical* shit ever, I don't know what is. However, Gen X currently carries the highest average balance at around $45,095. We millennials...well, we don't even come in second. It is hard to believe, but baby boomers have the second largest amount of average debt at $40,512. Absolutely shocking, as baby boomers are the generation that rallies the hardest *against* student loan forgiveness. Where do millennials fall on the list? Third, at an average balance of $38,877. Pretty interesting fact, but let's peel the stat onion back another layer.

Due to various systemic barriers like the racial wealth gap, it is none other than Black students taking out the most student loans to obtain a bachelor's degree. And what happens after graduating? As per the Federal Reserve, four years after graduating, Black students continue to trail behind their white counterparts with a remaining balance that is twice as large.

While women, in general, hold two-thirds of the outstanding student loan debt in the United States, Black women carry the largest average balance overall. On average, women graduate with almost $22,000 in student debt, compared to the average $18,880 that men hold. Black women, however, carry an average of $44,880, while white, Hispanic, and Asian women respectively carry $40,170, $38,890, and $40,400.

I sat down with Nika Booth to discuss her remarkable six-figure debt-payoff journey and her thoughts on the student loan forgiveness plan under the Biden-Harris administration.

As someone who has earned PSLF (public service loan forgiveness) through the adjusted requirements announced in 2021 (and guiding hundreds of others in the process to do the same), I wanted to hear how student loan forgiveness has impacted Nika's personal finance journey. Nika stated, "I get emotional just answering this question because for so long, I've carried the burden and weight of my student loan debt for most of my adult life. This debt has followed me around every day. It's influenced the way I've felt about myself and how I believed others would view me if they knew exactly how much debt I was in. I've kept it from family, friends, and even from partners in serious relationships."

I'm a firm believer that two things can be true at one time. So yes, blanket student loan forgiveness would benefit those currently making six figures who took out student loans to fund their college career. This is true. It is also so true that student loans disproportionately affect minorities. Marginalized communities' monthly budgets are substantially burdened at a much costlier rate after graduation due to student loan repayment that often causes a delay in significant financial decisions such as saving, investing, or purchasing a home. Three key factors to building generational wealth.

The Institute on Assets and Social Policy revealed, "Within twenty years of starting a college education, the typical white borrower will have almost 95 percent of their balance paid off; the typical Black borrower will still owe 95 percent of their principal balance in the same time frame." It is clear which demographics would benefit the most from student loan forgiveness and it is not rich white people.

GOOD DEBT VS. BAD DEBT

I know...I've spent a hell of a lot of time discussing student loans even though everyone doesn't have them. This is true, so in the spirit of providing accessible intel for everyone, let's shift our attention toward debt in general. Pop quiz!

Quickly—someone tell me the difference between credit card debt and a mortgage? *plays *Jeopardy* theme song as you shout out as many answers as you can* *Buzz!* The answer is *shame*. People with credit card debt are shamed and deemed to be irresponsible, whereas people with mortgages are usually seen as intelligent wealth builders. Fun fact: they both fall into the consumer debt category.

The arbitrary terms "good debt" and "bad debt" are often used to assign blame or to celebrate people's financial circumstances. The story goes a little something like this: If you have student loan debt or a mortgage, then you must be an upstanding citizen securing a viable generational asset while funding the advancement of your education. Good debt! If you have credit card debt or payday loans, you are living beyond your means and have a financially irresponsible lifestyle. Bad debt! Both sentiments fail to accurately portray the personal finance spectrum in a nuanced manner.

It is not uncommon for people to charge their tuition and ancillary school fees to a credit card, especially if for any reason it is not possible to secure a student loan. People with older parents, particularly first-gen Americans, will often take out personal loans to cover medical care for their family members. The 2008 recession was a strong reminder to many that a mortgage is very much *still* debt that can destroy any semblance of stability if you are financially overextended. As the housing market currently continues to spiral into pretentiously overpriced chaos, now is just as good a time as any to remind y'all: having *too* much house can lead to the same financial burdens and outcomes as spending *too* much on a credit card.

Accepting the concepts of "good" and "bad" debt as common rhetoric detracts from the diverse lived experiences of every human being on this planet. Personal finance is not only personal but is quite often messy AF and will never fit neatly into the stale archaic prepackaged finance bro boxes we've all come to know and hate.

Like I so casually mentioned in the intro, if one thing holds true, America runs on Dunkin' and debt. There are 329.5 million people living in the United States. Collectively, 80 percent of the population has debt totaling $14.96 trillion. According to a 2021 CNBC report, the average American has $90,460 in debt, including student loan debt, mortgages, credit cards, and personal loans. With mortgage debt excluded, the average consumer has $38,000 in debt. If my math serves me right, that is approximately 263.6 million different people carrying a balance of $38,000–$90,000. Doesn't it just sound beyond absurd to trivialize every one of their unique financial experiences into "good" and "bad" debt?

Without further ado, it is time that I address the elephant in the room. Debt does not holistically nor accurately indicate the level of financial literacy people possess. Don't get me wrong; it can tell you certain things about what people know or don't know about money in general. However, assessing someone's debt profile is an assessment of their access to two of the world's most important privileges: time and money. Using credit card statements or student loan balances as financial gauges does not leave enough room to truthfully calculate a person's financial responsibility through such a myopic lens.

Yes, we know this formula is what credit scores are made of and how new lines of credit are extended. We get that, but here's the thing. The unfortunate ugly truth is the concept of "good" debt is tied to appreciating assets that have become synonymous with higher-income earners. When higher income earners take on debt it is viewed as a smart way to leverage more wealth during their personal finance journey. The wealthier you are, the more likely it is that you will carry debt, and the easier it will be for you to get out of that debt. You have the luxury of time and money on your side. You are always playing the game with the upper hand.

Americans in the top 10 percent of income earners have a median of $222,200 in debt. Their average credit card debt is approximately $12,600, according to the 2021 Federal Reserve reports. Income earners in the bottom 25 percent have less than $20,900 in debt. They have less debt, yes, but because their debt profile consists of suboptimal financing and does not typically consist of an appreciating asset like a home that debt is considered "bad." The important piece missing in this dialogue is that access to "good" debt is often attached to a circumstantial privilege that is not equitably accessible to all. People with lower incomes are less likely to qualify for mortgages and have a higher chance of building credit through credit cards due to relatively less stringent qualifications.

If you've previously used "good" and "bad" to identify different types of debt, it's okay because I have done the same in the past as well. That was because I didn't understand what I was implying, and I didn't have the appropriate verbiage to voice what I was trying to explain. But now that I know, I want you to be informed too.

Installment debt comes from installment credit, where the consumer is given a lump sum of money (think: mortgage, car note, student loans) and fixed scheduled payments are made until the loan is paid off in full. Then, *boom*, the account is closed, and the installment is done. Revolving debt occurs when a set credit limit is provided to the borrower that they can spend in parts or all at once. Think of it as a revolving door because you're essentially using the same money repeatedly when you spend and repay the funds you have spent. The most popular type of revolving credit comes directly from credit cards.

In both cases your debt can be secured (backed by an asset) or unsecured (not backed by any collateral). What does that mean in regular talk? A secured installment loan would be something like a mortgage for your home. Your house is the asset that is being used as collateral, and if you don't pay your mortgage on time, they can eventually seize your home. That's why and how foreclosures happen. Your student loans are unsecured installment loans, because as much as we joke about Sallie Mae coming to pick up the degree we aren't using, there is no true asset that can be taken from you as repayment if you miss your payments. This is when wage garnishments occur.

You've got the student loan tea, and you've got the proper debt terminology, but what you don't have yet is the proper toolkit in place to tackle your consumer debt. You've been patient enough.

TACKLING CONSUMER DEBT

Twenty percent of Americans use at least 50 percent of their income to repay their debt, while 13 percent of Americans expect to be in debt for the rest of their lives. Cue the Iyanla Vanzant meme, please: *not on my watch!* I 100 percent believe that debt, no matter the type, is a beast that needs to be tackled head-on. With approximately 80 percent of Americans carrying consumer debt our task today is to focus on the impacts of revolving debt and the next steps needed to wipe it out one credit card bill at a time.

The big scary truth: American consumers are more indebted than ever. The August 2022 Federal Reserve Consumer Credit report revealed that outstanding US consumer credit has reached historic levels.

What do we consider historic? Oh, just a measly little ol' $4.68 trillion. This is an increase at a seasonally adjusted annual rate of 8.3 percent. Revolving credit (i.e., credit cards) saw an 18.1 percent increase, while installment debt (i.e., mortgages and student loans), also known as nonrevolving debt, increased at an annual rate of 5.1 percent.

That is a lot of freaking debt! To the untrained eye, it may appear that people are spending way more and irresponsibly racking up debt in record numbers. Are there people that use Apple Pay like it's Apple footing the bill? Hell yeah! Are there people who walk into Target and let Target tell them what they need? Yep, no list, just vibes. No one can deny that there are people who habitually spend beyond their means and wind up in large amounts of debt. I can pay for a meal in seconds by scanning my face with my phone and it will be delivered directly to my doorstep. I don't have to move off the couch; I don't have to drive to a restaurant; I don't even have to grab my credit card. There is no sense of delayed gratification and no true inconvenience during the process. That is why the additional costs and fees do not often act as a deterrent because look at all the time I'm getting back. Treat yo' self to level 10!

It is easier than ever to spend without thinking, especially with digital payment products like Apple Pay and Google Pay that make it so you never even have to physically see your credit card. Out of sight, out of mind. If you scroll on social media platforms long enough, the algorithm is going to do its job and show you all the things you never knew you wanted but now can't seem to live without. "TikTok made me buy it" is a *very* real thing, and I've got three pairs of *those* leggings in my closet to prove it. IYKYK.

Remember what I said about facts? Two things can be true at once. One side of the consumer-debt coin can be tied to overspending, surely. The other side, however, cannot be overlooked. There are people who have consumer debt as a means of survival. You step outside, breathe in some air, and *boom*, your account has two hundred dollars less in it because you had the audacity to merely be *outside*. You think you're doing something by staying in? *Psych!* That comes with a two-hundred-dollar indoor existence fee as well. It is expensive to live, and only getting pricier by the minute. Inflation is at an all-time high, wages have not kept that same energy, and unexpected emergencies are always here to remind you how hard and fast life can shift from comfortably coasting to drowning.

Case in point: medical expenses have increased by 33 percent in the last thirty years, while income has only grown by 30 percent in the same time frame. As I write this book in a country without universal healthcare during the second year of a global pandemic very few of us saw coming, you can see where I'm about to go with this. Health insurance isn't covering nearly enough of what is being charged for medical procedures, and when you're hit with rising unemployment and massive waves of layoffs, health insurance very much becomes a crapshoot. Seeking medical care is rarely a choice, and nearly one in four Americans have medical debt between $5,000–$9,999. According to a 2021 LendingTree survey, 35 percent of Americans with medical debt are using some form of revolving debt to pay off their medical bills, while 33 percent use their savings.

Debt is not and should not be a dirty word, as oftentimes it is the only option. The stigma of irresponsible financial behaviors tied to debt is harmful to those who are actively doing their best to rectify the situation regardless of the circumstances that caused the debt in the first place. At the end of the day, debt is debt no matter what it looks like and most of us have it. Uh, hello…it's my namesake! So regardless of how you acquired your debt, the five steps to tackling that debt below are shamelessly curated to support your debt-payoff journey.

STEP ONE: LOOK AT THE WHOLE PICTURE

Much like the steps you took in Chapter 1 to create your budget, you're going to need to know exactly what you're working with. You're not starting from scratch, though, because you did that in Chapter 1! Pull out that paperwork, baby; we are double-dipping and stepping back into our financially vulnerable state for a moment. It's just you and me here, so there's no need to panic.

Remember when you added up all your liabilities to calculate your net worth? Let's take another look at your total debts. We're going to sit down and look at them closely this time, not just the balances. For each debt you have, write down the balance, minimum payment, monthly due date, and current interest rate. Your paper or digital documentation should look something like this:

DUE DATE	REMAINING BALANCE	MINIMUM PAYMENT	CURRENT INTEREST RATE

Step one done? Great, head on down to step two; you've got everything you're going to need!

STEP TWO: CHOOSE WHICH DEBT TO TACKLE FIRST

Being overwhelmed on your debt-payoff journey is a normal human reaction and is bound to happen. As the resident crier in my friend group, I am not ashamed to say I cried many a tear when paying that trifling heifer Sallie Mae her money back at 16 percent interest. To help you get ahead of your frustration and anxiety, the wisest thing to do after you've looked at your entire debt picture is to choose which debt you're going to take on first. It's a cute idea to say you're going to pay it all off, but cute is hardly ever practical, and cute surely isn't going to get that debt paid off.

Are you going with the snowball method and tackling the smallest balance, or are you taking on higher-interest debt first? There are pros and cons for either method, just like with most things in life...it'll depend on what works best for you. There's no denying the mental relief you feel, even if just temporary, when you close the door on a loan. It is exhilarating and often motivates you to keep pushing forward at full speed. If you know you need bursts of endorphins with quick wins to keep you motivated on your journey, then the snowball method is better suited for your needs. If you want to focus on paying the least amount of interest in the long run, the debt avalanche method should be your go-to. Whichever route you take, make sure it works for you and not for anyone on the internet. Your favorite influencer's favorite way does not matter here, I promise you.

STEP THREE: SET UP A PRACTICAL TIMELINE FOR YOURSELF

Emphasis on practical. Paying off debt as quickly as possible is a huge priority for many and there is nothing wrong with that, especially with the economy acting up and doing way too much right now. Do not over-prioritize your debt payoff for the sake of everything else in your life. It is not sustainable and can be dangerous if you do not have other financial pillars like an emergency savings fund in place.

The best way to set up a practical timeline is to start with the timeline provided by the credit provider first. This timeline will be based on the monthly minimum with no additional debt added to the current balance. Once you know their timeline you can use it as a springboard to make your own.

Why is it so important to make your own? Because you can control and adjust it whenever you need to. You are in the driver's seat. Once you have a timeline in your mind, you can work backward to figure out exactly how you're going to get there. Write down this purpose statement as your reminder of that:

I will pay off my _____ debt in _____ months
(name/type of debt you're focusing on)   (amt of time)

by paying _____ extra every _____ .
(amt of time)   (frequency)

STEP FOUR: MAKE ROOM IN THE BUDGET TO PRIORITIZE YOUR DEBT-PAYOFF JOURNEY

This is not a revolutionary step, but it is a crucial step if you want to take back your life in a timely manner. Once you've looked at the whole picture and set up your timeline, you are going to want to work backward in a way that allows you to make extra payments when possible.

It does not have to be every single month, but making extra payments when you receive gifts, bonuses at work, a raise, or your tax return are key opportunities to save money, buy back time, and free up more money in your budget long-term. When you look at your entire financial picture, are there areas in your budget you can cut or scale back to increase the amount of extra money you put toward your debt (because remember you have to pay the minimum to avoid going into default)? Can you make that extra payment every month? Every two months? Twice a year? It all counts, and it all makes a difference, so do not feel discouraged if you can only make one extra payment a year. The internet will have you believing everyone is a master at paying off large amounts of money in short periods of time.

Nika Booth has paid off nearly $80,000 of credit card debt, and when I asked her what is one thing she wished more people understood about the process, she stated, "I wish more people understood the mental and emotional challenges. Specifically, when witnessing the celebrations of debt payoff on social media. Yes, it is rewarding but paying off debt isn't glamorous. It takes a lot of hard work and there's often much sacrifice and personal struggles that happened along the way." Do not be fooled by the glitz and glamour of what everyone else appears to be doing. Paying down debt takes discipline and requires adaptation. It does not require it to look sexy to the public. Do ya thang the way you need to do it.

STEP FIVE: AVOID NEW DEBT (ESPECIALLY HIGH-INTEREST DEBT)

Credit providers thrive off the interest your debt accrues. They are banking on you taking as long as possible to pay off your debt so they can profit as much as possible. This is why they make the minimum payments so low. It's not because they are worried about payments being an affordable part of your budget. *No!* They're setting a trap!

Avoiding new debt is easier said than done, so it is going to take some skillful maneuvering. The skillful maneuvering will make quite an impact on your timing and execution. Will it be annoying? Perhaps. Is it worth it? Absolutely! "It's impossible to climb out of debt while digging yourself into debt at the same time. I knew that if I was serious this time, I couldn't keep doing the same shit that got me into debt," Nika stated when asked what she wished she had known earlier in her debt-payoff journey.

What does skillful maneuvering look like holistically? Minimizing how often you use and carry a balance on your revolving credit accounts. It also looks like refusing to open new lines of credit. You don't want to put all your energy into tackling one debt only to create another elsewhere.

Hot Tip: If you must use a credit card, use *only* one and pay off the new charge in total. This is going to take some discernment on your part, but I have faith in you. You will have to decide whether this purchase is a want or truly a necessity. Is it a necessity that can wait until you have the cash to fund it? Ask yourself the real questions that are often uncomfortable to answer before you take your next step.

There's a lot to unpack when it comes to debt payoff, and your brain may feel like it's doing backflips right now. That's okay; my brain is currently doing the same. We will not leave this chapter feeling defeated. Not a chance. We will end instead manifesting positive energy using my favorite mantra. In the wise words of Cardi B, say it with me, all together now 1...2...3: "I just checked my account, turns out I'm rich, I'm rich, I'm rich."

PART II: I MAKE MONEY MOVES

—

THE ROAD TO FINANCIAL INDEPENDENCE

CHAPTER 5

GET RICH OR INVEST TRYING

In 2015 I opened my first individual investment account with Capital One and bought my first stock: Netflix. It was right after their 7:1 stock split and I paid around ninety-six dollars for one share. Every couple of months after that, whenever I felt the urge, I would randomly purchase a few random shares in companies that I really liked *and* could afford. This included more shares in Netflix and others in Snapchat, Twitter, Fitbit, Verizon, and Etsy. If it was a public company I used or liked with shares that cost less than a hundred dollars, you could count me in. Of course, I *lost* a shit ton of money, and in hindsight realized this was the dumbest investment strategy on the planet.

You would think the tales of my ignorance end there; they most certainly do *not*. Three years after I purchased my first Netflix stock for ninety-six dollars, I sold all my Netflix shares, about eight of them at $260 apiece. I walked away with about two thousand dollars so I could buy furniture for my house. I thought I was doing the right thing, the smart thing. I avoided taking on new debt to furnish my home, and I made a killer profit, right? *Wrong!* Two years after I sold all my shares, Netflix's valuation skyrocketed during the pandemic and individual shares were now going for about $495 each. That means if I held on to those same shares I bought in 2015, I would have seen a 415 percent return. Instead, I have a couch purchased with Netflix shares that I now hate and want to replace. Life...amirite?

Thankfully the plotline to this absurd money story took a much smarter turn as I learned more about investing in the market. I shifted from investing in individual stocks—terribly, I might add—to low-cost index funds and ETFs. My investment portfolio stands at six figures (about $150,000, give or take a dollar) despite the bear market the world is currently navigating. In seven years, I went from a painstakingly ignorant novice to a rather knowledgeable long-term investor with a portfolio in place to grow to $1.5 million at the time of retirement, even if I never invest another dollar ever again.

Only 1 percent of the global adult population has a net worth of one million dollars. Seventy-five percent of US millionaires are white, and 13 percent are Black or African American. As a Black woman with a master's degree, statistics show that I have a 6 percent chance of becoming a millionaire. Personally, I've always been fond of achieving what is not traditionally expected of me. It brings me great pleasure to prove people wrong. I don't care what the numbers show or how the stats lean; I will be the first millionaire in my family. And I don't want that just for me. I want that for you too. So let's get into the intricacies of how to get it done.

FUTURE MILLIONAIRE LOADING: INVESTING 101

Have you ever spent hours in a Google spiral trying to figure out how millionaires made their millions? It's an exercise I highly recommend doing but not at two in the morning when you should be sleeping. Speaking from experience, even if you feel locked and loaded, ready to fix your entire life before sunrise, just go to bed.

While I may not have fixed my entire life Iyanla-style during my Google spiral, I did learn a thing or two that helped cultivate my current investment strategy.

Things I Learned During My Two-O'clock-in-the-Morning Millionaire Google Spiral

What I learned: Most millionaires have their assets in retirement accounts like Roth IRAs, traditional IRAs, and 401Ks. Financial planner Andrew Herron, founding partner of Stone Pine Financial, reports about 70 percent of his typical millionaire clients keep their assets in retirement accounts, 5 percent in cash reserves, and about 25 percent in other investment accounts.

- **What I took from that:** The internet will have you believe that your strongest path to wealth is through flashy day trades and options, but that is false. The unsexy, boring retirement accounts are truly where it's at.

What I learned: Most millionaires have no debt outside of mortgages and they keep their lifestyle spending to a conservative minimum.

- **What I took from that:** Keep an eye out for lifestyle creep. The more money I make does not mean I need to increase my expenses.

What I learned: Approximately 79 percent of millionaires are self-made, while 3 percent inherited their wealth. The most common careers held by millionaires: engineering, accounting (CPA), law, management, and teaching. Where did these folks go to school? Investopedia reports nearly two-thirds of American millionaires (62 percent) went to public or state schools.

- **What I took from that:** Becoming a millionaire isn't easy but it is not an accomplishment only reserved for the elite. It is achievable even for a teacher who didn't graduate with a 4.0 GPA from an Ivy League school.

The most important fact I learned: You need to have a long-term strategy that focuses primarily on diversified assets. You're not trying to time the market; you're enjoying time *in* the market, and there's a big difference.

- **What I took from that:** Make investing decisions that will benefit my future self without putting all my eggs in one basket. Don't try to jump into the market to get rich quick when you see excitement about a stock (*coughs*, I'm looking at you, GameStop and AMC) because if you're hearing about it, it's likely too late or at the very least too speculative. Stay the course, follow through with your strategy, and let compound interest do its thing.

The investing style described at the start of this chapter is a clear example of someone (that *someone* being me) with zero strategy, just vibes. I was investing my money without doing an ounce of research and making short-sighted decisions that did not shield me from extreme market volatility. Presently as a long-term index fund enthusiast, my investing strategy is *actually* a *real* strategy rooted in research and diversification. Plus, Warren Buffet told me I'm doing a good job, and as one of the best investors in the country, I consider that personally to be a high five of approval.

Okay, he may not personally have told me I'm doing a good job, but my investment strategy is his favorite investment strategy so...ergo, same difference. Warren Buffet is one of the world's wealthiest investors, and at ninety-two years old, he possesses a $107.2 billion net worth. That's billion with a big B, and he always shares the same sentiment about his preferred investing style: "If you aren't willing to own a stock for ten years, don't even think about owning it for ten minutes."

Buffet has been vocal about his long-term buy-and-hold investment style publicly for years. When you adopt the "forever" mentality, Buffet mentions that becomes one of the best investments you can make. Taking on the set-it-and-forget-it approach after investing in low-cost index funds such as the S&P 500 gives you the greatest advantage you can hope to get from the market. If Buffet is easily using compound interest and dividend reinvesting to his benefit, I sure as shit don't mind doing the same.

As the unbelievably talented yet egregiously tardy Lauryn Hill once said, "It could all be so simple." Investing does not have to be difficult, and you don't need thousands of dollars to get started. The best way to get started truly is to start. If you continue to wait for that perfect moment when you feel "ready" or when you think you know *everything* you need to know, you will *never* start. Marc Russell, owner and founder of "BetterWallet," sees this as the biggest mistake investors make at the start of their investing journey. He states, "When starting their investing journey people often wait until they feel 100 percent comfortable. Like anything in life, you'll never be 100 percent perfect at it. You will suck at it initially. Embrace it. Getting good at anything takes practice and plenty of missteps. Waiting until you feel 100 percent comfortable limits the most important factor in investing; time."

Once you've got a handle on investing basics, you can enjoy your time *in* the market, which will always be one of your most valuable strategic inputs. Marc goes on to add, "my guidance is to use tools like YouTube or online courses, to round your knowledge of investing in index funds then when you feel comfortable enough to start investing, start small. Then, work your way up to larger contributions. This is how you build your investing *muscle*."

So that is where we'll begin, with the basics to help strengthen your investing muscle.

THE BASICS

We'll begin with one of the common questions I see in my comments consistently: "Where do I start?" I like to answer that question using the order of operations. Please excuse my dear aunt Sally, a.k.a. PEMDAS, always clarified what we were supposed to do and in what order, making ninth-grade algebra just a smidge more bearable than it was. The investing order of operations does the exact same.

Though it may not have a fancy acronym like our dear ol' classic PEMDAS, the method still thwarts the madness. If you are looking for where to start, what accounts you should have, and how much money you can contribute annually to each year, you are in the right place.

WHERE DO I START?

- Identify your investment goals (one long-term and one short-term are enough) so you can set up a realistic timeframe and understand your risk profile (more on that in a moment).

- Decide if you want to be an active investor with passive qualities—you do it yourself but follow a simple set-it-and-forget-it routine. Or you go the managed route where you get to be completely hands-off but will be paying more in fees.

- Pick the type of investment accounts you'll be using in your investor journey. More than one account type is common, but you don't have to try and have more than one right away.

- Open the account. *Duh!*

- Choose the investments you'll be making that align with your investment strategy and your risk tolerance. The best strategies will also provide diversification. Think stocks, bonds, real estate, etc.

Identifying your investment goals is as simple as identifying your overall financial goals. What do you want to achieve financially, in what time frame, and why? Do not make it more complicated than it has to be.

For example, my long-term investment goal is to have a two-million-dollar investment portfolio by the time I retire in thirty years. This long-term investment goal helps me create a plan and a short-term goal that can help bring me closer to my end goal. Short-term goal: Max out my Roth IRA this calendar year. *Simple!* No bells and whistles are needed unless that's your thing.

Understanding your risk profile will also help guide you during your goal setting because it will help you manage expectations. The more risk-adverse you are (like me), the longer your investment goals will take to achieve, and that's okay. This is a marathon, not a sprint.

So you've got your goals, you understand your risk profile, and you're unsure whether you want your assets actively or passively managed. It truly is a matter of preference. I manage my assets myself and it does not take much of my time, energy, or effort. I automate wherever I can, and I do not obsessively check my accounts. In addition, I primarily purchase index funds and ETFs for the long term so there's no need to have an active manager doing that when I can do it for free. Prior to going the active management route, if you are truly at a loss and don't want to immediately go at it alone, I suggest starting with a Roboadvisor first. This way you get some of the perks of an actively managed account without some of the higher-costing fees that other brokerages may charge. For a list of my suggested Roboadvisors, hit the resource section found at the end of the book!

With all the heavy lifting behind you, it is now time to pick the type of investment accounts you'll be using.

Order of Operations, Round Two

ACCOUNT	WHY SHOULD I HAVE THIS ACCOUNT?	MAXIMUM ANNUAL CONTRIBUTION
1. Emergency Savings Fund	Life happens fast AF and you don't want to land in debt because of an unforeseen emergency.	No maximum contribution (aim to have three to six months of living expenses saved).

2. Employer-Sponsored Plan (i.e., 401K, 403B, 457)	An employer-sponsored plan is your next step. If it is offered, at the minimum you should attempt to invest enough to earn the company match. This is the only guaranteed return you'll ever have in the market.	The 2023 max contribution for the year is $22,500. People who are fifty and up are allotted an additional $7,500 catch-up contribution, which allows for $30,000 invested annually.
3. HSA	Your health savings account is a tax-advantaged investment tool that helps you cover the costs of medical expenses. You can also invest your HSA in the market just like any other investing account.	$3,850 for an individual and $7,750 for family coverage. Those fifty-five and up can contribute an additional $1,000 as a catch-up contribution.
4. IRA	Once you've got your first three accounts set up and you're comfortably contributing, opening an IRA (traditional or Roth) is your next step as the dope investing ninja you are. Your IRA can provide you with another tax-advantaged account (if you go the traditional route) or tax-free growth on your gains (if you go the Roth route). The choice is yours. The best thing to do once you've reached this step is to consider maxing out your 401K, HSA, and IRA before moving into the fifth and final step.	The 2023 IRA contribution limit saw a cost-of-living increase of $500 bringing the annual investment total to $6,500 and $7,500 for those fifty years and up.

5. Individual Brokerage	The last step in your investing journey will be an individual brokerage that you open with a brokerage of your choosing. These accounts have no contribution limits and can be used as a supplemental support to your other accounts.	Your individual brokerage will have no contribution limits. You can invest as much or as little as you'd like.

If I tried to acronym this, we'd get EEHII. Clearly not as effective as PEMDAS and lacks the cute jingle to make it stick to memory. So, I suggest earmarking this page so you can quickly access the chart as an added resource in your investment journey. What comes next?

OPENING YOUR FIRST ACCOUNT

If you are not enrolled in your employer's sponsored plan, you know where I'm going to point you to *first*. If you already have a 401K or comparable plan, then move into an HSA if you are eligible. If you don't meet the eligibility requirements to qualify for an HSA, the next best step would be to open an IRA.

Your employer-sponsored plan does not allow you to pick the brokerage you will use, and that's okay. For your IRA you get to choose the brokerage you'd like to do your investing with. Here are three quick questions to ask when you're trying to decide which brokerage to use. Word to the wise: Similar to choosing an HYSA, you don't need to make a big fuss about it. If the brokerage meets your needs on a basic level, don't spend too much time overcomplicating the process.

Questions to ask when looking for a brokerage:

- Does the brokerage offer the type of investment account you're looking to open?

- What fees are associated with the account you're looking to open and the types of investments you'll be making?

- Does the brokerage have a proven, reliable track record?

Opening your account will likely take ten to fifteen minutes and generally won't require a lot of money to get started. Most brokerages have simplified the process. You'll need to enter identifying information and deposit or transfer funds before you can start investing.

INVESTING

We've reached my fave part...the *fun* part, of course! Well, it's what I consider the fun part—the research. Oh, you thought I was going to say the investing, right? Here's a secret I want to share with you and only you: they go hand in hand! I'm willing to go out on a limb here and say your best, most exciting investing moments will be the moments you sign into your account and see your gains. There's something about seeing all that green that sits exactly right with all of us. But it is your research that will help you get to those exciting investing victories. It is your research that will help you stay on the generational wealth path and achieve millionaire status. So, you see, future millionaire, the research *is* the fun part!

Don't get overwhelmed! You don't need to spend hours reading any and every prospectus in the world. I know that suggesting a complex or overly extensive research routine would ultimately act as a deterrent, thus ending your investing journey and *ruining* your life. Okay, maybe not ruin, but I would completely understand if you rolled your eyes, shut this book, and passionately yelled into the ether, "Ain't nobody got time for that." Our lives are jam-packed with one adulting requirement after another. The name of the game here is KISS: Keep investing super simple.

As a long-term index fund investor, there are four main things I concern myself with when researching an index fund:

1. **Fund Issuer:** Who is issuing the fund? The easiest way to figure this out is to Google "fund issuer of X index fund." For example, the popular index funds VTI and VOO are issued by Vanguard (you can usually take a guess on the fund issuer based on the letter the index fund begins with, but this isn't always the case). Another example would be FXAIX, which is issued by Fidelity, whereas QQQ is issued by Invesco.

2. **Expense Ratio:** How much is this fund going to cost you annually to own? I like to keep as much of my money as possible, so I like to invest in index funds with low expense ratios. VTI has an expense ratio of 0.03 percent, which means for every $10,000 I have invested in VTI, I will pay $3.00. The lower the expense ratio, the better!

3. **Holdings:** What companies are tracked by this index fund or ETF? This is important to research ahead of time to ensure true diversification. There are many similar index funds and ETFs, so you don't want to invest in two funds that are tracking the same exact companies. This is called fund overlap and takes away from your diversification efforts. For example, investing in both VOO and VTI wouldn't provide you with the amount of diversification you think you'd be getting because you would have an 85 percent overlap.

   The best thing to try and do when selecting the funds you are interested in is to look into funds that track different sectors of the market so you cast a wider net. And as a final measure, I use ETF Research Center (etfrc.com) whenever I want to check if I'm experiencing any major fund overlap between the two funds I'm investing in.

4. **Long-Term Performance:** How has the index fund performed in the last five to ten years? Has the fund underperformed or outperformed the market?

When I first started my research, I mainly used Yahoo Finance to provide all four details and saved the information I found in my notes app. It was the simplest way for me to understand what I would be putting my money into without reading through long documents are trying to figure out confusing terminology. No fancy spreadsheets or complicated research journals. I continue to use Yahoo Finance as my first research stop when I'm curious about a particular fund and depending on where I am, my notes app is still my primary note-taking resource.

INVESTING WITH DEBT

I have reached Coast FI/RE. This means that if I never invest a single dollar ever again, I will still have over $1.5 million dollars in my investment account when it's time to retire. While I'll be expanding further on this further in Chapter 6, it's important to note here as well. Why? Because I would not have been able to achieve this if I did not invest while I was paying down my student loans. A decision I cannot take full credit for.

My work mom is to thank. At my first full-time teaching job, she recommended opening a 403B as an additional retirement account outside of my pension. As stubborn as I know I can be, I listened to her, opened the account, and started with a 3 percent contribution. I would go on to listen to her two more times regarding increasing my contribution with every pay increase and changing my allocations to be less conservative.

Twelve years later these actions unknowingly secured my place as a future millionaire at retirement. If I had waited to be debt-free to take these same actions, I would not currently have a six-figure investment portfolio and would have lost out on seven years of time in the market.

You know my fave vibe: two things can be true at the same time! Investing while you're in debt can impact the trajectory of your investing journey immensely, but your bills must be paid. You have to pay the minimum payment on your debts no matter what or risk damaging your credit score and other significant financial repercussions. The decision about what to do with any remaining money is where the gray area arises. There are finance gurus on the interwebs that believe investing should be your final frontier after all debt is paid off, and I simply don't agree. As with everything it will depend on the circumstances of your situation. Your financial responsibilities will differ, and your goals will change.

However, there are several questions to consider if you're stuck trying to figure out whether to accelerate your debt payoff or invest while you're paying off debt.

- **Do you have an emergency savings fund?** A leaking roof and a flat tire do not care about your debt-payoff journey. A flooded kitchen and emergency root canal couldn't care less about your investment goals. I know you're tired of hearing me say it, but your emergency savings fund should be a primary focus because an unforeseen emergency can have a cataclysmic impact on your finances and derail the progress you've worked hard to achieve. You can't ask for your extra debt payments back from your loan provider if your engine craps out on you on a random Tuesday afternoon. You want to avoid falling into a pattern of taking on new debt when unexpected expenses arise. Prioritize at least three months in expenses to give yourself a healthy buffer.

- **How much extra money do I have?** Your budget is set so you should be able to answer this question easily! You can't invest or pay off debt without extra money. After all your bills are paid, how much money do you have left over? Do you have enough to split between saving, investing, and debt payoff? Using your SMART goals from Chapter 1 will help you decide on what to prioritize with your extra cash.

- **What type of debt do you have?** Do you have low-interest debt, like student loans or a mortgage? Do you have high-interest debt like a personal loan or credit card debt? If you have low-interest debt (typically 7 percent or lower), it is not a bad idea to try to invest while paying off your debt. Since this debt is not costing you much and is below the average rate of return of the stock market, it would make sense to capitalize on the potential gains you could make by investing that extra money instead. Whereas if you have high-interest debt (typically above 10 percent) it would make more sense to throw your extra cash at your debt.

I sat down with Marc Russell, a foster-child-turned-full-time-financial-educator who put himself through college and paid off $80,000 of debt after graduating. He has taught thousands of families how to manage their money the right way. As the owner and founder of BetterWallet, he teaches people around the world how to make money work for them so they can build true generational wealth. As a licensed stockbroker and financial advisor, Marc openly shared his experience investing while paying off debt and offered a suggested strategy for anyone looking to invest while struggling with debt.

Marc suggests, "Consider starting with the 'free' money first. If you work for a company who offers an employer sponsored retirement plan like a 401k, 403b, etc. you likely have what they call an employer match. An employer match is when your employer matches your contributions to your retirement plan up to a certain percentage. For example, you put in 4 percent of your salary per year and your employer matches it with another 4 percent. That's 8 percent of your income going toward your retirement annually. Consider this a two-for-one deal that can significantly turbocharge your retirement investing."

Similarly to Marc, the only investing I did toward the beginning of my debt-payoff journey was in the 403b I begrudgingly opened at the suggestion of my work mom. This account is not only the largest part of my six-figure portfolio, but it also helped me reach Coast FI/RE. Don't sleep on the small contributions during your debt-payoff journey; every bit counts! Marc expands on his strategy using his employer-sponsored account during his debt-payoff journey, "When I was paying off debt, that was the only investing I did. Once I became debt free, I significantly increased my retirement contributions well beyond my employer match. In my journey, I knew that I had $80,000 of debt which at the time was projected to be paid off by November 2020. Once I added in my monthly retirement contributions (up to my employer match), that date pushed back to the end of 2021. I was comfortable with that because I wanted to have a decent retirement portfolio *and* be debt free."

I finished paying off my student loans in 2018 and jumped right into a mortgage in 2019. So, when I opened my individual investment account in 2015, I knew that I would be affecting my debt-payoff timeline. This is something I was cognizant of and planned for after two years of only focusing on my debt payoff and my 403b. I was ready to take on another account, but there is no rush or requirement to do so if you're not comfortable. Marc suggests, "Be sure that you know your specific debt-free date using the endless number of free calculators online and budget in your monthly investing goals. Investing could set your debt-free date back a few months or years, but as long as you're comfortable with the time reset, go for it!"

BFFR: AVOIDING THE HYPE AND THE SCAMS

I'm gonna be honest here: The market is *full* of people trying to make as much money as possible in the shortest amount of time possible. They do *not* care about your well-being or your retirement account. Another unfiltered truth: Long-term investing is not sexy; it is not flashy and takes a great deal of resolve to ride out the ebbs and flows of the market. When you look at your 401K or IRA it simply doesn't have the pizazz that options, forex, and day trading offer. The short-term growth is nothing to write home about, and the withdrawal restrictions make retirement investing boring AF in a world that thrives on immediate gratification. Cue in exhibit A: "It's my money and I want it now."

When I step on my soap box to scream the benefits of long-term index fund investing, I know that the promise of turning $5,000 into $50,000 in a week is a much louder and more interesting conversation. Your 401K will never get your blood pumping the way options and day trading can. No one would choose to turn down $50,000 right now with the promise of $50,000 in ten to fifteen years. Especially for those who are struggling to make ends meet, the opportunity to make beaucoup bucks right away is tantalizing. So, I get it. I really do. And I'm still about to rip this bandage off.

BFFR: Be F&$*#g For Real. We have been on the mean streets of the internet far too long to still fall for money schemes and scams that prey on the financial insecurities of the public. We've all seen those Instagram pages with the stock market emojis in their profile, and the bots in the comments raving about the life-changing altruistic service that said profile provided. Those same scammers love to reach out with opportunities, especially opportunities for people who don't have a strong understanding of the market. What does the opportunity usually entail? The opportunist exploiting the vulnerable, and the victim being left a little poorer than when they started.

Let's look at a few BFFR investment-related opportunities that you need to be aware of.

DAY TRADING

If you've ever seen the Eddie Murphy and Dan Aykroyd classic *Trading Places*, you know exactly what day trading consists of. Hella risk and hella *hype*. And if you haven't seen it, I suggest you add it to your must-watch list immediately.

On the BFFR scam scale, day trading at its core is *not* a scam. It is also not investing. Instead, we'll categorize it as a part of the market that centers on hype. Day traders buy and sell stocks or other assets during the trading day so that they can profit from the fluctuation in prices. Day trading requires quite a bit of time and energy as well as a strategic forethought. This strategy is usually informed by technical analysis of price movements, a.k.a. not beginner friendly. If you tend to be risk-adverse like me, you may want to sit this type of trading out. Looking for financial accessibility? To the tune of the oh-so-vibey Lil' Uzi Vert, "This ain't what you want." Day trading typically requires a minimum equity of $25,000 in capital.

It would be easy to think, *Wow, Melissa. You've got a little haterade in your blood; there are professionals who make a lucrative living as day traders.* This is true, so I will leave you with this one shiny additional truth: In comparison to long-term index fund investing, day trading has a historically low margin of success. Various studies reveal an average success rate of 5 to 20 percent, and 75 percent of day traders quit after two years. In a *Business Insider* interview, Sean Bandazian, investment analyst for Cornerstone Wealth, said it best: "People should understand that there are exponentially more people that lose money trying to catch lightning in a bottle...the obvious issue with the get rich quick mentality is it usually involves taking massive concentration risk in a volatile asset."

FOREX

Forex really had its scammer day in the sun when the pandemic started. Suddenly, everybody and their mama was a forex trading broker. Like day trading, forex itself is not a scam. Forex, also known as foreign exchange trading, is buying and selling foreign currencies to try and make a profit. Foreign exchange is *highly* complex and risky. The US Securities and Exchange Commission conducted a study of forex traders and revealed harrowing facts.

Of all forex traders, 70 percent lose money every quarter on average, and over the course of twelve months traders will typically lose 100 percent of their money. *Yikes!*

As if those stats weren't frightening enough, cue the scammers. Forex scams came in two predominant waves. The first holds true to the classic, "Give me five dollars and I'll turn it into five thousand" that we all know and love. Forex "expert" investors will slide into your DMs and tell you about all the people they have helped turn a profit. You send them the funds, and they string you along for a few weeks, showing you just how much your money has grown. When do you ask for the profits and your initial investment to be returned? They either vanish or ask you for more money to cover taxes and fees. They were never trading your money and you were never making a profit. Do not click any links they send to you to avoid any security breaches in your sensitive personal accounts.

The second variation of the forex scam is a little more devious. The trading experts will once again reach out with an "opportunity" to copy their trades. They will require you to sign up and make a deposit with a forex brokerage, which is usually a scam paying them a commission after your deposit is made.

It's safe to say, forex is not a beginner's playground and is not an opportunity you want to jump on from someone approaching you on Instagram.

CRYPTOCURRENCY

Make no mistake, I fully embrace and anticipate change. I know cryptocurrency is here to stay and it is interesting to see its integration into our everyday lives. But my risk aversion wouldn't allow me to write this chapter without mentioning the amount of volatility, fraud, loss, theft, and cybercrime that currently comes with the cryptocurrency territory. With looser regulations as a part of the appeal, there are no real investor protections. All investing comes with risk and investing in cryptocurrency is extremely speculative. It is wise to treat it as such as you venture into it.

LIFE INSURANCE

Whew, the life insurance salesmen are going to be mad about this one. I went back and forth about whether to even include this piece here, especially since we'll be diving further into life insurance in the estate-planning chapter. However, life insurance has strangely become entwined in the investing narrative on these TikTok and Instagram streets, so why not! I'm going to keep this short and sweet: life insurance is important! It is important; it is so, so, *so* important! I have repeated it three times, yet I know there will be a troll or ten that will purposely misinterpret this paragraph anyway.

Many life insurance plans are available, and as of late, there has been an onslaught of not-so-honest insurance salesmen promoting life insurance policies riddled with enormous fees as investment tools. Whole or universal life insurance policies are *not* meant for everyone and do not need to be offered to everyone. That's all I'm gonna say on that...for now (*yes,* I am smirking menacingly).

THE LIGHTNING ROUND

This chapter is meant to whet your investing palate; think of it as the appetizer. I want you to use it as your starter kit to get comfortable interacting with the stock market. The next few sections of information are going to be a part of what I call the lightning round. This is information I wish I had known much earlier on that helped me understand what all the old white men on CNBC were talking about while I was on the treadmill at the gym. Earmark and highlight as you see fit!

COMMON INVESTING MISTAKES

CHASING TRENDS

Investing can get boring if you follow a long-term strategy, so it's easy to get sucked into the razzle-dazzle of investment trends popping up all over social media. Don't let FOMO catch you and your pockets slipping.

CONSTANTLY CHECKING YOUR PORTFOLIO

Look, I get it. When the market is up, we all want to grab our screenshots to share our gains publicly, and conversely, when the market is down, we want to slide down the wall crying. You cannot check your portfolio every day and hope to keep your sanity. Remember why you started investing and stay the course. Try checking in on your portfolio quarterly instead.

INVESTING MONEY YOU NEED

You should only be investing money that you do not immediately need. That means you should have a separate cash reserve to help you avoid relying on your investments. The market can be volatile and there are no guarantees. So no...do not invest your down payment money for your future home if you're going to need it in the near future.

UNCLEAR INVESTING GOALS

You need a why to help you set up your investment portfolio properly. Without clear investing goals, you won't have a clear understanding of the assets you'll need to secure, and you'll likely end up making other investment errors that will cost you time and money.

INVESTING INCONSISTENTLY

You will have better returns if you engage in dollar-cost averaging over the long term. I know the ups and downs of the market can be difficult to watch, especially when you're seeing a bunch of red. Do not panic. This is what the market does; this is what the market is always going to do. By dollar-cost averaging, you are strengthening a positive financial habit and lowering your average purchase price.

PAYING TOO MUCH IN FEES AND COMMISSIONS

Always pay attention to expense ratios, commission fees, management fees and maintenance fees. A small, consistent leak can still sink a ship. One of your main objectives should be to keep as much of your money as possible. Over time "small fees" add up. Keep an eye on what you're being charged and why.

FAILING TO DIVERSIFY ENOUGH

This is a common investing mistake that is easy to identify and resolve. A truly diversified investment portfolio will contain different assets across many industries. Basically, don't put all your eggs into one basket. Low-cost index funds and ETFs will make diversification easier than picking out individual stocks.

TRYING TO TIME THE MARKET

If anyone could successfully time the market, they would not only be ridiculously wealthy, but they would also be a psychic. Trying to time the market is a fool's errand that will cost you more money in the long run. Don't try and "get in when prices drop." Just start. Your future self will thank you.

NEGLECTING TO START

The best way to get started investing is to get started. The best time to get started investing is *now*. Marc of BetterWallet states, "The biggest mistake investors make when starting their investing journey is that they wait until they feel 100 percent comfortable. Like anything in life, you'll never be 100 percent perfect at it. You will suck at it initially. Embrace it. Getting good at anything takes practice and plenty of missteps. Waiting until you feel 100 percent comfortable limits the most important factor in investing; time."

LACK OF PATIENCE

The BFFR section was a clear warning about what happens when people lack patience when it comes to investing. You must be patient and let the market do what it is going to do. Easier said than done, but if you find yourself looking toward "get rich quick" alternatives, you will find that you're putting your finances at great risk. Remember, time *in* the market! You're laying the generational wealth foundation for lifetimes to come; it takes time.

NOT ACTUALLY INVESTING MONEY

This is a *big* one! Oftentimes, people will transfer money into their Roth IRA and think that it's invested. That is the first step, but the *critical* step is investing the money you have deposited into the account. If not, you're letting your coins sit in cash instead of in stocks and bonds. The last step when you open your IRA is to use the deposited money to purchase investments. Otherwise, you're leaving tons of money on the table!

INVESTING FAQS

WHAT IS A STOCK?

A stock is known as an equity or security that represents fractional ownership in a company. Individual stock units are known as shares. When you purchase a company's stocks you are purchasing a small piece of that company called a share.

WHAT IS THE STOCK MARKET?

The stock market is where shares of public companies are bought and sold. The terms *stock market* and *stock exchange* are usually used interchangeably. Often you will also hear people refer to the S&P500 as the stock market. Don't let this trip you up. This common reference occurs because the S&P500 is one of the OG indexes that tracks the movement of the overall market. Since it is a market capitalization weighted index, it is used as one of the best gauges for prominent American equities' performance. *Uh, layman's terms, please, Melissa.* The S&P500 tracks the five hundred leading companies in the US, so by extension it is a pretty good indicator of how the stock market is doing overall.

WHAT IS THE DIFFERENCE BETWEEN SAVING AND INVESTING?

Saving involves putting money away in a safe place to be used later. Investing is purchasing assets with the aim of growing your money as those assets increase in value. It is wise to save money that you will need in less than five years, whereas it is wiser to invest money you don't immediately need.

HOW MUCH SHOULD I INVEST?

You should invest an amount that supports your investing goals and doesn't disrupt your financial health. As your financial circumstances evolve, the amount you can and should invest will change. The important thing to remember is you can get started investing with as little as ten dollars and dollar-cost averaging will help build a strong investing habit.

WHAT ARE COMMON TYPES OF INVESTMENTS?

Stocks, bonds, mutual funds, and ETFs.

WILL I PAY A LOT IN FEES?

You do not have to pay a ton of fees to invest in the market. Low-cost index funds and ETFs will help keep fees at a minimum. If your brokerage charges commissions or you choose to have an actively managed account, the fees will eat into more of your earnings.

WHAT IS MARKET CAPITALIZATION?

This investing term refers to how much a company is worth as determined by the stock market. It is the total dollar market value of a company's outstanding shares of stock. There are three market cap distinctions in the market: *large cap* refers to companies worth $1 billion or more. Companies like Apple, Google, and Microsoft are considered *large-cap* stocks. *Mid-cap* stocks refer to companies worth $2 billion to $10 billion, and *small-cap* stocks are any companies worth $300 million to $2 billion.

WHAT IS A BROKERAGE ACCOUNT?

A brokerage account is an account that allows you to purchase and sell investments.

HOW DOES COMPOUND INTEREST WORK?

Long story short, compound interest is magic. Compound interest allows you not only to earn interest on your principal but also on top of your interest. This is why time in the market is so crucial. You're allowing your interest to gain more interest and that, as I said, is simply a magical sight!

SHOULD I OPEN A ROTH OR TRADITIONAL IRA?

This depends on one main thing: do you want to save on taxes now or do you want to save on them later? If you go the traditional route, you will have a tax advantage now since you'd be funding your IRA with pre-tax dollars. This would lower your taxable income in the present day. If you go the Roth route, you will be funding your IRA with post-tax dollars that will grow tax-free. That means when you withdraw at the time of retirement you will not have to pay taxes on your gains. People choose the Roth route if they feel they will be in a higher tax bracket in the future.

WHAT IS A ROBO-ADVISOR?

Having a living, breathing financial advisor is pricy, and investing on your own can be a bit overwhelming when you first get started. A robo-advisor is a happy medium. They provide automated investment services using algorithm-driven planning. When you sign up for an account with a robo-advisor, you'll likely have to answer a series of questions so that they can familiarize themselves with your goals and financial situation. After that, the algorithm does its thing and offers advice while automatically investing for you. I share my robo-advisor suggestions in the resources at the end of this book.

Now that you've reached this point, I want you to stop and do something for me. Whether you want to call it a homework assignment or an action item, you have to get it done. I'll *know* if you don't! If you haven't started your investment journey yet, I want you to take one step today to get started. It can be something as small as researching an index fund you want to invest in or opening your first brokerage account. If you're not enrolled in a 401K at work, it can be as simple as reaching out to HR to learn how to enroll. By taking one step today, you're setting your future self up to reach financial independence and one step closer to future millionaire status!

CHAPTER 6

THIS GIRL IS ON FIRE

Take a moment right now to imagine what financial independence looks like. Now that you can picture it, answer the following questions for me. In your financially independent life, what are you thinking about? What are you feeling? Are you doing things you've always wanted to do? Does it feel like an unattainable dream? What freedoms will financial independence afford you? How will your quality of life impacted as you thought about your era of financial freedom?

Though it may seem like it, these questions are not rhetorical. Yes, financial freedom is going to obviously have a positive impact on your day to day. However, financial independence does not solely focus on the day to day. It's unlikely anyone would argue that having an ample amount of money at your disposal makes things easier 100 percent of the time. Despite this universal truth, being rich is relative and financial independence looks different for every individual. A recent CNBC survey uncovered 80 percent of Americans said they need to earn at least $100,000 a year to feel rich. While 80 percent seems like the vast majority does agree on what financial independence looks like when it comes to income, it's important to peel back the layers on the stats at hand.

- 61 percent of Americans currently earning less than $100,000 would feel rich earning between $50,000-$150,000.

- Whereas only 7 percent of Americans currently earning more than $100,000 would feel rich earning the same $50,000-$150,000 income range.

- 52 percent of those earning more than $100,00 stated they would need more than $200,000 annually to feel rich.

- 18 percent of Americans who make less than $50,000 would feel rich earning between $50,000–$99,000, while only 2 percent of Americans who make more than $100,000 would feel the same income range.

Your current economic circumstances and income play a significant role in determining how you define financial comfort and financial independence. So yes, when I ask you what financial independence means to you, I want you to stop and think:

- What does my most financially independent self look like?

- What do I do with my time? Even better, what do I no longer do with my time?

- How do I feel? How do I think about the world?

- Where do I go? Where do I stop going?

Financial independence has the power to evolve the intricacies of your life, and FIRE can help you get there. The acronym FIRE was popularized in 1992 by Vicki Robin and Joe Dominguez in their book, *Your Money or Your Life*. It is a term used to express the Financial Independence, Retire Early (FIRE) movement. FIRE strategically accelerates your path to financial independence and will require you to have a strong "why" to build and support your day-to-day financial routines.

The FIRE movement has evolved over the last thirty years to incorporate different versions to meet the needs of various lifestyles, but at its core it is the practice of saving and investing in a way that allows for earlier retirement than the traditional path permits. FIRE often gets a bad rap because when practiced in an extreme manner oftentimes leads to unhealthy deprivation to meet target investing and saving goals. However, extreme deprivation is not the only way to reach FIRE; in fact, it's my least favorite way. So let's look at the different paths you can take to financial independence and what they'll require of you.

FIVE TYPES OF FIRE

Whenever I discuss FIRE with anyone, I always get two questions: "Is FIRE for me?" and "What would I do if I retired early?" The first question is a bit harder to answer, so I'll answer the second first. FIRE is not just about retiring early.

The concept of retiring has been coupled with old age because the traditional retirement age is sixty-five years old. Yes, at the ripe young age of sixty-five you are eligible to receive your full Social Security benefits, which at this rate will likely provide you with the most lavish lifestyle seven dollars can buy.

If you're concerned that you won't know what to do with yourself if you retire early, think about the alternative. The current average yearly Social Security benefit for sixty-five-year-olds in 2023 is $30,708 or $2,559 a month. You calculated your monthly expenses in Chapter 1; can you live the life you have right now with $2,500? Can you live the life you want with $2,500 a month? Wise future millionaires do not plan to rely solely on Social Security at retirement, and you are a wise future millionaire.

When it comes to FIRE, my focus isn't on retiring early; instead I prefer to use the term *work optional*. FIRE is a financially liberating path that makes working a choice and not a requirement. If comfort and flexibility are what you're after, then FIRE is for you! I'm chasing FIRE so I can get to that FU money way faster so when people ask, "What are you going to do if you retire early?" I can simply respond, "Whatever I want whenever I want."

Though I do believe everyone would benefit from practicing FIRE, I don't think everyone needs to practice it in the same manner. Financial freedom means different things to different people, and personal finance is just that: personal. So of course, it makes sense to have options when it comes to FIRE. All types are going to require the following in varying degrees:

- **Discipline:** No matter the type of FIRE you align with, you must take a disciplined approach to your finances to meet your goals. Discipline does not necessarily mean deprivation. It's important to clarify this immediately. Will you have to give up some things? Maybe. Will you have to give up everything? Absolutely not. Your level of discipline will make quite a difference.

- **Your Numbers:** With the work you've completed in previous chapters, you should have a pretty firm understanding of your current numbers. Let's expand that picture further. By now you know what you have in your accounts, but what do you want or need in your accounts to comfortably become work optional? You'll find many ways to calculate that number, but as someone who stands firmly against overcomplicating anything, we're going to go with the simplest calculation method. The simplest way to calculate your FI (financial independence) number is to take your annual expenses and multiply it by 25. For example, if you need $100,000 a year to cover your lifestyle needs you would aim to save $2.5 million for retirement. In Chapter 11 we'll further discuss how to account for inflation, and how to withdraw your money on an annual basis. But for now, let's stick to **_annual expenses x 25 = FIRE_** as our base calculation equation.

- **A Plan:** Lastly you'll need a plan, preferably an automated plan, but a plan, nonetheless. Your plan will define your strategy. I like to work backward whenever I need to create a plan. Start with your end number in mind and create the plan from there. What do you need to do weekly, monthly, and annually to reach your short-term target goals and long-term financial goals? What's important when creating your plan is that you want to be realistic and flexible. Sometimes the plan will need to change. It's okay to have a contingency plan if your initial strategy doesn't go exactly as planned. Never forget that life is gonna life no matter what we have planned.

TRADITIONAL FIRE

The OG version of FIRE front and center has led the way for many people to become financially independent way before sixty-five!

How to Calculate Your FIRE Number

The traditional FIRE method takes the simple equation:

ANNUAL EXPENSES X 25 = FIRE

and provides you with your financial independence number.

Once you've calculated your FIRE number, your next steps will involve increasing your investment assets while keeping your expenses low. How you navigate the process of achieving traditional FIRE is truly based on your discretion, but the main factor besides increasing investments is avoiding lifestyle creep. Any additional income you make is saved or invested, and large splurges or major personal purchases are kept to a minimum. The lower your expenses remain, the more you can direct to your savings and brokerage accounts so you can hit FIRE quicker. Those who practice traditional FIRE also focus on increasing their income to help accelerate the process.

FAT FIRE

I'm not going to mince words with you here; this version of FIRE is aggressive and is *not* easily attainable for the average person. Most people who successfully achieve Fat FIRE have a high annual income source and are pursuing a FIRE number of $2.5 million or more.

How to Calculate Your Fat FIRE Number

The Fat FIRE equation has a bit of a twist in comparison to the traditional method. Your Fat FIRE number takes:

YOUR YEARLY SPENDING X 25 = FAT FIRE

This FIRE strategy involves saving and investing aggressively without necessarily tightening those purse strings. People who adopt Fat FIRE do not typically operate on a tight budget nor do they downsize their current lifestyle. A major Fat FIRE pro is the considerable financial flexibility you gain in retirement since you have preemptively prepared to cover expenses for a higher cost of living. The appeal is clear, but the process takes longer to achieve than other FIRE variants.

Fat FIRE is far easier to achieve as a six-figure earner than for someone who earns a lower income. According to the US Bureau of Labor Statistics, the 2022 median salary is $54,132 a year, so unfortunately six-figure salaries are not yet the new norm despite what the internet would have you believe. Does that mean that the 83 percent of people who earn less than six figures should just give up? No, not at all. It will, however, require one of two things:

1. A strategic road map to earn that six-figure income.

or

2. The acceptance that you may have to work a little longer before you can retire.

Even with all the magic of compound interest it will still take an extended period of time to hit your Fat FIRE goal if you cannot aggressively fund your portfolio.

LEAN FIRE

If you're a self-proclaimed minimalist, then Lean FIRE is definitely for you. You can think of Lean FIRE as traditional FIRE's minimalist sibling.

How to Calculate Your Lean FIRE Number

By now we know the equation is going to include expenses and that little multiplication symbol is going to pop up to give us our end game. Correct with a little razzle-dazzle. Because Lean FIRE is a slimmed-down version of traditional FIRE, you are calculating your monthly expense target. Typically, those who seek to successfully achieve Lean FIRE live on $25,000–$40,000 annually, depending on their household dynamic. On average someone practicing Lean FIRE will decrease their monthly expenses to $3,400 or less. So let's do some math using the following equation:

ANNUAL TARGET EXPENSES X 25 = LEAN FIRE

For someone with a target monthly expense of $3,400, their annual target expenses equal $40,800 (FYI: this would be considered the heavier side of Lean FIRE). Their total Lean FIRE number would be $1.02 million. If an individual were on the leaner side of Lean FIRE and had a monthly target expense rate of $2,500 ($30,000 annually), their Lean FIRE number would be $750,000.

With Fat FIRE you have the freedom to splurge on luxury items on your road to financial independence, whereas Lean FIRE requires a frugal, minimalist approach.

What I enjoy most about Lean FIRE is it makes financial independence accessible to the everyday person. Fat FIRE, though appealing, can feel unattainable for those that do not earn a higher income. Lean FIRE draws its appeal with the promise of time. Individuals who want to buy back their time quicker find that Lean FIRE is the way to go to avoid extending their financial independence beyond their desired timeline.

If the sound of Lean FIRE speaks to you, remember that your strategy will differ from traditional and Fat FIRE practices. There will be decisions you have to make to achieve that lean lifestyle, such as moving to a LCOL city, moving in with a family member or significant other to save on housing, and putting off large ticket purchases like a house or car. Another significant life decision many Lean FIRE enthusiasts consider is choosing not to have children. It is not impossible to be a homeowner, own a car, or be a parent if you choose to practice Lean FIRE but it is more difficult. Both the expected and unexpected financial requirements associated with all three can make it difficult to stick to a restricted budget or minimalist lifestyle.

And *this* is why we have options! If one doesn't work for your needs, there's always an alternative.

BARISTA FIRE

And here we have option four: the FIRE variant for my people seeking financial independence and still wanting to work in some capacity. Barista FIRE is a happy medium that isn't quite traditional, not entirely Lean, and dabbles a bit into Fat. It's got that "just right" perfect porridge vibe for people who want to practice FIRE and still have the benefits of employment like health insurance and supplemental income.

How to Calculate Your Barista FIRE Number

Like the previously mentioned variants, you always start your calculations with your traditional FIRE number. Remember that's **annual expenses x 25 = FIRE.** Your next step is to estimate the potential salary from a side gig, part-time or full-time job that you will continue to work. Then subtract your annual expenses from the salary you'll be earning. Last step, multiply the supplemental income needed by 25, and that is your Barista FIRE number.

That was a lot of verbalized math steps, so I understand if it made your head spin. Here's a simplified breakdown so you can visually see how to put the equation into practice.

- **Annual expenses** = $60,000

- **Traditional FIRE number** = $1.5 million

- **Estimated side hustle/part-time work income** = $30,000

- **Remaining expenses not covered by supplemental income**: $30,000

- **Barista FIRE equation** = uncovered expenses x 25 ($30,000 x 25)

- **Barista FIRE number** = $750,000

I'm no mathematician, but a savings goal of $750,000 seems more attainable than $1.5 million. Barista FIRE is an opportunity to pursue financial independence, give up your traditional nine-to-five, and decrease the pressures that come with living solely on your investments. Y'all know by now I have an immense risk aversion, so Barista FIRE is the interpretation of FIRE that personally hits the sweet spot for me. By incorporating supplemental income and health insurance there's a layer of security Barista FIRE offers that other interpretations of FIRE do not.

So why isn't everyone pursuing Barista FIRE? Well frankly, sometimes you don't want to work or side hustle anymore and that is well within your rights. What you gain in mental or financial security, you may give up in time. With every interpretation of FIRE, you will have tradeoffs you must make, so it's important to consider what you want your financial independence to look and feel like.

Ask yourself the following questions if you are considering pursuing Barista FIRE:

- When I retire from my full-time job, what will I do for health insurance?

- Am I currently working a job that I genuinely enjoy? Or is my current career mentally and emotionally draining on a consistent basis?

- Will I be able to live a fulfilling lifestyle with low expenses?

- Is there another low-stakes part-time job or monetizable side hustle that you would enjoy doing as an alternative to your current nine-to-five?

Dependent on your answers you will be able to decide whether Barista FIRE is the route you'd like to take on your path to financial independence.

COAST FIRE

Earlier in the book, I mentioned I reached Coast FIRE, so let's get into exactly what that means. Coast FIRE doesn't mean immediate financial independence, nor does it mean you can retire early. *Say what?* I know, I know, how could a type of FIRE in the FIRE chapter of all places not lead to financial independence or early retirement? Coast FIRE, also affectionately known as Coast FI, is an important indicator that you're on the right track.

Reaching Coast FIRE means that you have invested enough money early on to reap the full benefits of compound interest by sixty-five, a.k.a. the traditional retirement age. You've done all the hard work upfront and now, for lack of a less punny word...get to *coast.* If you've been on personal finance TikTok long enough you have heard people say, "If I never invest another dollar in x years I'll have x amount of dollars." If you follow me on any social platform you've definitely heard me say it before as well.

What's important to remember when striving to achieve Coast FI is that you will still need to work once you've hit your target investment number. While the other variants of FIRE give you some form of early retirement, Coast FI doesn't operate quite the same way. The main appeal of frontloading your investments is the freedom you gain after reaching a huge financial milestone. You no longer have to save for retirement and can use that extra money for other ventures.

The specific investment threshold needed to reach Coast FI will depend on none other than your traditional FIRE number. However, most financial experts agree that hitting six-figure territory in your investment portfolio is that magical moment that signifies you have successfully transitioned into Coast FI.

HOW TO CALCULATE YOUR COAST FIRE NUMBER

You know where our calculations always begin—calculate your traditional FIRE number. Now we get into the most intricate calculations on the FIRE spectrum. FYI, there are tons of plug-and-play digital Coast FI calculators that will take the mathematical pressure off your plate. Even though I hate doing math, I still like to understand how the numbers work themselves out. This calculation outline is strictly for informative purposes only; soft life your way right into those digital calculators whenever you can.

Calculating Coast FI consists of three steps. You've already done the first (calculated your traditional FIRE number). The next step requires the compound interest formula: **A = P * (1 + n) ^t** to calculate your Coast FIRE number. You set "A" as your traditional FIRE number, jot down the amount of time you have left until you reach the traditional retirement age, and choose an annual growth rate. Typically, if you're investing in the S&P500 you can historically expect to see an annual return of 10 percent over an extended period of time. I, however, like to err on the side of caution and use much more conservative rates like 7 or 8 percent to account for potential down years.

If step two is getting confusing, let's clarify where we're at so far. Our compound interest formula has us plugging in the following information and solving for "P."

- **A** = your traditional FIRE number
- **P** = principal (initial amount you'll need to reach Coast FIRE: this is what we're currently trying to calculate in step two, so you're solving for P)
- **n** = annual growth rate (between 6 and 10 percent)
- **t** = time in years (how many years do you have before you reach traditional retirement age)

Example Time!

One thirty-five-year-old future millionaire in the squad has $40,000 in annual expenses and wants to retire at sixty-five years old. Their traditional FIRE number is one million dollars ($40,000 x 25), and they have thirty years' worth of compounding to get there. Though the S&P500 has traditionally returned an average of 10 percent over the long term, for our purposes we'll use an 8 percent instead. Now we plug and play the numbers to calculate the Coast FIRE number.

- $1,000,000 = P * (1 + 0.08) ^\wedge 30$

- $1,000,000 = P * (1.08) ^\wedge 30$

- $P = \$199,062$

Our thirty-five-year-old future millionaire would need to have $199,062 invested right now to successfully Coast FIRE themselves into their financially independent number by retirement.

What's the third step? If you're looking to achieve Coast FIRE, once you've figured out your Coast FI number, you now have a goal to work toward. Your third step is implementing the necessary investment steps into your financial routines. If your Coast FI number is $150,000 and you have $50,000 currently invested, set long-term and short-term goals to keep your $150,000 target in focus.

Goals and the steps to reach those goals will differ but can include things like:

- Increasing the contribution to your employer-sponsored retirement plan (that's your 401K, 403B, or 457)

- Opening an IRA (traditional or Roth is up to you)

- Investing in an HSA (if you're eligible)

- Dollar-cost averaging your investments consistently into your taxable brokerage account

- Using your sign-on or annual bonuses as a large investment opportunity

- Directing 30–50 percent of your side hustle funds into your investment portfolio

HOW TO SET YOUR MONEY ON FIRE

So far, you've got the pros, cons, formulas, and calculations associated with FIRE and its variants. You may even have a headache with all that math we just had to endure together. I promise not to do that again! However, what I haven't shared with you just yet is how to actually get started.

CALCULATE YOUR FIRE NUMBER

The first thing I want you to do if you haven't stopped reading to do so already is to calculate your FIRE number. Even if you have no interest in following any FIRE lifestyle or you don't plan on retiring early, it is still important to know your numbers, and your financial independence number is a big one!

CONSIDER IF FIRE IS FOR YOU

Now, I've asked you quite a few times in this book to be completely honest with yourself, and this is going to be one of those times. FIRE, even with all of its variations, may not be effective for you and that is okay. You may finish reading this chapter and decide that the FIRE movement just isn't your cup of tea. Let's be real here—it can at times feel restrictive and more than a little obsessive. That doesn't mean if you decide not to seek out FIRE you can't be on your future millionaire wealth-building flow.

FIRE guardrails maintain two main foci: saving as much as possible and limiting new debt. These are powerful financial guardrails, but they are not always possible for everyone at all times. There are barriers, systemic and otherwise, that can stand directly in the way of practically achieving FIRE. In addition, forcing FIRE when you don't have the capacity to do so can be catastrophic to your motivation and ability to prepare properly. FIRE can also create massive FOMO, especially if you choose to practice Lean FIRE. I recommend three things to consider before you dive into any type of FIRE.

- Discuss your financial goals with your loved ones. This will help you not only express your goals and vision for yourself in the future, but it will also help both you and them manage expectations. There will undoubtedly be lifestyle changes that impact you as well as them such as attending birthday celebrations, taking vacations, going out, etc. The conversations will serve as a litmus test indicating how prepared you are to take on this task and how much support you'll have along the way.

- Consider the pros and cons of what your new lifestyle will entail. Write down a pro/con list if you wish and think about the following questions: will you be able to comfortably adjust to certain expenses being removed or minimized? Are you truly okay with sacrificing certain experiences for an extended period of time to reach your FIRE number?

- Ask yourself what you are doing this for. Why do you want to partake in the FIRE movement? What are you trying to achieve? Make sure the answers to those questions are crystal clear because they will be your "why." They will be the North Star you return to when doing the financially responsible thing isn't appealing.

DECIDE WHICH TYPE OF FIRE IS FOR YOU

Okay, you've decided that FIRE is for you; now it's time to choose which type of FIRE you'll be practicing. Here's a quick pro/con comparison since I made you do all that math earlier.

TYPE OF FIRE	PROS	CONS	HOW MUCH DO YOU NEED TO INVEST?	CAN YOU QUIT YOUR JOB?
Coast FIRE	• You don't need to worry about whether you'll have enough saved for retirement. • Once you hit Coast FI you can use the extra money for other lifestyle expenses. • An easier target to reach than your full FIRE number.	• Even when you hit Coast FI you still have to keep working. • You need a lot more time on your side. The earlier you start the easier and less money you'll have to invest.	Usually between 25–50 percent of your FIRE number	No
Fat FIRE	• Fat FIRE allows for more of a comfortable or luxurious retirement. • Your budget has a bit more wiggle room for larger purchases. • Not only are you work optional, but you become location independent and can live in HCOL cities.	• You will need to save a lot of money, which can take quite some time to achieve. • Can tempt you to splurge and live above your means.	$2.5 million or more	Yes

Traditional FIRE	• Gives you the opportunity to achieve financial independence before traditional retirement age.	• May be a bit restrictive as you focus on saving as much as possible for retirement.	$1 million– $2.5 million	Yes
Lean FIRE	• Works well for people who want to or live a minimalistic lifestyle. • Much lower and accessible FIRE number. • You become work optional the quickest with this version of FIRE.	• Can be a bit restrictive since Lean FIRE is usually restricted to $3,300 in monthly expenses. • Lean FIRE does not work well for people with children, a mortgage or other large monthly expenses. • Can require relocation if you live in a HCOL city.	Less than $1 million (dependent on your annual expenses)	Yes

| Barista FIRE | • You can reach Barista FIRE much quicker than traditional FIRE since the threshold is lower.

• Allows you to transition out of a high-stress job and into more appealing work.

• Your part-time job helps offset your expenses and can provide you with health insurance. | • Just like with Coast FI you still have to work. You can work less, but you still have to work.

• Depending on how far you are from your FIRE number you may have to work/side hustle for a long time.

• Finding that side hustle or part-time job that fulfills you can be difficult. | Usually between 50–100 percent of your traditional FIRE number | No |

CHOOSE YOUR STRATEGY

The last pieces of the FIRE puzzle are your actionable steps. As I mentioned earlier, this will look different for everyone because we are individuals who navigate our personal finances differently. But I'll never leave you to figure it out yourself. Here are a few recommendations for financial routines to add to your FIRE strategy.

- **Decrease your expenses:** No matter which version of FIRE you choose to follow you are going to want to decrease your expenses, so you have more of that glorious gap (the money left over after you've covered all your big girl, big boy, or big nonbinary bills).

- **Increase your income:** Whether that's by job hopping, landing a promotion and a raise, or side hustling, you'll want to increase your income to help accelerate the amount of money you can save for retirement. Healthy reminder: when you increase your income, see tip one: decrease your expenses. Do not fall victim to inflating your lifestyle, a.k.a. lifestyle creep. The key is to continue to increase the amount of money you have remaining at the end of each month.

- **Invest with intent:** To achieve goals you've never achieved before; you must do things you've never done before. You can't expect to invest more if you don't intentionally do so. That means following the investing order of operations back in Chapter 5. Start with your employer-sponsored plan up to the match, then shift your focus toward maxing your IRA and HSA. Once you've hit the max in both of those accounts, pivot back toward your 401K or 403B and max that out as well. By that point you will have invested a little over $30,000 for the year, a moment to stop and celebrate. If you've still got more gas in the investing tank, then turn to a taxable brokerage to continue your path.

Think back to what you imagined financial independence would look and feel like at the start of this chapter. Recall what you were doing, where you were, and what you were feeling. Hold on to that moment for just a second longer. Now set it on FIRE.

CHAPTER 7

SIDE HUSTLE & CHILL

Come in close; I want to share a secret with you. There is not a single wealthy person in existence that gained financial freedom with one income stream. Before you roll your eyes and tell me you already knew this, let's stop and think about it for a moment. How many finance books, articles, or social media posts have you seen that provide a similar variation of the following cookie-cutter money advice: "to buy a house or save more money you need to cut those seven-dollar lattes out of your life." Not only does that feed directly into a scarcity mindset, but it also implies that the path to wealth is made up of nonstop sacrifice. Do you really think Jeff Bezos, Elon Musk, and Mark Zuckerberg became billionaires because they pinched their pennies and made coffee at home? Let's be supercalifragilisticexpialidociously for real here. Steve Jobs did many unconventional things to build wealth, but I guarantee you homemade coffee wasn't one of his wealth-building hacks.

Here's the reality when it comes to money and building wealth. Yes, it takes a remarkable amount of discipline and focus to manage money properly and gain financial freedom. If you don't have the right mindset and routines in place to effectively manage ten dollars you won't magically be better at managing a hundred or a thousand dollars. You know what else it takes to build wealth? More money. Your mindset, though a crucial piece to the wealth-building puzzle, will not be the primary factor that leads to generational wealth. The primary factor that leads to wealth is money. There's no way around that indisputable fact.

A 2018 CNBC article revealed that 65 percent of self-made millionaires had three streams of income, while 29 percent had five or more. Having multiple streams of income is a logical financial routine to implement into your wealth-building strategy. I don't know about you, but around here I love things that make sense. During economic volatility one stream of income is not always reliable, especially if the source of that income is negatively impacted for whatever reason.

If the pandemic showed us nothing else, it horrifically highlighted how quickly one source of income can become no source of income. Having more than one way to secure the bag is not only imperative to building wealth but also a protective measure to help you sustain your lifestyle should an unexpected life change occur.

Basically, the millionaires out here are putting us on to free game by showing, not telling, and I love me a lucrative show and tell. We never want to put all our eggs in one basket, and after stressing the need to diversify your portfolio in Chapter 5, I'd be a huge hypocrite if I didn't keep that same energy here. We have no choice but to diversify.

HOW TO BUILD MULTIPLE STREAMS OF INCOME

There are two considerations to keep in mind as you prepare to create multiple streams of income. The first step to building anything is to know your options. There are seven main categories that define the types of income you can hope to earn.

TYPE OF INCOME	HOW TO EARN THIS TYPE OF INCOME
Dividend Income	If you invest in the stock market, you become part-owner of the companies you buy shares from. That also means you earn dividends from those companies (think of it as a reward for being a part-owner). A company will distribute its profits to its shareholders usually on a quarterly basis. The more shares you have in a company, the larger your dividend will be. You can use these quarterly payments as a source of passive income or reinvest your dividends to continue to grow your investment portfolio.
Capital Gains	This type of income is earned through buying and selling assets where you make a profit. In fancy-schmancy investing terms, that profit is called a capital gain. So if you buy a share of a company for $200 and sell that share for $250, your capital gain is $50.

Interest Payments	If you have any type of debt you already understand how interest works. Lenders make a ton of additional income on the interest we pay on the money we have borrowed. It works the same way for us as consumers, on a smaller scale. Putting your money in a savings account (preferably a high-yield savings account), opening a certificate of deposit (CD), or purchasing a government bond are three ways you can earn interest payment income.
Business Income	Even if you don't consider yourself a business owner or entrepreneur, you still earn business income if you dabble in various side hustles. Often, side hustles become the catalyst for business ideation and execution, so don't sleep on your potential earning power or opportunity to turn your side hustle into your main hustle.
Earned Income	Though all income is technically earned, this is the income you make from your everyday nine-to-five. It's what I like to call ol' faithful because you know that every two weeks, that check is deposited into your bank account.
Rental Income	Rental income sounds like it should be any income that stems from renting out just about anything. Though that is not technically incorrect, for our intents and purposes we will go with the more commonly accepted understanding of what it means to earn rental income: owning and renting out an investment property. So if you own a building or a home that you purchased to generate income, you are earning rental income. It is important to note that though rental income can be steadily lucrative, it does require a substantial initial investment on your end because...well, duh, you have to make a large investment to buy the property.
Royalties	This type of income is a passive income stream that you can generate by creating a product and charging people or businesses a fee to use it. For example, musicians who create a song are paid a royalty fee whenever that song is used in a movie, show, video game, etc.

HUSTLE CULTURE: IS IT DEAD OR REBRANDED?

By this point in our literary journey together, you're aware that I paid off $102,000 in student loans over five years while working as a high school English teacher in New York, an immensely high cost-of-living area. You know the what and the why, so now it's time to share the how.

In 2013, as a teacher with a master's degree and an additional thirty-credit differential, I was making a smidge more than $60,000 a year. After taxes and deductions, I'd bring home about $2,600 a month. The goals I wanted to reach were set, the timeline was mapped out, and the plans were in motion. I inhaled every episode of Diddy's *Making the Band* and inundated myself with every #Girlboss #BossBabe book I could get my hands on. If I had to operate on two hours of sleep, walk to Junior's for cheesecake, and eat nothing but $0.99 honey buns for dinner every night to prove my dedication and hustle, I would.

It is not a shock how easily I adopted the hustle culture mentality and turned it into an annoyingly overbearing full-time personality. The ingredients were already in the pantry. When you mix West Indian first-generation overachiever with first-born daughter and sprinkle a dash of toxic 2013 girl-boss energy, the result is bound to be a burnt-out, unhinged disaster.

Outside of illegal activities and sex work, there was no side hustle that was off-limits. Can't make it home to walk your dog? Oh, of course I can help! I'm a canine connoisseur and it just so happens I can walk 'em even better than Cesar Milan, dog whisperer extraordinaire! Need a tutor for your kids' educational advancement? You got it. I'm free nights and weekends. Four-hour focus groups? Yes, I'll be there right after my two-hour tutoring session. Taste tester? Mystery shopper? Count me in! I'm with all the shits.

The more I hustled, the more miserable I became. At the time, my mental health was declining rapidly, and honestly, I didn't care. Taking my day-to-day feelings into consideration wasn't a priority because I kept telling myself that the misery was worth it as long as I reached the goal. It was my fault I was in this mess, so it was up to me to get out of it by any means necessary. The level of shame and embarrassment I felt as a college graduate with two degrees who couldn't afford to move out of my parents' house consistently played in my head on loop. It was my driving force, and nothing else mattered but the hustle.

Hustle culture was, is, and always will be bullshit. For a more prophetic definition I shall use the words of a more prophetic speaker. Joe Ryle, the director of the four-day week campaign, defined *hustle culture* as "work dominating your time in such an unnatural way that we have no time to live our lives." It is a culture that benefits capitalism through systems that reward and glorify busyness as the ultimate sign of productivity. The more you do, the more valuable you are, it seems. The more you do, the more your hustle is taken advantage of. A 2021 survey published by the ADP Research Institute revealed one in ten employees across seventeen countries have been putting in more than twenty hours of free work per week, averaging 9.2 hours of unpaid overtime weekly. As I said, hustle culture was, is, and always will be bullshit.

We've been inundated with hustle culture way before the term was packaged up nicely into think pieces on the internet. I was eight years old when Jay Z told me you can't knock the hustle. A whole decade before Rick Ross and Lil' Wayne told me to hustle hard. Enter the endless amounts of films that lean heavily into the hard-worker trope including a highly involved, self-centered shark of a character that puts their job before anything, thus risking and jeopardizing every relationship in their lives. You add a drizzle of gender-study-worthy girl-boss toxicity and every variation of The Devil Wears Prada springs to mind. We're not new to this.

However, the 2008 Great Recession certainly played a special part in the aggressive acceleration and amplification of the "rise and grind" mentality in younger generations. With the growing popularity of social media increasing our visibility into other people's lives and the tough economic climate, millennials felt an immense pressure to work longer hours and take on more side gigs as a means of survival. At that time, when many people were facing layoffs, foreclosures, and financial insecurities, prominent social media influencers, businesspeople, and motivational speakers were spewing the grind culture rhetoric at all-time highs. Elon Musk, the CEO of Tesla, and newly appointed Twitter overlord, notoriously stated, "nobody ever changed the world on forty hours a week." Were you doing enough to not only ensure success but ensure you could also afford a roof over your head? The hustling-harder dynamic shifted into hustling out of necessity to cover basic expenses, pay off debt, and save for specific goals that their full-time jobs could not financially cover.

There is no denying that doing the most in your professional or personal life can have tremendous financial benefits. Promotions, raises, annual bonuses, and staying employed during massive layoffs, just to name a few. And what happens after that? *Burnout!* As a culture we have collectively shifted toward a deeper understanding of mental health and its impact on the emotional and physical self. Hustle culture as we knew it, was not sustainable for the long term. Besides a loss of work-life balance, the World Health Organization (WHO) conducted a study revealing that working more than fifty-five hours a week kills more than 745,000 people a year. The hustle quite literally has the power to take us out one medical issue at a time. Working excessively increases the risk of stroke by 35 percent and heart disease by 17 percent.

Over the last twelve years the economy waxed and waned as it so often does, and hustle culture experienced several transitional periods as well. We saw a rise in gig work as companies like Uber, Lyft, and Instacart popped onto the scene. MLMs continued to sucker in unsuspecting participants at unprecedented rates. Uh, LuLaRoe, anyone? But none would be truly as transformative as the forced transition COVID-19 would cause. The pandemic hit the reset button on many aspects of our everyday lives. As a society we collectively took a step back to rethink many of the social, political, and cultural practices we previously accepted as the norm. COVID-19 shined a much-needed spotlight on the frustrations and inequities involving the labor practices of the US workforce. We told corporate America to count their days, and we meant that shit. In the spring of 2021, forty-seven million Americans voluntarily quit their jobs, according to the US Bureau of Labor Statistics.

At the start of the pandemic, companies permanently closed their doors and massive layoffs ensued. The spiking unemployment rates were daunting, and people were rightfully afraid of what could potentially come next. Like with the Great Recession, hustle culture increased as a means of survival. Those who could keep their jobs felt an immense need to increase productivity to avoid future layoffs and increase their income streams in case they were impacted. Those who were thrust into unemployment picked up side hustle after side hustle to keep a roof over their heads and food on the table. The boundaries between work and personal life blurred quickly as people were navigating feelings of fear, guilt, and shame—three emotions often caused by the glorified comparative nature that hustle culture promotes. Nicole Cammack, PhD, clinical psychologist and CEO of Black Mental Wellness, states, "It can make you feel like 'Maybe this life I'm creating isn't enough because everyone else has so much going on.'"

The longer we haphazardly navigated through COVID-19, the more the labor force evolved. In the spring of 2021, amid strong labor demand and low unemployment, the relationship between employers and employees reached a boiling point. The frustrations employees felt at the start of the pandemic remained pent up due to uncertainties in the job market. The pandemic also intensified the need for work-life balance and flexibility. 2020 brought about a tremendous amount of pain and loss, which has caused many people to reevaluate hustle culture and swap it out for healthier work-life balance opportunities instead. The role of work in people's lives ultimately shifted as more people reconsidered the nonstop grind and reevaluated priorities.

It is undoubtedly a different world, and many employers struggle to acknowledge that. There has been a clear shift in perspective as people's tolerances regarding work have changed. As fears around COVID-19 decreased and robust demand increased, frontline workers, parents, caregivers, and women experienced the brunt of burnout.

The Great Resignation has been a culmination of many factors and has led to notable action. Companies have created more attractive work environments to keep their current talent pool and attract new employees as well. Extensive benefits packages, flexible scheduling and hybrid or fully remote work became popular selling points to current and potential candidates as well as actual competitive salaries. For example, in 2021, McDonald's increased hourly wages for current employees on average by 10 percent while increasing entry-level wages between eleven and seventeen dollars an hour. They went on to improve their benefits package to add in emergency childcare, paid time off, and tuition reimbursement.

The effects and impact of the Great Resignation have reverberated through the labor force for over a year most visibly in employee benefits. But does this mean that hustle culture is dead? The latest quiet quitting trend may imply so, but I think not. A 2022 LendingTree survey revealed that three in ten employees are participating in quiet quitting, which is the act of doing the absolute bare minimum at work. Of that group, 57 percent claim their work-life balance has improved.

Which of course makes sense. Once you stop doing work outside of your job description, you will obviously have less work on your plate.

In theory, I'm all for doing your job and nothing more to avoid being taken advantage of. In reality, I know better. Quiet quitting is a privilege that most certainly is not afforded to people of color. In a world where Black and brown children are taught (cue Papa Pope's speech on *Scandal*), "You have to work twice as hard to get half as far," the notion of scaling back at work is laughable. If we're looking for ways to promote work-life balance and negate hustle culture this isn't a practical route. Quiet quitting negatively impacts other employees far more than the CEO and can be immediately ended at the employer's whim. And where does that leave the quiet quitter after they've been loudly laid off? Immediately hustling and grinding to find sustainable income. And then? Proving their productivity and value from a new cubicle in a new building in corporate America. I'm all for doing the job that pays you and doing it well without harming your mental health. However, the quiet quitting trend does not remove you from the hustle culture hamster wheel. It perpetuates it.

With the constant evolution of the job force, I can confidently say hustle culture is not going anywhere. It will look different and it will evolve, but it will never be dead. That isn't a bad thing. A little bit of hustle never hurt. The important thing to remember when side hustling, creating multiple streams of income and navigating your finances, is to manage that hustle. Be cognizant of whether you're operating at level 10 or level 100. Here are a few ways to identify, alter, and manage that hustle culture mentality so you're being productive without burning out.

HOW TO BREAK FREE OF HUSTLE CULTURE BEHAVIORS

I was doing the absolute most when I started paying off my student loans, and it was detrimental to many aspects of my life. I thought nothing of it because that's the path that made sense to me. I thought I had to deprive myself of everything and work day and night to reach my debt-free goals. Obviously, I was absolutely wrong, and I wish someone had told me there was a different way, a better way. I hope to be that voice of reason for you here.

Vulnerable honesty moment: While I do wish someone would have stepped in to tell me to relax, I'm not sure I would have listened. Though I managed to get it together eventually, this wasn't the last time that I'd find myself doing the absolute most to prove my worth. Though I am getting better at discouraging my internalized hustle culture rhetoric, I'm still a messy, chaotic, beautiful work in progress. I give myself grace to be just that. So as you read these next few lines, just know they're here to support you, but it's okay if you cannot switch off hustle culture behaviors overnight. You also are a beautiful work in progress who deserves grace.

- **Have regular check-ins:** Set aside some time to monitor your energy. Check in with yourself and be honest about how you are feeling. If you're feeling like you're close to burning out, some things have to change to prevent that. Identify what is causing those feelings of burnout so you can start targeting how to address them.

- **Schedule rest and things you enjoy:** This is the hardest for me to do, especially when I have a long laundry list of tasks to complete. Schedule some time for yourself to do nothing or something you love. No questions asked. That time is for you.

- **Set clear boundaries:** This is at work, at home, and anywhere else. Set clear boundaries for yourself and don't let anyone cross them. That includes yourself.

- **Make a priority checklist**: You are not Santa Claus, so please don't check the list obsessively. Make the list so you know what you must get done and prioritize. Sometimes I put things on the list as a lofty goal or a reminder, but I note whether it needs to get done right away. This way if I don't get it done, I'm mentally okay with that. The priority checklist also lets me know if I'm taking on too much. If my list has twenty things on it, they cannot all be a priority. Cap your list between five to eight to help you hustle with intention.

- **Give yourself grace:** I can't stress this enough! Your goals are important. Your job, family, tasks, and life are important! But they cannot operate or function properly if you're not at your best. Give yourself grace if you make a mistake, overbook, or don't hit a target in time. You will get it done.

PASSIVE INCOME IS A MISNOMER

I would like to go on record and vote to change the term "passive income" into "eventually passive income." When I discuss passive income opportunities on social media or with my clients, I choose to take the path of brutal honesty to manage expectations. Passive income is da bomb, point blank, period. I know I've violently dated myself with the usage of archaic slang but at my big ol' age, it would be cringe AF to use the Gen Z equivalent and even cringier if I used it incorrectly. I'm shamelessly a '90s kind of girl, and you're just going to have to accept that.

Swiftly moving on, passive income streams not only give you a seat at the multiple-streams-of-income table, if set up properly, they also have the potential to become a long-term income source you can capitalize on without ever lifting another finger. The catch? It isn't that simple, and just like rental income, there tends to be a huge initial investment on your end. Whether that investment is your time or money, creating a stream of passive income is hardly ever simple or passive.

Can you make money in your sleep with passive income? Absolutely. Will you lose a little bit of sleep before those passive income streams start flowing? Quite possibly. Case in point, one of the most popular passive income suggestions is to start a blog or create a digital product. As someone who has done both, let me tell you something: it is *not* as easy as YouTubers and social media influencers make it seem. Though I don't think they are purposely trying to be misleading, I want to be the first to keep it all the way 100 with you in these influencer streets. There are many active foundational steps that must first occur before you're pulling in six figures from your blog or digital product.

When I started my first public blog in 2013, it took me at least a year to make any money at all. I spent hundreds of hours writing blog posts, creating social content, learning SEO, building an engaged social media audience, and applying for brand deals, all while working full-time and side hustling part-time. That first year I made *zero* dollars. When I did eventually start making money from Google's AdSense program, my site traffic was so low I was only reaching the minimum hundred-dollar payout threshold every few months. Eight hundred–plus blog posts and a decade later, I consider my blog to be a consistent stream of passive income. But I will never downplay the amount of time, energy, and money that went in to get it to that point.

One of my largest streams of passive income while paying off my student loans was the revenue I earned from selling my lesson plans and unit plans online. To all my teachers, past, present, or future, you know the amount of work that goes into building out lesson plans and unit plans. The handouts, pacing, objectives, state standards, and grouping. On average it took forty to fifty hours to build out a four-to-six-week unit plan with lessons, activities, handouts, and assessments. I usually taught five to six units a year *per* prep! Which means if I taught two different grade levels, which I did, I'd create twelve units total for the year, an equivalent of six hundred hours or twenty-five days of lesson planning. I don't know about you, but nothing sounds passive about six hundred hours of work to me. Though I 100 percent agree, this isn't an "I think teachers should get paid more" gripe session. This is a preemptive reality check.

At the height of my lesson plan–selling era, I had forty to sixty assets in my digital store and was making $10,000–$12,000 a year. This passive income stream was critical in my debt-payoff journey because it gave me back my time and gave me options. My earned income now had breathing room. I could scale back on multiple time-consuming side hustles and use my teacher checks for expenses and savings. Of course, I could jump on social media and talk about how easy it is to make an extra $10,000 a year selling lesson plans. That type of post would get a ton of engagement. Way more engagement than a post sharing how little I slept because I spent six hundred hours creating the lessons, and hundreds more hours creating the marketing strategy and customer funnel to push traffic to the storefront. Yes, I did reach a point where I was making money in my sleep, after missing out on a shit ton of sleep first. This will not always be the case for every passive income stream you build; in fact, it may never be the case for you. However, it's important for me to share the good, bad, and ugly possibilities so that when you're in the trenches you remember one thing: keep pushing because it is absolutely worth it.

Even though I've been out of the classroom for over a year and removed a large majority of the assets in my storefront, I still make about two thousand dollars a year from the remaining lessons and units on the platform. This is the true beauty of passive income. It's the gift that keeps on giving, and that gift is freedom. The freedom to work from anywhere, take time off, spend time with your loved ones, and rest when you need to. Though we've heard time and time again that "money can't buy happiness," I respectfully disagree.

I've paid over three thousand dollars in copays and healthcare fees this year alone, and that is with the support of a six-figure tech job, an FSA, and what most would describe as really good health insurance. I am happy AF to have the funds to manage my healthcare needs, a feat that is unfortunately a privilege instead of a social norm. The Bureau of Labor Statistics recently revealed that the price of food increased by 10.6 percent, with grocery prices specifically seeing a sharp 12 percent increase. Comparatively wage growth has not managed to keep pace, and hovers at an average of 5.8 percent. A head of lettuce has seen a larger raise than the average member of the US workforce. I'll give you a moment to sit with that.

I know the late great Notorious B.I.G. told us with more money comes more problems, but I will gladly take the problems that come with having more money as opposed to the problems that come with having less of it. Money gives you the opportunity to freely interact and engage with the things, experiences, and people that make you happiest. So I'm going on record and saying yes, money does buy happiness. At the very least, it buys you food, and more tacos have never made me unhappy.

Passive income may not be 100 percent passive all the time, but there is an undeniable value surrounding its potential impact on your financial life. I still stand firmly behind the fact that passive income is da bomb and worth the initial investment. Does that mean you go out and throw your money and time into any half-baked idea simply because an internet guru said this is the fastest path to wealth? *No!* Over here we get our ducks in a row so we're over-prepared for what's to come next. So...what *does* come next?

SIDE HUSTLING 101: WHAT'S YOUR VIBE?

You already know I've had a wild ride that involves a wide gambit of side hustle experiences. In the end I ultimately scaled back my audacious hustle hard routine to two side hustles: selling my lesson plans/unit plans and blogging/creating content. I could do both from the comfort of my bed and didn't have to spend time I didn't have commuting to a specific location to make money. Though they were both time-consuming, these two side hustles were amplifications of what I was already doing daily.

FINDING THE SIDE HUSTLE THAT'S RIGHT FOR YOU

Side hustling expert and personal finance content creator Selma C. doubles as a full-time special education teacher who paid off over $41,000 of debt in 2.5 years on a $37,000 salary. How'd she get it done? Side hustling with finesse and nuance to propel her debt-free journey. Selma states, "There's but so far below your means you can live, but when you learn to increase your income, you can increase your chances of becoming financially free. I started side hustling more seriously in 2020 when I decided I wanted to be debt free. I knew I loved my job, but I also knew it wasn't paying me enough. After an honest conversation with myself I realized my debt freedom won't come from this one source of income. I had to find a way to make more money to reach my goals and I've never looked back!"

Here's a statement that deserves a huge Michelle Tanner eye-rolling *duh*: everyone is not good at everything. *Duh!* Which is why everyone cannot successfully monetize every side hustle on those popular YouTube videos or perfectly curated Pinterest lists. No matter how easy they say it is to make a hundred dollars a day, if the side hustle does not play to your current abilities, strengths, or skill set, it is not right for you. Everyone may not be good at everything, but everyone is good at something.

For several hours Selma and I commiserated about our side hustle journeys while simultaneously balancing full-time jobs that often demanded immeasurable amounts of time and energy outside of the school day. What did our stories have in common? We did the absolute most and chose side hustles that internet folks told us were "simple and easy" without taking our skills and bandwidth into account. I proceeded to ask: "From one educator to another, I know it can feel like there simply just aren't enough hours in the day to get our teaching jobs done. My side-hustle journey started off chaotically, and there are so many things I wish I had done differently. What would you say is the most impactful first step people should take when seeking to build multiple streams of income?"

Selma stated, "The first impactful step is to take inventory on the current skills you have and see how you can monetize them. Many people think side hustling requires new skills and it doesn't. The everyday administrative assistance is a great segue into becoming a virtual assistant. The teacher that makes great lesson plans and graphics for her class can sell those to supplement her income! The introverted personality can deliver packages and never has to interact with anyone. Start where you are and what you know! There is an income stream for all skills."

Personal finance is a personal experience just like your side hustle journey will be. Your budget will only thrive if it fits your lifestyle needs and money goals. Your side hustles will thrive if they fit your skills and lifestyle criteria. What are some criteria you can consider? The "Bitch I'm Budgeting" founder goes on to explain, "The first thing I did was assess the current tools and skills I had that would make me money. I realized my car, phone and experience in the education field were all great starting points. During the pandemic one of the first things I realized was how fast delivery side hustles were taking off. People weren't leaving their homes to grocery shop or get food. I started with one of the easiest side hustles to sign up for which was delivering food and groceries for people. I would work my regular nine-to-five and then side hustle from six to nine in the evening and would make about $200 to $250 a day! I found side hustles that would be easy for me to do after work and wouldn't eat up too much of my time. Most delivery side hustles only require a car or bike and my smartphone. You always want to use what you have within your reach before acquiring new skills to make money."

WHAT'S THE ROI?

As you seek to increase your income streams, this is a question I want you to keep at the forefront. What is the return on my investment? This isn't only about how much money you're earning; this question embodies your entire side hustle experience. Once you've taken the time to assess your skills and outline your criteria you have to determine the holistic impact. Map out what the entirety of the side hustle will entail on every level and how it will impact your financial goals. If that sounds way too daunting just to deliver groceries it doesn't have to be. Here's how you can easily calculate a potential side hustle's ROI to determine if it is the right fit for you.

- **Skill set required:** What skills do you need to complete this side hustle? Do you already possess these skills, or will you have to take time to learn them? If you do need or want to learn the required skills, how long will that take and how much will it cost?

- **Money goal:** What is the monetary goal you're hoping to reach with this side hustle? How long will it take you to reach based on compensation? This will vary based on the side hustle. For example, if your goal is to make an additional $250 a week tutoring, what is your hourly rate and how many clients will you need a week to reach that goal? Delivering groceries on Instacart? How many hours on average will you have to work to hit the same $250 goal?

- **Interests:** Am I interested in this side hustle on a passionate level or is this a means of simply making more money? Be very honest with yourself here! It's okay if you're not passionate about the potential work you'll be doing, but this is something you want to know beforehand to manage your expectations around the experience.

- **Demand:** Is this side hustle in demand? Is it solving a major pain point for people? Is there a ton of competition? Are there numerous places or platforms you can use to find customers or opportunities to make money?

- **Convenience:** How convenient is this side hustle going to be in your life? Will you have to commute, or can you do it remotely? Can you set your own hours or is there a predetermined schedule?

- **Time invested:** Do you have the time in your schedule to commit to a set number of hours daily? Weekly? Monthly? More importantly, does the available time you have in your schedule allow you to make a substantial amount of money to bring you closer to your money goal? Time is a valuable resource that should not be wasted. If you can only work one hour a week and only make fifteen dollars, is that worth the hassle?

- **Anticipated costs:** How much money will this side hustle cost you? For example, starting a blog is a way of making passive income, but it takes *time* and *money*! The amount of time and money will vary but you'll still need to invest in a domain, potential hosting fees, and other small expenses that can add up. Another non-digital example is gig work like Instacart or Uber Eats, which require some form of transportation. Be sure to calculate the cost of gas or car maintenance needed if you choose this as an additional income option. Wanting to passionately jump into a side hustle is noble, but it is important to be practical as well. If the anticipated initial investments will take some time to recover, factor that into your ROI.

Now it's your turn! Use this graph to identify a side hustle you've been interested in or researched to determine if the ROI is worth your time, effort, and energy. Don't forget the resources at the back of the book have my favorites and if you're stuck on side hustle ideas and platforms, I've got you covered!

SKILL SET REQUIRED:	
MONEY GOAL:	
INTERESTS:	
DEMAND:	
CONVENIENCE:	
TIME INVESTED:	
ANTICIPATED COSTS:	

I HAVE MORE MONEY, NOW WHAT?

First off, congratulations because this is a great problem to have. How's the line go? "Birthdays was the worst days, now we create a plan 'cause we thirty," or whatever Biggie said. Your additional streams of income need to be planned for just like your first stream of income. We're not about to Walter White our money away. *Every* dollar has a job around here y'all.

Your relationship with money will evolve, your financial goals will change, and your budget should keep up. Outside of putting money aside for Uncle Sam because we absolutely do not play around with taxes, you'll have to determine how your additional income will be used. Will you be sending all your side hustle money directly to your debt? Is it being used to build your emergency savings fund? Invest? Buy a spaceship? A little of all three?

At the start of my side hustle journey, I put all my additional income into a sinking fund and used it to pay the principal on my student loans at the end of each year. By doing this, I updated my budget so my earned income could be used for bills, savings, and fun money. As my teacher salary grew, my budget was updated again to reflect that. This kept me focused on my money goals but also shifted my perspective on deprivation and how I would side hustle moving forward. I became money-minded logically.

Toward the end of my conversation with Selma, I asked her about the impact of side hustling on her relationship with money, and I was pleasantly surprised to hear, "Side hustling has changed my life! It has shown me I can use my current skills, tools, and resources to create so many new streams of income. You don't need new skills to make new money! In 2020 I made $23,000 side hustling and in 2021 I made $45,000 by leveraging my car, phone, and current profession! Side hustling is still something I do just in a different form now! Money is a tool I use to make more money and I utilize it with a more logical mindset."

At the beginning of my side hustle journey, I became the spokesperson for, "If it don't make dollars, then it don't make sense." I was willing to paper chase and do everything I could to get that bag. But once I grew into a smarter side hustler, I learned the best way to make dollars is to *only* do what makes sense. There is no "don't make dollars." There's always money to be made. Your approach, your strategy, that's what makes the real life-changing money. Intention, practicality, and execution—that's what secures the bag!

CHAPTER 8

JUST HOLD ON... WE'RE BUYING HOMES

I am currently typing this chapter from my dining room table as water leaks from behind my kitchen tiles. Not enough to destroy anything, but just enough that I automatically know that the solution to this problem will be expensive. Am I panicked? Meh, a smidge. Am I surprised? Not even a little bit. Oh, the joys of homeownership will teach you quickly it is *always* something. The effortless gift that never stops giving. And never stops taking, so make sure your budget is strapped up because it's about to be a fucking bumpy ride.

I bought a house before I was ready. Surprise, surprise. You've been here long enough to know that this isn't actually a surprise to any one of us, is it?

Let's do a little activity together, shall we? Take a deep breath, clear your mind, and answer the following for me: What are the top three images that come to mind when you think about the American Dream? Most people's answers will vary, of course, but I'm willing to bet that during our short exercise, most of you pictured a house. In fact, *The New York Times* recently reported that "74 percent of Americans say owning a home is a higher measurement of achievement than having a successful career, raising a family, or earning a college degree."

Whether you pictured the all-too-familiar white picket fence or a more modern take, for the vast majority, no matter your age, race, gender, or sexual identity, the American Dream is rooted in homeownership.

In October 2018, I used $40,000 as a down payment for my first home. By January 2019, I closed on that home and moved in the same day. A ton of shit happened in between (*coughs* I made my final student loan payment), but the feelings I felt on those two days are the most impactful in this story.

That's because I was filled with nothing but regret and dread. I didn't have a clear vision of what I was doing, why I was doing it, and who I was doing it for. I tried to convince myself repeatedly that I was doing it for me, but in reality, I wasn't. All I knew for certain was I had started the process, so I had no choice but to finish it.

First gen'ers, listen to me clearly: You are allowed the grace and mercy to do or not do things in your own way and in your own time. You want to know why? Because no one is going to pay for your mistakes or missteps but you. And I don't know about y'all, but I'd much rather pay for a mistake I wholeheartedly wanted to make than pay for a mistake I was pressured into.

From the moment I closed to the present day, I haven't stopped learning new lessons, figuring out shit as I go, and trying to DIY everything. Truth moment for both of us right here: We cannot DIY everything; some projects must be DBP (done by a professional). I absolutely made that acronym up, just now, so don't try and steal it! Patent pending, or whatever all the cool kids say on *Shark Tank*.

Handing over any amount of money has always made me think twice. If it's more than a dollar, I go through several rounds of "Do I really need this?" before pressing add to cart. If it's less than a dollar my suspicions are raised, and I wonder about the profit margin on such an inexpensive item. Obviously *too* much *Shark Tank* in the blood. It's safe to say I think about most if not all my purchases thoroughly before making them. And yet, something about writing out that $40,000 check and handing it to my lawyer felt way different than any type of hesitation I had felt before.

It was eerie hesitation I felt when I walked out of the co-op board interview with my approval letter in hand. I was on a nonstop-moving train charging forward, and slowing down was not an option. Deadlines had to be met, paperwork had to be filled out, and every person involved had to get their cut. In retrospect, it only felt this way because I didn't ask questions. I didn't take the time to make myself comfortable with this major life change that would require a lot more adulting than I was prepared to complete. Asking questions would have saved me time, energy, and most importantly, *money*! Those questions would have naturally slowed that train up and given me the time to process before making any life-changing decisions. Ask questions. Always ask questions.

THE HOUSING CRISIS IS REAL AF

HOW DOES A RECESSION AFFECT THE HOUSING MARKET?

The recession is a *hot* topic right now for many different reasons. The stock market has been at the red wedding for the majority of 2022; gas and groceries are feeling like luxuries due to inflation; and the Federal Reserve interest rate hikes have pushed us right into another unprecedented historical time. At just above 7 percent, US mortgage rates have hit a twenty-year high. All of this as we stare down the barrel of a looming recession that has yet to be officially announced but is absolutely being felt in every facet of our financial lives.

Right now, as I write to you, we're not currently in an official recession. By the time you have this book in your hands, we may in fact be in the thick of it or already on the other side. Who knows? Either way, it is important to know how recessions typically impact the housing market and how a housing crisis makes it even worse.

For the sake of clarity let's first define exactly what a recession is, so we can all be on the same page about why they are so scary. The National Bureau of Economic Research defines a recession as a period of widespread economic decline that lasts for more than a few months. Formally speaking, as per the ITR Economics dictionary gods, a recession is, "a period of temporary economic decline during which trade and industrial activity are reduced, generally identified by a fall in GDP in two successive quarters." Informally, recessions suck because at the basic human level, the wealthy get wealthier while life gets so much tougher for the everyday hard-working professional. Unemployment tends to increase, wages usually remain stagnant, inflation remains predominant, and uncertainty is at an all-time high. The housing market does not go untouched during the economic volatility taking place.

By definition, a housing crisis occurs when affordable housing becomes scarce. The counter to a housing crisis is often referred to as a housing bubble. And if we tilt our heads and squint our eyes, we can recall a faint distant memory of the 2008 housing bubble that faced a cataclysmic pop. At the basic root of real estate and housing, everything is connected to the financial concept of supply and demand.

Based on historical patterns, a recession will usually slow down the housing market. This common trajectory occurs because during a recession there is less demand for a home. Simple enough. People typically cannot or are not looking to purchase a big-ticket item like a home during economic downturns. If you're a homeowner, you potentially face the realities of losing equity as the housing market weathers the storm. If you're attempting to become a homeowner, a recession may be a favorable time to purchase if you have the capabilities to do so and meet the necessary qualifications.

However, as we say in the investing world, past performance is not indicative of future results. Each recession may have similarities, but the outcomes in regard to the housing market do not always historically track. The 2008 recession played out differently from the 2020 recession. And as we potentially slide right into another recession a little more than two years later, we can see that past performance is not indicative of WTF is going on in the housing market right now.

The price of everything is all the way up, including the average cost of a home. It is hard to say any one thing is to blame, but the housing crisis plays a huge part in the increase of both rent and prospective homeownership. As previously mentioned, we expect a level of predictability when we are in a recession or a pending one is on the way. Less demand, lower prices—makes sense, right? More people are generally pushed into renting during a recession because money is tighter, fear is higher, and the necessary homeownership qualifications become more difficult. This makes the demand for rental properties increase, which traditionally causes rent prices to increase. 2022 stepped in and said hold my beer.

Nationally, the cost of rent in 2022 went up by 8.8 percent compared to 2021, averaging a median of $2,002 a month. States like Florida, Delaware, New Mexico, and Oklahoma have seen approximately 20+ percent year-over-year state increases, with the national average wage growth hovering at 6.2 percent. The rent is too *damn* high, and our checks are not keeping up! How much has the average home increased this last year? *Thirty percent* between 2020 and 2022. Yep, you read that right; that was not a typo. Rent is skyrocketing and the price to purchase a home has also drastically increased to an average of $428,700 in the first quarter of 2022.

The housing crisis we witnessed in 2022 is a byproduct of the 2008 recession that has further been exacerbated by COVID-19 production and supply delays. Fewer homes were built, and with the drastic interest rate decrease in 2020, we accidentally finagled ourselves right into an unexpected housing boom. Remember, supply and demand drive a huge portion of the housing market's outputs. It is unclear what this pending recession may do to worsen or correct the current state of real estate. Much like the stock market, it is truly impossible to time the housing market accurately. The best metric to use is your financial security and abilities. When you decide to buy a home, especially during uncertain economic times, you are taking a calculated risk that may not have an immediate ROI (return on investment) in the short term. Factor in your lifestyle, do your research, and think long-term. This will be significant if not the most impactful method to navigating economic uncertainty and homeownership.

UNPACKING THE PROCESS

Before we dive into the all-so-elusive process of purchasing a home, let's set the record straight on a few real estate myths first, shall we? Despite what the real estate gurus on TikTok say, owning a home is not all rainbows and butterflies. It also is most certainly not the only way to build wealth. There are millionaires that rent their primary residence, and there are homeowners who are financially struggling. So if millionaire status is what you're after, I'm here to remind you that reaching that destination does not have one direct path.

MYTH ONE: THE VALUE OF YOUR HOME WILL ALWAYS GO UP. EQUITY, EQUITY, EQUITY!

Uhh...the 2008 housing bubble and financial crisis would like a word, please. Though 65 percent of US homeowners believe the value of their home will continue to rise over the next ten years, the value of your home does not *always* increase.

There are two main factors that significantly contribute to property value: location and the housing market. Both of those factors are not something you can directly control. Of course, you can control where you live, but you can't control the external factors in your neighborhood, like what your neighbors do to their homes or how far away your home may be from public transportation. What else impacts your property value?

We may not want to keep up with the Joneses, but we do have to keep up with how much they are selling their homes for. The price of comparable properties in the neighborhood will influence the value of your house as well. For the most part, if you look at recently listed homes in your area or how much a home has just sold for, you will get a general sense of how much your home is worth. The downside to this is during a seller's market, home prices will often take on an inflated price point due to the basic rules of supply and demand.

The neighborhood where the home is located is an additional factor that weighs heavily on your property value. What does that mean? An appealing neighborhood will have accessible proximity to quality schools, grocery stores, entertainment, places of worship, major highways, and public transportation. These factors tend to influence buyers to pay higher prices for real estate in certain areas compared to similar homes that don't have that same access. Most people don't want to move into a neighborhood with a high crime rate and poor-performing schools. The better the neighborhood seems, the higher the property value.

As a homeowner, when you hear the saying, "There goes the neighborhood," symbolically that usually translates to a slow external leak you don't have the ability to put an end to. That slow leak can look like many things but overall is an indirect outcome that directly causes the value of your home to decline.

Recessions flow in waves, the stock market flows in waves, and so does the housing market. In fact, the economy is the cause of all three interconnected financial waves. If you're in the market to buy a home right now, or you're just window-shopping on Zillow, you're probably experiencing a seller's market. That is when supply (available homes) is low so the prices of homes skyrocket because demand has not wavered. The opposite, a buyer's market, is when there are tons of homes available and less demand, thus driving the cost of homes down.

As with all money things we discuss here, we always use nuance to iron out some of the details. The common economic concept of supply and demand is not new to us. We've mastered that since we were in elementary school selling and trading Pokémon cards. When it comes to homes, it is not that simple. Supply and demand play a big part in which way the market swings, but macroeconomics also plays an even bigger role here.

When the Federal Reserve slashed interest rates at the start of 2020, the median sale price of a home, according to Zillow data, was $266,300. It was cheaper to borrow money, and mortgage rates were appealing to those looking to become first-time homeowners. Two years later, with increased interest rates and a strained supply, January 2022 brought about a 58.9 percent increase. The median sale price grew to $423,300.

I know what you're thinking. *Okay, Melissa. This seems like property value is going up if the sale price is going up.* It would appear that way for sure! The market, whether housing or stock, will always correct itself. To do that, it must swing in the other direction. The people who purchase their homes during this seller's market for $400,000 or refinance to cash in on their equity, face the real potential reality of seeing the value of their homes decrease. This can especially become financially concerning for people who have mortgages with variable interest rates. Your monthly payment increases, you're paying more in interest, and you do not have the equity to borrow against that you thought you had because the value of your home is no longer $400,000.

Besides the uncontrollable factors that impact the value of your property, many times increasing that value will usually require a steep financial investment on your end. That doesn't only mean large renovations, but it also means routine maintenance and repairs. According to a 2019 NAR remodeling report, "Replacing a roof can run over seven thousand dollars, while an HVAC system could set a homeowner back more than eight thousand dollars." It's not always about building a new fancy kitchen or bathroom, which is what we love watching on those HGTV remodeling shows. Sometimes (dare I say it, most times), maintaining and increasing the value of your home includes the unsexy task of maintaining the home itself.

Long story short, does the value of your home appreciate more often than not? Prior to 2008, that answer would be a loud, resounding *yes!* Now we approach that question with more reality splayed across our purview. Historically, the housing market hasn't swung from one end to the other as often or as volatilely as the stock market has. It has typically followed an upward trajectory that has made real estate investors feel like they are making safer investments. However, all investments come with a layer of risk. If you are in the market for a home or two, your best strategy is to move forward with what you can afford and keep in mind that the prices of homes do not *always* increase.

MYTH TWO: ALL YOU NEED IS THE DOWN PAYMENT AND CLOSING COSTS

I am currently in the library and have let out the biggest LOL just typing out myth #2. This is the furthest thing from the truth. Yes, down payment and closing costs are a substantial part of the process, but they are not the only part. You will need what I call "buffer money" during the process. This will cover fees, applications, inspections, renovations, furniture, and whatever ad hoc expenses arise as you get closer to your closing date or immediately after you've moved in.

MYTH THREE: RENTING IS THROWING AWAY MONEY

Owning a home is a great accomplishment that I do not take lightly. As I type this paragraph from my kitchen table, I truly feel fortunate that I can call this space mine. However, I do not mince words when I say home ownership is also hands down one of the hardest things I've ever done. I was unprepared, overwhelmed, and uncertain about everything every step of the way that entire first year. Is that the normal vibe for most first-time homeowners, I don't know, but I kept my big girl pants on at all times to deal with what seemingly felt like one catastrophe after the next.

I may have felt differently or had a different experience if I had gone from my parents' home into an apartment that required less adulting on my end. At the end of the day, paying for housing should *never* be considered a waste. If you are stuck on the fence and trying to decide whether you should rent or own, ask yourself the following questions and *really* answer them!

FIVE KEY QUESTIONS TO HELP YOU DECIDE IF YOU'RE READY FOR HOMEOWNERSHIP:	MY ANSWER:
Why do I want to be a homeowner? Is this decision for you because you want it or is this decision to please others?	
Where do I want to live, and do I want to live there for five or more years? Buying a home is a huge investment, and if you're unsure of if and where you want to plant roots, answer that honestly for yourself first.	
How do I start the process? What is the first step you would need to take to start your homeownership journey? [**Cheat Code:** If you don't currently know, you'll def know by the end of this chapter.]	
What do I need to have prepared to continue the process after I've started? Do you have the documentation needed to qualify for a mortgage? [**Cheat Code:** The list near the end of this chapter is a great resource to guide you through all the docs you'll need.]	
What is the entire process going to cost me? Calculate the average necessary down payment, closing costs, and other fees needed to buy a home in the areas you're looking into.	

Cost is a real homeowner factor that is often glamorized until you're neck-deep in it. There will be none of that here; we're going through the real realities!

WHAT DOES IT REALLY COST?

Being a homeowner comes with a slew of fees even before you close. The down payment and closing costs are usually the two main foci of conversations centered around buying a property. I get why; they will be a huge chunk of your costs before you move in, so we must talk about them. Since they are so heavily discussed, I'm going to skip that part. There are many other things you need to also consider and financially plan for when you're preparing to start your homeownership journey.

This list of fees is not exhaustive, but it is in fact exhausting to think about, so let's take a breath together before we proceed.

FEE	AVERAGE COST
Mortgage Application	$200–$500
Closing Costs	3–6 percent of the home's total value
Appraisal Fee	$600–$2,000
Origination	0.5–1.0 percent of loan amount
Credit Report	$20–$30
Title Fees	$75–$200
Home Inspection	$300–$500

The fees mentioned above are averages that vary based on location and your specific lender. So it makes sense to have a separate account where you budget money separately to cover fees. What's a smart amount to set aside? As a general suggestion, budgeting three to four thousand dollars to cover processing and document fees is a wise first step. Two alternate suggestions that will give you a better estimate are:

1. Research the average cost of these fees in your area.

or

2. Ask the lender directly.

You can speak to a customer service representative in the mortgage department and ask them directly what they charge for these services.

The last suggestion will also give you a good idea about which fees you can potentially negotiate and which fees are set firmly. Remember to always ask questions. If you are uncertain about a certain fee and want clarification, have the service provider or financial institution explain the purpose of the fee in a way that makes sense until you can fully explain it yourself.

WHAT ABOUT INVESTING IN REAL ESTATE PROPERTIES?

So you want to house hack, huh? In the hilarious words of Dunder Mifflin employee Kelly Kapoor, "I have a lot of questions; number one: *how dare you?!*" Just kidding. Investment properties and house hacking have grown a well-deserved but traditionally misguided and misinformed bad rap because of the housing crisis that has been inflamed due to the rise of Airbnb and similar business models.

To clarify, we (and I speak for myself only) are not opposed to ethical investment properties or ethical house hacking. That means you would also be an ethical landlord. To deem investment properties and house hacking as the root cause of the housing crisis is unfair and not 100 percent true. But we (again, just speaking for me here) are opposed to unethical investment properties that create hazardous living conditions or make it difficult for people to gain access to affordable housing. Do we see the difference?

Why the uproar then? Well, because with great power comes great responsibility, and many people stop seeing people and start seeing green when it comes to purchasing investment properties. Luxury housing and Airbnb rentals are now a dime a dozen and have priced many people out of neighborhoods they have lived in their entire lives. When you buy a building and triple the cost of living to increase your profit, you can see why we think you're moving real shady.

For those that are interested in going the ethical investment property route, we (I) are still rooting for you! In fact, I took the time to chat with Ali and Josh Lupo, collectively known as "The FI Couple," to discuss how they paid off $100,000 of student loans in three years with a household income below $80,000, while also investing in real estate. Through their goal to become financially independent in their thirties they spend most of their time teaching beginners all things real estate and personal finance through their social media platform.

As real estate and finance educators, when asked what they felt was the biggest misconception many people have about using real estate as a means of building wealth, they stated, "There are so many myths and misconceptions regarding real estate investing, and unfortunately this makes real estate less accessible to everyday people—simply because they think it's not realistic for them. While not *everyone* should invest in real estate, some of the most common misconceptions that we see are: you need to put 20-25 percent down to buy real estate, you need to come from money (or be rich), or you need to be handy in order to invest."

Ali and Josh went on to share their initial experience entering the investment property world after realizing these misconceptions were in fact just that. "You can purchase an owner-occupied building (two-to-four-unit property) with as little as a 0-5 percent down payment. When we started in real estate, we had a negative net worth, over $100,000 in debt, and neither of us were making more than $50,000 a year—yet we were able to qualify for loan products."

Investment properties are different from a primary residence or a second home. They are taxed differently, usually have higher mortgage rates, and the mortgage qualifications will also vary.

The FI Couple and I wholeheartedly agree on this last reminder, whether you're on the path to primary residence ownership or an investment property: "We cannot stress financial preparedness enough. Real estate investing is not for the faint of heart. Unexpected expenses can (and will) come up. When you purchase a home, you are signing up for the financial responsibility to maintain and upkeep the property to a level where it is safe and comfortable for tenants. It is very important to not only have personal savings and reserves, but also rental savings and reserves."

MY FAVORITE HOMEOWNERSHIP SECRETS

These may not necessarily be secrets so to speak, but these tidbits of information are a healthy mix of things I wish I knew prior to purchasing my home, and things that in my humble opinion are not openly discussed often enough. Knowledge is power, and if you're in the market to buy a home right now I want you easily armed with all the knowledge you'll need to make an informed decision, without having to read articles on page two of Google. Because we all know you're really down bad if you reach page two on Google.

SECRET ONE: PROFIT & EQUITY ARE NOT THE F$%^&#G SAME

I didn't realize how many people were confused about what equity actually was until I ended up on homeowner TikTok. Equity is one of those fancy-for-no-reason buzzwords thrown around whenever anyone talks about buying or owning a home. At its core, equity is just an opportunity to take on new debt using your home as leverage. In simple basic terms, equity is the difference between how much your home is currently worth versus how much is left on your mortgage. Quick math time: If your home is worth $400,000 and you have $200,000 remaining on your mortgage, then your equity is $200,000.

Homeowners often use their equity in one of three ways: a home equity loan, a home equity line of credit, or a cash-out refinance. Typically, people will borrow against their home's equity to make renovations on the house, which in turn can potentially further increase the value of the property, or they will use their home equity loan to purchase another home. All three manners in which you can tap into your equity will usually have a lower interest rate than a personal loan or credit card. This is a fan favorite when it comes to leveraging debt to build more wealth. The secondary property is then ultimately turned into an investment property that is either rented out or flipped for profit. Why or how do people mix equity up with profit? Whether it is simple misunderstandings or purposefully misleading information we're clearing it up now.

Equity and profit are not interchangeable and do not mean the same thing. To calculate how much a homeowner has profited, all expenses must be considered. This is where it gets blurry for many, but I'm here to unblur the bigger picture. The difference between the price you bought your home and the price when you sell your home is not the profit. Some people frame it that way because it just sounds so much sexier than reality.

Wanna do some more math? Let's! If you buy your home for $400,000 and when you sell your home, you sell it for $500,000 you have *not* made a $100,000 profit. How much have you paid in interest on your mortgage? How much have you spent on renovations? For our mathematic purposes, we'll say you made $20,000 in renovations, and paid $40,000 in interest. Subtract both of those from the $500,000 then proceed to subtract the amount that you paid (that's the $400,000). Following the rules of basic addition, though your house's value increased by $100,000, this is not what you've made from the property. Your profit here in this scenario would be a bit less than $40,000 after other fees are assessed.

Equity is important and can be a game-changer for many, but it is not free money, and it is not the profit you can hope to earn if you decide to sell your home.

SECRET TWO: CAPITAL GAINS TAX IS A VERY REAL THING

One of my favorite things my father always tells my brothers and me: "You can always come home." It has always given us a sense of comfort and support whenever we had to do scary things, got ourselves into trouble or realized we made a huge effing mistake. After my first month in my house, I was ready to cash in that offer, call it quits, and return to my parents' house with my tail tucked between my legs. I was done. So done that I started to look into movers and realtors to reverse this terrible mistake I thought I had made.

That's when I learned the real nature of capital gains taxes for homeowners. Though I was familiar with capital gains (profit) and how they're taxed when it comes to the stock market, I didn't know that similar rules applied to house and property sales. If you sell your home or property less than one year after you purchased it, your short-term capital gains are taxed as regular income at a much higher rate. Those house-flipping TV shows conveniently leave out that unsexy fact.

You can be expected to pay as high as 37 percent on your short-term capital gains, whereas if you own a home or property for more than a year you are taxed at a much lower rate of 15–20 percent dependent on your income tax bracket. There are several exemptions regarding capital gains tax when it comes to the sale of a primary residence, but those come with another caveat: You must have occupied the residence for at least two of the last five years.

Most people don't buy a home as a primary residence and expect to live there for less than a year. It would truly be an immense waste of time and energy to do so. However, things happen. Life happens! And while I stuck it out and adapted to the new responsibilities of homeownership, it would have been nice to know that a potential early exit strategy would be taxed at an egregiously high rate.

SECRET THREE: AN INVESTMENT PROPERTY AND PRIMARY RESIDENCE DO NOT OPERATE THE SAME WAY

If anyone tells you that the home you're planning to live in full-time is an investment, please give them a copy of this book, direct them to this chapter, and point to the section discussing real estate properties. It is not the same thing. Your primary residence *usually* will not be a huge source of profit unless you're renting out spaces in that home. And in that case, you're sticking your pinky toe into the investment property pool instead of traditional primary residence status.

Renting a spare room on Airbnb every now and then does not make you a full-blown landlord; let's not get ridiculous here. But if you are planning on using your home solely as a place to live, it is your primary residence and it should be discussed as such. Don't let real estate TikTok bully you into thinking your primary residence is going to be a cash cow. An investment property is one thing, and a primary residence is another! That's why they have two different names, *duh!*

SECRET FOUR: YOU DO NOT HAVE TO ALWAYS PUT DOWN 20 PERCENT... BUT THERE ARE THINGS YOU'LL NEED TO KNOW

Back in the day, many, many moons ago, the common expected practice when it came to starting the homeownership journey was to have at least 20 percent of the total cost to hand over as your down payment. There were several reasons behind this thinking. Firstly, the more you put down, the smaller your mortgage will be and the lower your monthly payments will be. Immediately that was a huge selling point. The second reason people held on tight to the 20 percent rule was to avoid PMI.

Private mortgage insurance (a.k.a. PMI) is a fee you may be required to pay if you have a conventional mortgage and own less than 20 percent equity on your property. This insurance is meant to protect the lender, *not* you, so if you do fall behind on your mortgage you could still be in danger of foreclosure. It's all about risk and liability. The bank sees your smaller down payment as a liability that you may not actually be able to afford this home. Kind of f—d up when you think about it, right? Why would they even approve me for this much if they think I can't keep up? Either way, the PMI is tacked on in addition to your monthly mortgage until you have paid down 20 percent of the loan. Outside of the typical monthly premium, at closing you may be offered an upfront premium payment or have an upfront + monthly premium option.

The conventional mortgage route leaves many things to be desired as it often excludes many people who want to be homeowners but do not meet the stringent qualifications. Enter the FHA loan, a government-guaranteed loan that improves homeownership accessibility by offering more favorable terms than their conventional counterparts. Approval for a Federal Housing Administration (FHA) loan has its own set of requirements depending on the specific type of loan you're seeking.

An FHA loan usually requires the borrower to be a first-time homeowner and possess a 620+ credit score and proof of income. What's the down payment look like? Typically, you'll get a loan that requires 3.5 percent down instead of the conventional 20 percent that shuts out many working-class people from achieving their American Dream of homeownership. What's the catch? All FHA loans will have a PMI in addition to the mortgage.

Some people are often discouraged by these two options, but here's the real tea! Your down payment will determine your LTV (loan-to-value) ratio. This ultimately determines your interest rate and your monthly mortgage payment. The bigger the down payment the better, *but* your down payment is *not* the end-all-be-all. If you are ready to be a homeowner and cannot afford a larger down payment, using an FHA or other specialty programs for first-time homebuyers is a sound decision to take.

Many people choose to put down less so they can remain liquid as the process continues. Remember it's not just down payment and closing when it comes to buying a house. You will need money for the move and you will have to pay for insurance, taxes, potential repairs, etc. Having more cash on hand is never a bad idea especially given the unexpected financial demands that come along with homeownership. Your lifestyle and financial circumstances will dictate the mortgages you are eligible for and choose to accept. The process doesn't have to be wrapped up in a 20-percent-down-payment ribbon, and often your financial circumstances evolve. Taking on a loan with PMI today doesn't mean you can't pay more on your mortgage to speed up the removal of that PMI down the road.

SECRET FIVE: PROPERTY TAX IS A BITCH

As a gentle reminder, owning a home is *not* only a monthly mortgage. A slew of costs come with being a homeowner that never goes away. Property taxes are one of those costs. This cost is what I call a civic-duty fee. Your property taxes may not directly impact you on the daily, but they are a holistic benefit to your neighboring society. From funding schools to street repairs, even after you pay off your mortgage, you will still have to pay property taxes on your home. Worst part: Property taxes tend to increase consistently, because if there's one thing the cost of living is going to have the audacity to do, it's increase. So just when you've mastered your budget like the professional budgeting badass that you are, a property tax increase is always going to be around the corner, waiting to throw you out of whack.

Property tax increases aren't something you can necessarily control. There are many factors that determine when and how much an increase is going to be, so the best thing you can do is prepare, even when you feel like you can't prepare.

This means one of two things:

1. Make sure you have a three-to-six-month emergency savings fund to help you stay afloat if you experience any sudden property tax increases.

2. When you're searching for a new home, be sure to look up the average property taxes in the area. You will find many similarities, even if it isn't an exact number. This will at least give you an idea of how much you should aim to have saved before moving in.

SECRET SIX: YOU WILL BE FINANCIALLY EXPOSED...HERE'S HOW TO PREPARE

My best friend recently told me she's never felt more exposed than while she was pregnant because all sense of privacy is out the door. Believe it or not, the process of purchasing a home is a similar exposure, just financially and without the blood and cervical dilation at the end.

If you thought you just had to have a great credit score and a down payment to breeze through the process, I am sorry to break the news to you. For you to get your dream house, you have to lay it all out there for everyone involved to see.

Banks are not out here giving people $500,000 loans without ensuring they are making a good investment. They want the full picture of who you are as a borrower before they lend you a single dime, and unfortunately a good credit score alone isn't going to cut it.

For a financial institution to even consider approving you for a home loan you're going to need the following documents:

TAX RETURNS	The mortgage lender will usually ask you to fill out form 4506-T so they can directly request a copy of your tax returns from the IRS. Be prepared to disclose your tax returns for the last one to two years.
PROOF OF INCOME	Initially the bank will want to see that you have proof of income from the last month or so. Yes, your tax returns will show them you have income, but think of that as a holistic financial picture. Your paystubs or W2s give them an idea of your monthly earnings so they can determine how much you can additionally afford to pay.
BUSINESS DOCUMENTS	If you're a business owner or contractor, you will need to show your profit and loss statements year to date. Business owners typically have a few more hoops to jump through than regular nine-to-fivers so be prepared for more paperwork if you are an entrepreneur.
ASSETS	You will need to show proof of all your assets, including bank statements for your savings accounts, stocks, bonds, and retirement accounts.
LIABILITIES	Just like they want to see all the things you have, mortgage lenders also want to see all the money you owe. Your debt-to-income ratio plays a part in how much you get approved for. This is because the bank will consider how much more debt they think you can handle based on your income.
CREDIT HISTORY	This isn't a document you'll have to prepare in advance, but it's a piece I want you to be aware of. They will run your credit, hard-inquiry style, to learn about your credit history and credit health.
PHOTO ID	This I guess can go without saying, but you will need an active photo ID. Your license, state ID, or passport will do the trick. They want to know you are who you say you are.

CONFIRMATION OF PROPERTY	If you have purchased a home before you will have to show proof of ownership or proof of sale if you no longer own it.
BANK STATEMENTS	You will likely have to show bank statements from the last thirty to ninety days, so the mortgage lender has a clear snapshot of the money coming in and out of your account consistently. Hot Tip: When it comes to spending, saving, or taking on new debt, you don't want to make any big changes to your normal financial routine that will look strange or stand out while you're in the process of buying a home. Be mindful that the process can move quickly, and you don't want to be turned down or questioned about unusual financial activities.
GIFT LETTERS	If any of your friends or family members have gifted you money toward your down payment or closing costs they will have to provide a formal letter stating how much they have gifted you and confirm that it is indeed a gift and not a loan.
RESIDENTIAL HISTORY	You're going to need proof of all the locations you've lived in over a predetermined amount of time. Some banks require one to two years, while others are looking for a more extensive history of three to seven years.
EMPLOYER CONTACT INFO	If you don't want people at work in your business, too bad. You will have to give up your employer's contact information (usually HR or your supervisor) so they can confirm you are gainfully employed.
EARNEST MONEY SOURCE	The bank wants to make sure everything is on the up and up. After you've made your down payment, you must essentially prove that the large sum of money came from a legitimate source. If your down payment came from your savings account, you could use your bank statement as proof. If it came from elsewhere, you'd have to prove that as well.

It is quite a hefty list so if you're getting ready to purchase a home or just thinking about it, start organizing these documents and place them in a safe place you can easily access.

SECRET SEVEN: APPRAISAL AND INSPECTION ARE DIFFERENT. HIRE YOUR OWN INSPECTOR.

This is a *big* one! When I was in the thick of the purchasing process, I thought everyone worked for me. *Wrong!* The older, wiser version of me questions why would I naively think that the real estate agent, the bank-appointed appraiser, or the HOA would have my best interest at heart? You will be the only one with your interests at heart, so hire your own people and don't be afraid to get second opinions. I made the ridiculously silly mistake of not hiring my own inspector, and I paid gravely for that mistake.

My house was appraised by the bank; you can't buy a house without taking that step. It is *not* the same as having the house inspected—there's a difference. The difference here is you pay an appraisal fee to the bank, and they will have an unbiased professional come out to make sure the bank isn't getting the shitty end of this deal. The appraisal determines the fair market value of the property (that's how your equity increases or decreases). The same factors we discussed earlier that impact your equity will be what the professional will be using during the appraisal process.

A home inspection on the other hand determines the condition of the home and identifies any areas that need repair or will need repair soon. So that leak under the kitchen sink I found the week I moved in, the sloping floors that had to be repaired for $5,000, or the structural issues with the bathroom that cost me $11,000 would have been brought to my attention before I handed over my $40,000 down payment. Stupid move on my part, undoubtedly! This was my error and my error alone. Why? Because I'm traditionally cautious with my money, I ask a ton of questions, and I Google ridiculous things for hours on end. I should have done my due diligence. But instead, I let my ego kick in. I was so consumed with finding a place before the end of the year, I let the "shine" of an affordable two-bedroom in a nice neighborhood overshadow my common sense. I assumed the appraisal would be enough. Don't do that!

You can choose to have the home inspection completed before you even put an offer on the table, whereas with an appraisal those typically occur once you're in the middle of the process and your down payment has already been snatched up.

It is a beyond wise decision to hire your own inspector. It is costly, yes; however, when it comes to a huge investment like a house, better safe than sorry. That second set of eyes that you're paying three to five hundred dollars for can potentially save you hundreds of thousands of dollars. Once you've had your potential home appraised, this is the sweet spot where you can renegotiate the asking price or decide to entirely walk away from the property to avoid any costly pending repairs.

SECRET EIGHT: ACCOUNT FOR THINGS YOU'VE NEVER ACCOUNTED FOR

The first time I attempted to cook breakfast in my house for myself, I realized quickly that my kitchen was not my mama's kitchen. You ever tried to make pancakes without butter or a spatula? How about trying to make dinner and all you have are cereal bowls, salt, pepper, and plastic straws in your cabinets? Besides two years living on campus, I lived with my parents my entire life. Though I pitched in tremendously as an adult, certain things that were always readily available I assumed would magically appear in my home too. Sadly, it just doesn't work that way.

If you're moving into your new home, especially if you'll be living on your own for the first time, create a buffer for the unaccounted. This is for small ticket items that don't cost much but will add up along the way. You'll be buying most things from scratch unless you have a housewarming, and even then, you'll still want to have that buffer to ease some of your tension and anxiety, which tends to lead to overspending.

SECRET NINE: FURNITURE IS EXPENSIVE AF...PLAN ACCORDINGLY

You know how we all have collectively at one point talked a little shit about furniture wrapped up in plastic. I would just like to go on the record and say, I get it, I may not like it, but whew, do I get it! Somebody should have told me this a little more aggressively—whatever your furniture budget is, it is likely not enough. Honestly, it doesn't matter if someone did try and tell me. I wouldn't have believed them until I saw it with my own eyes.

I have graciously spent most of my life inhabiting the furniture that my parents so kindly provided to me for free. I am also going to take the time out right here, right now to say I am so sorry, Dad, for every window blind that someone in the house broke (wasn't me, though) while trying to open or close the window. Them thangs cost more than I ever could have imagined, and when I broke two of mine after throwing a Nike slide at a house fly, I grew an even bigger appreciation for the masking tape and staples that repaired them.

Furniture is unbelievably expensive, and with inflation inflating the way it is, I can only imagine because I refuse to look at current prices of items that I already thought were out of pocket back in 2018. I'm looking at you, Urban Outfitters. Couches, nightstands, coffee tables, kitchen tables, and desk chairs shockingly all cost a shit ton more than five dollars—the price I feel everything should actually cost.

When I started looking into furnishing my home, I had grandiose visions and set aside two thousand dollars. Yes, you can all let out a collective chuckle that I was trying to furnish my entire home with only two thousand dollars. I needed to buy a bed, a mattress, a dresser, a kitchen table, chairs, a couch—you know, the basics, and I thought I could do that all with two thousand dollars. I'm sure with tremendous creativity and ingenuity there are plenty of people who could make that happen. I, however, was not one of those people. That two thousand dollars did not go far, even with all of the seemingly frugal budget-friendly steps I took.

In the end I spent closer to $3,500, which many people still find remarkable that I was able to furnish my entire house for so little. At the time I didn't think $3,500 was a steal at all, especially because I budgeted for two thousand dollars. Yes, even after all of my money mistakes in my twenties, after all of my money triumphs and successes in my early thirties, I still can blow my budget. The journey isn't linear, y'all, not even by a long shot!

Whether you think I spent too much or the right amount, here's what I did to keep the costs as low as possible:

1. My family pitched in and helped me move my things from my parents' house to mine. I did not hire professional movers because I didn't have any large items that I was moving from one place to another. I wasn't taking my childhood bed, wasn't stealing my parents' couch (though I thought about it after I saw the prices in these streets), and only took my clothes, shoes, small personal items, and books.

2. I started shopping for furniture during Black Friday sales. I scored a two-hundred-dollar discount on my bedframe and drawers because I was the first one to walk into the furniture store on Black Friday. There were a couple of other deals that I was able to capitalize on to bring some of my costs down: bed sheets and towels were on sale, my mattress was on sale, and I got a great deal on my kitchen table and chairs.

3. The stores I chose to shop with were in line with my budget. I bought most of my furniture from places that are franchises and lead with affordability. That means IKEA and Target were my home. I used my credit card points wherever it made sense (Target mostly) and chose to build all of the furniture I bought from IKEA myself. (I will never do that again.)

4. I threw a housewarming party a few weeks after I initially moved in and had a registry for pieces that either were too expensive or that I simply forgot I needed. This helped me save on pieces as well when people opted to give me gift cards so I could purchase something later when I needed it.

5. Though I didn't thrift or purchase used furniture, this is absolutely something that you can do to cut costs and get great unique pieces in your home. Facebook Marketplace and Craigslist are the two sources you can use to start your search for local pieces. This is also

a great starting point to sell your old or gently used pieces to help offset a move or refurnish your current space.

6. And as *always*, sinking fund that furniture! There are larger pieces that I wanted that I simply could not afford or they weren't an absolute necessity. I created smaller sinking funds that gave me some time to put money away for a future purchase without adding an unnecessary purchase to my card that I wouldn't be able to pay off at the end of the month.

As I approach year four in my home, I have learned that although I now know so much, I have so much more to learn. Homeownership evolves constantly and comes with challenges and victories. It is not an easy choice to make and not a choice to be taken lightly; however, it can be a solid choice that leads to beautiful outcomes. During the final few moments of our conversation, I asked Ali and Josh to think back to their first investment purchase and what they wished they had known before closing. "The entire process of buying your first property (whether it's a primary residence or investment) is scary. You're likely spending more money than you ever have before, and that alone can be very daunting. The biggest obstacle we faced was our own self-doubt and fear. Whether you live in the property or not, real estate is a business, and you are the CEO."

PART III:

STARTED FROM THE BOTTOM...NOW WE'RE WEALTHY-*ISH*

CHAPTER 9

TAKE CARE: ESTATE PLANNING 101

About four years ago, my father tricked my mother and me into taking a field trip with him to a cemetery. If you're wondering exactly how one tricks somebody into visiting a cemetery, just know Target and Starbucks were involved. When we pulled into the parking lot, he happily announced he was making the final payment on the two plots he bought for himself and my mom. While my mother didn't seem shocked at all, I was immediately taken aback.

He jovially walked through the double doors that led to a surprisingly more cheerful office than I expected to see, given the fact that we were at a cemetery. After about ten minutes of paperwork and the final credit card swipe, the customer service agent asked my father if he'd like to visit the plots. Um, excuse me? I signed up for a stroll down aisle A4 and a strawberry acai lemonade, not an impromptu cemetery tour on a Saturday morning.

After ten minutes of navigating a poorly drawn "map" leading to my parents' plots, we arrived at the destination. My mother's first reaction? "Oh, we're under a tree; we'll have shade. That's nice." Uh, ma'am, you can't be *dead-ass* right now. My father's response: "Yeah, you're right; that's nice. Who are we next to?" (*glances over at other tombstones*). I'm sure you can imagine my face at that moment. If not, insert your favorite gif that visually demonstrates unabashed confusion. Yes, that gif, that was me.

Before I could ask what was going on, my father started talking about the receipts, documentation, and location of the plots. He was adamant that my brothers and I should know where all of his paperwork was located when it came time to use it. The whole conversation and experience felt grim AF. Once the unintentionally traumatic field trip came to an end, he did keep his end of the deal and happily drove us to our respective happy places as promised.

Four years after our morbid field trip, I couldn't tell you what that cemetery is called, where in New Jersey it's located, or where any of those documents are. I wasn't paying enough attention to the conversation; I didn't want to because it made me uncomfortable and sad. My discomfort created the illusion of time, which prevented a necessary conversation.

First dose of reality is, as the eldest daughter, that moment on that day in that cemetery with my sixty-one-year-old father was important, and I dropped the ball. Second dose of reality: We do not have the luxury of time on our side like we think we do. The time to prepare and plan for tragedy is *not* when tragedy occurs; it is before. Last bit of reality: Frankly speaking, tragedies are expensive. There's no gentle sugar-coated alternative way to say it. Nine times out of ten, they are also usually unexpected. An unexpected high-ticket expense tied to an emotionally triggering life event is going to require a substantial amount of time and energy. A plan can be a preliminary assistive measure that eases certain stressors when tragedy eventually does occur.

WHAT IS ESTATE PLANNING?

Today as we celebrate my dad's sixty-fifth birthday, I've stepped firmly into my first-born-daughter duties as I adamantly try to get both his and my mother's estate in order. I'll be the first to admit it sounds fancy AF to say, "I'm getting their estate in order," but if we're going to continue to be dead-ass with each other, *estate* is just a fancy word for "all of my shit." If you'd rather call it "getting all of my shit together" planning, I won't fight you just as long as you get it done.

Both of my parents have what I'd call a skeletal estate plan. They have a few things in order, but nowhere near enough of an effective estate plan. For all intents and purposes, their shit is not together. Between them they have life insurance policies, pensions, retirement accounts, bank accounts, small investment accounts, vehicles, and possibly a living will. Neither my brothers nor I actually know where any of those documents or accounts are currently housed or the login information to access any of their digital accounts.

Long story made incredibly short: they have the necessary items that need to be planned for so their wishes can be accommodated. Even shorter story, the plan hasn't been planned. Hopefully by the time you reach the end of this chapter, I will have successfully helped both of my parents develop an estate plan worthy of their lifetime achievements and efforts. At the least, let's hope my brothers and I know the passwords for their email and bank accounts.

WHAT'S THE BIG DEAL ABOUT ESTATE PLANNING, ANYWAY?

A variation of this question is often asked because estate planning is often associated with wealthy people. The term *estate* feels like a big lofty idea, when estate planning is simply a security measure that makes life easier for your loved ones should you pass away or become incapacitated. Truth moment: estate planning is just as, if not more, crucial for the everyday middle-class worker as it is for Bill Gates. Why? When tragedy strikes it is an absolute misfortune for everyone involved at any income level, but the financial burdens of tragedy hit quite differently when you have millions in the bank versus when you're living paycheck to paycheck. At the least, think of an estate plan as taking the guesswork out of highly stressful and emotional times.

WHEN & WHO SHOULD ESTATE PLAN?

Now that we've gotten past the idea that estate planning is only for the wealthy, I'd kindly like to also toss out the idea that it's only for the elderly. I'm of the mind that any and every person eighteen and up should have at least the bare bones of an official estate plan in their adulting arsenal. This starter estate plan should then be updated every three to five years as you progress further into your career and obtain various assets. You may think you have nothing to plan for right now, but you have more than you realize.

I'm not naïve enough to think that eighteen-year-olds are going to suddenly start flocking to their nearest financial advisor to start estate planning. Though Gen Z is arguably far more financially cognizant than generations past, asking an eighteen-year-old to sit down and choose their beneficiaries or power of attorney is a tall ask, even for the profoundly progressive bunch. So, if you're an eighteen-year-old reading this book right now, shout out to you! Second, I understand your hesitation and lack of planning; it's normal. If you're older than eighteen, still shout-outs going straight out to you heavily. I'm also proud of you for taking your personal finance journey seriously. Now let's kick that soon-to-be estate-planning ass into full speed ahead.

Whether you're a young, fresh, novice adult walking into a closet-sized apartment or a suburban homeowning parent, you'll want to pay attention to these life events as indicators that you should already have your estate planned or you need to update your estate.

ESTATE PLANNING TRIGGERS

(signs you should have an estate plan/need to update your estate plan)

- **Savings Account:** We start right here! If you're this far into the book I know you've got a whole budget, spending, and savings plan, so I know for a fact you've got a savings account. This also means your estate planning journey can begin right here! You will want to designate a beneficiary to have access to those funds in the event of your passing. Having a designated beneficiary will ensure that your money goes to the person/people or cause of your choosing without delays or difficulties.

- **Homeownership/Additional Property Ownership:** The name of the game is preparing your loved ones to take care of business when you're no longer capable of doing so. To avoid lengthy probate proceedings, you'll want to have a will that specifically outlines who will become the new owner of your home and any additional properties you own. *Probate* refers to the process of validating a will and administering your estate plan. Think of every movie or TV show you've seen where the family has gathered to hear the Last Will and Testament read, only to lead to a shocking revelation. That is the tail end of probate, but the process involves a few more legal steps. Without a proper estate plan, your probate can be overseen and managed through probate court. They will ultimately have the final say on where your money and assets go, so if you want your home to be passed to your children or turned into a museum, you must explicitly state that.

- **Death:** It may not be the first thing that comes to mind when a loved one passes away, but if a close family member or friend who had a huge part in your original estate plan is no longer capable of doing so, your estate plan needs to be updated to reflect that. If not, your estate will find itself in lengthy probate court proceedings, and no one wants that!

- **Retirement Accounts:** This was a step I skipped for a long time when I started my teaching career and I wish I could tell you it was for a better reason than pure laziness. Much like your savings account, when you have established and funded a retirement account you should also assign a beneficiary in the same breath. It took me five years and numerous reminders from my union rep to finally declare a beneficiary for my pension and 403B. How long did it take me? Three minutes!

- **Marriage:** If you just tied the knot you will want to update your estate plan to include your partner. That means you're not just updating your will or the beneficiaries listed on your accounts, but you will also have to decide whose name(s) are on what accounts and what happens to your assets in the unfortunate event that one spouse or both pass away.

- **Divorce:** Like marriage, a divorce is going to require another estate plan update. Whereas in marriage you are coupling assets and deciding what to do as a unit, in a divorce you must ensure that your spouse's name is removed from all documentation as a viable beneficiary. I don't know about y'all, but I'd be upset watching my ex get his hands on my 401K as I strut through the pearly gates. Honestly, I'd have no choice but to consistently haunt him because my pettiness would not allow anything less.

- **Becoming a Parent/New Additional Children:** This is a major life moment that triggers one of the biggest estate planning updates you'll likely encounter. Once you become a parent for the first time, and every additional time after that, it would behoove you to update your plan in a timely manner. Outside of beneficiary updates, you will also need to think about guardianship. Speaking for my Caribbean people only, we love choosing solid godparents who can step up in times of tragedy. However, you'll still want to make sure you legally elect a guardian in a will and notify the person of your election. The last thing you want to do is surprise someone with legal guardianship of your children in the same breath they are mourning a loss. Whether you're in a relationship or not, ensuring financial, physical, mental, and emotional security for your children is an absolute necessity that must take precedence in your estate plan.

- **Inheritance of Money or Assets:** If you've recently inherited money or assets, that means someone who really loves you properly estate planned with you in mind. Now it's time for you to do the same. Update your estate plan to include the newly acquired money and assets.

- **Grandchildren/Births in the Family:** As I got older, I realized quickly that my nuclear family is not the only group of relatives I'd have to keep in mind when estate planning. If my currently nonexistent but potentially on-the-way children decide to have children of their own, this is another estate planning trigger that may require a necessary update. My brother's potential future children also will have a seat at the *Millennial in Debt* estate plan when they arrive on the scene. If any pivotal family births occur, it may be time to log in to your digital accounts and account for their arrival.

- **Business Owner:** Have you seen the HBO show *Succession*? I haven't, but I've Googled the plot a few times and I can't help but think a lot of the conflict could be remedied with a stronger estate plan. Granted, I've never seen the show, so take my review with all the grains of salt you can find. If you're a business owner, you don't want those *Succession* problems, so you're going to need to think about what happens to your business after you're gone. Who is going to take over? What regulations do you want to preemptively employ? All really important things to think about as you update or create your estate plan.

ESTATE PLANNING BASICS: THE TEN-STEP CHECKLIST

So far, I've spoken briefly about certain moving pieces involved in estate planning. Selecting beneficiaries is a big step; creating a will and selecting guardians for your children are also big steps. But these aren't the only actions you'll need to take to have a fully planned estate.

Here's a quick hit list of what you'll want to consider when preparing a solid estate plan:

- Establish guardians for any living dependents you may have (this could be done in a will).

- Appoint or update your beneficiaries on your bank accounts, retirement accounts, and life insurance plans.

- Assign power of attorney and healthcare proxy that will uphold your healthcare wishes and make decisions on your behalf when you are unable to do so.

- Create a will in which you choose your power of attorney, designate a healthcare proxy, and specify how and to whom you want your assets and money distributed.

- Create a trust if you have quite a few assets (like property or investments). There are various trusts you can choose from to meet your needs and ensure your assets are properly distributed.

- Make funeral arrangements and make them well known. My father was definitely on to something when he tricked us into going to that cemetery that day. If you don't want to plan out your funeral, I completely understand; it is a dark task. It is still a wise choice to have loose skeletal plans outlined for your loved ones to have some form of guidance. Do you want an open casket, do you want to be cremated, do you want to be buried in a particular state or country? All of that matters and will take some of the guessing game out of the process for your family members.

As the list has revealed, a couple of steps must be taken to comprehensively create an estate plan. It doesn't mean it has to be daunting, overwhelming, or anxiety-inducing. Some steps may be simple and take one to two days to complete. Other steps may take a few weeks and more of your time and energy. Remember they are steps and meant to be taken one at a time. So whenever you find yourself overwhelmed or stuck in your head trying to plow through the moving pieces, take a deep breath and stop. This is not a race; there are no gold stars. You are proactively preparing to take care of the people you love the most even after you're gone, and you want to do it right. A practical timeline to create a fully comprehensive estate plan could truthfully take two to three years. Set a practical timeline for yourself that tackles one task every few months.

To ensure your efforts don't go in vain and your timeline is met, we need an outline to support your plan. Use the following checklist as a key player in your estate planning strategy.

ONE: ITEMIZE YOUR STUFF

The best place to start your estate planning journey is to take stock of your tangible items. That will include things like your car, home, jewelry, art, investment properties, and other personal items. Don't just make a mental note, and an iPhone note isn't going to cut it. You'll need to formally itemize your belongings with actual pen and paper. Shocking, I know! If you're a digital junkie like I am, you can use a spreadsheet or Word document that you'll later print a hard copy of.

- **Add your nontangible assets:** Once you've itemized your physical assets, add your nontangible assets to the list. This will include your investment accounts, checking and savings accounts, life insurance policies, and health savings accounts.

- **Tally your debts:** This is a step I know you've already completed from Chapter 1, so it shouldn't take you more energy than grabbing your budget and savings plan. A solid estate plan will itemize not only your assets but also your liabilities. The last thing you want is a lender contacting your loved ones about debts they didn't know you had and aren't sure how to handle.

- **Make copies of documentation and store it safely:** Everything you have itemized will have or should have documentation that details their value. This will look like bank statements, home appraisals, and statements for other financial accounts. For any assets that do not have a direct valuation, you will have to estimate the value of the items. Once you have your paperwork together, make at least three copies. One copy will go to your estate administrator, the second copy should go to a loved one, and the third will be your copy. The documents should always be kept in a safe place, so it is a good idea to invest in a safety deposit box or one of those fireproof/waterproof at-home safes.

TWO: REVIEW YOUR ACCOUNTS

Your nontangible accounts will need a once-over to ensure that the information is accurate and up to date. Different types of financial accounts will operate differently, so don't be shy about asking as many questions as you need for clarification. I can't stress this one point enough; your bank accounts and individual brokerage accounts will need a death designation. Without a death designation, the funds in these accounts will unnecessarily be a part of a dreadfully drawn-out probate. Let's not do that! Contact your banks and financial institutions to assign or update your transfer-on-death designation. It is also likely that you can do this virtually in your online accounts.

THREE: SELECT AN ESTATE ADMINISTRATOR

You will need to select a responsible estate administrator who will take the lead after you have passed. An estate administrator is in charge of administering your will to ensure your final wishes are made public. It can be anyone you choose, but it is vital they can carry out your wishes. People often initially think that an immediate relative or spouse should be the estate administrator but that is not always the case. A qualified individual will be in a healthy mental state to make decisions, so if emotions related to your death will cause unstable decision-making, they may not be your best option.

FOUR: DRAFT A WILL

Think of a will as a guidebook. Without it, the government gets to decide how your assets will be distributed based on state laws. It will detail what you want and don't want after you are gone. It is easy and inexpensive to draft a will with or without the assistance of a professional. Modern technology has made it so you can write your own will in less than an hour using online services. If you have a more complicated estate, an attorney can help you draft a will for around $800–$1,000, depending on the complexity and your geographical location.

Once the will has been completed, sign and date the document and have it notarized and stored in a safe place. Your safety deposit box or at-home safe are two ideal locations. Most importantly, inform your estate administrator and another person you trust where your will is located. No one is trying to play "Where's Waldo" in times of distress.

FIVE: BRING IN THE PROFESSIONALS

There is a common theme in the homeownership, retirement, estate planning, and tax chapter that you may not have noticed just yet. Let me clarify it: Do not try and DIY every aspect of your finances. It is risky to do so and usually does not work out in your best financial interest. Don't get me wrong; figuring out how to do things yourself is a vital part of your journey to becoming a financially literate badass. However, there's a time and place to DIY and a time and place to bring in the professionals. And I'm here to help you identify when to do which.

Can you estate plan on your own? Yes-*ish*. If you have a relatively small estate and straightforward wishes, a DIY online service may be all you need. For many of us, including my first-generation ass, the process of estate planning is a new concept. The intricacies are unknown; therefore, it is a good idea to put an estate planning team together that consists of an estate attorney and tax professional at the least. As your estate plan grows and evolves, the new complexities may also require you to tap into a financial advisor to help you determine if you are on the proper planning path.

Long story short: don't try to wing it.

SIX: CONSIDER ESTABLISHING A TRUST

Think of a trust as a container where you put your assets for your loved ones. Establishing a trust is a good idea for two reasons:

- A trust that is established properly has a high likelihood of protecting your estate from entering probate. Remember, probate is often a time-consuming and expensive experience for loved ones, so the more pre-planning you do, the better.

- A properly structured trust will also minimize the impact of estate taxes. After you pass, your estate will be taxed when it is distributed. Estate taxes are federal taxes, and the burden to pay taxes on any cash, real estate, or valuable belongings will fall directly on your beneficiaries. Once they receive their inheritance, they typically will have nine months after your death to pay those taxes. An irrevocable trust is an intelligent preventative measure you can take to prevent this from occurring.

If and when you decide to establish a trust, you will have a few options and an estate attorney is highly suggested to help you choose the right option for your specific needs. The three most common trusts that can be established are:

- **Irrevocable Trust:** This type of trust cannot be changed once it has been finalized. This trust lacks flexibility since you cannot make amendments or updates if you change your mind, but there is an added layer of protection against the IRS, lenders, and creditors.

- **Revocable Trust:** The revokable trust offers more flexibility than the aforementioned option. You can make edits if life circumstances require you to do so. You can also cancel a revokable trust before you pass away. After your death, this type of trust transitions into an irrevocable trust.

- **Charitable Trust:** A charitable trust gives you the option to donate money and or assets to a charitable organization. The beautiful part about a charitable trust is your assets are no longer considered your personal property. This means the organization will not have to deal with any potential tax issues or lawsuits, and absolutely no probates.

SEVEN: CONSOLIDATE YOUR ACCOUNTS

Listen, living life is a nonstop, energy-consuming process. We do not always have the time to make sure every I is dotted and every T is crossed. We do the best we can and as long as we're afloat on a macro level, we triumphantly proceed to the next challenge or opportunity. If I remember to eat at least two meals in a day, I consider that a win since I so often forget to even eat just once. So believe me when I tell you I understand why it is so easy to forget you have a 401K left behind with a toxic employer you're thrilled to have left behind. Consolidate as many accounts as you can to make it easier for your loved ones to access.

I wish I could blame it on anything besides pure laziness, but it took me ten months to successfully transfer my 403B into a traditional IRA when I left teaching. There are completely free services that will move your old retirement accounts from previous employers into one space, so you aren't paying an exorbitant amount of fees or leaving money behind.

EIGHT: WRITE A LETTER OF INSTRUCTION

This letter is going to detail a few things about your wishes, but it's also going to give your loved ones a starting point and the upper hand. Your letter of instruction should include:

- What kind of funeral arrangements would you like and what funeral arrangements have you already made? Funerals are expensive so if you have pre-funded any part of your arrangements, you'll want to let your family know.

- Make a note of your digital accounts and passwords. Most providers are not obligated to give your loved ones access to your accounts and they typically won't. That means any account (financial or otherwise) you have that you want your family to be able to access you should include login information in your letter of instruction. That can be for accounts like your PayPal, your social media accounts, email account, Dropbox, etc. As an alternative you can have your attorney close all your digital accounts.

NINE: CREATE AN "IN CASE OF DEATH" FOLDER/BINDER

Morbid, maybe. A good idea, yes. Your "in case of death folder/binder" should be kept in a safe space and include:

- Your letter of instruction and itemized list from step one

- Documents: loan documents, deeds, birth certificate, titles, etc.

- Life insurance policies

- Bank and credit card accounts

- Copies of keys to your home, cars, offices, safety deposit boxes, etc.

Be sure to inform your estate administrator and an additional loved one about the whereabouts of this folder. Hint: A copy of all of your important estate planning documents should ideally be kept in one space to avoid confusion and save time.

TEN: REGULARLY REVIEW YOUR ESTATE PLAN & MAKE UPDATES AS NEEDED

You will want to check in on your estate plan at least once every one to two years unless a major life event triggers the need to make changes sooner.

ESTATE PLANNING MYTHS

As we wrap up this absurdly grown-up chapter, let's remind ourselves of just what is fact and what is a fabrication of society's imagination. Seriously though, this chapter contains some of the most responsible adult words I've ever written. I can't believe someone let me adult by myself, let alone help others figure out how to also adult. When did I become the adultiest adult in the room? Gross! I digress...let's get to the bottom of these myths once and for all.

MYTH ONE: ESTATE PLANNING IS ONLY FOR THE WEALTHY

Though I think this chapter has successfully debunked this myth, there's no harm in driving the point all the way home. Estate planning is all about putting your affairs in order, so your loved ones have less stress to manage after you have passed away or become incapacitated. Leaving behind an organized comprehensive estate plan is not only thoughtful, but it is crucial.

MYTH TWO: YOU ONLY NEED TO MAKE A LAST WILL AND TESTAMENT

Another myth I no longer think you believe after we've spent time digging into what goes into a comprehensive estate plan. Think of a will as one level of a multilevel multiplayer game. If you're currently hungry like I am you can think of it as one tier of a multitier delicious vanilla wedding cake. Because yes, on a random cold Sunday evening in New York I am craving a slice of wedding cake.

Once you take steps to draft a will, I have another surprise for you—you may want to create a living will. Before you roll your eyes and suck your teeth, I want to inform you that a living will is just as important as a traditional postmortem will.

A living will, a.k.a. an advance directive, is a legal document that informs everyone involved what they can and can't do if you are no longer able to communicate your preferences yourself. This is also where you would also declare a medical power of attorney (a.k.a. a healthcare proxy) who will act on your behalf regarding healthcare decisions. A living will also afford you the opportunity to specify instructions about medical procedures and practices such as being kept on life support or the usage of breathing and feeding tubes.

You will also be able to declare a standard power of attorney. This person makes the decisions regarding your finances if you are not able to do so. Do not leave anything up to chance or the government when it comes to how you want yourself and your assets to be handled.

MYTH THREE: ESTATE PLANNING IS EXPENSIVE AND OVERWHELMING

Well, as someone often overwhelmed doing laundry, it is hard to truly say one way or another how overwhelming estate planning may or may not be. Will some parts be more intrusive and therefore more stressful than other parts? Absolutely. Is it overbearingly difficult? It doesn't have to be. Especially if you move through the ten-step checklist over an idyllic period of time and bring in a team of professionals to support your process.

The bigger myth here is that estate planning is a lavish expense. Estate planning is not a luxury; it is a necessity. The cost of an estate plan will vary because everyone's needs are different and thus everyone's estate plan will require different levels of support. On average a standard comprehensive estate plan with little to no complexities will cost between $800–$1,000. To bring some perspective into the mix, the average Amazon Prime member spends $1,400 annually buying a ton of shit they likely don't need. Raises hand sheepishly...add this average to my trips to Target and I easily could estate plan a few times over.

More complex estates that have a larger number of contingencies to keep in mind and assets to leave behind will see a steady increase in the average price of their estate plan. This can range from $3,000 to $10,000. I know, that is a big scary jump from the $800–$1,000 range, but you are not starting at the $10,000 starting mark. You don't even need to start at the $800 mark because budgets are real and $800 is not a laughable amount of money.

The best and smartest move you can make when starting your estate planning journey is to weigh your options. To weigh your options, you need to know what those options are. Here are things you already know:

- You can protect some of your assets (checking, savings, retirement) for free in less than ten minutes by declaring beneficiaries for those specified accounts.

- You also have an itemized list of your assets, both tangible and intangible, so you have a decent idea of what you'll need to plan for, and you'll update accordingly when you need to do so.

- Lastly, you know that you don't have to rush through each step immediately. You can take three- to four-month pauses between each step to learn more about your options or save for professional support. Don't be shy about asking for or seeking free consultations before committing to anyone.

- You can DIY the basics of your estate plan to get you started at an affordable price point. Legal service sites like Legal Zoom and Quicken offer basic packages to help you draft a will starting at eighty-nine dollars.

Start where you're comfortable and capable, but absolutely start.

MYTH FOUR: I NEED A MILLION-DOLLAR LIFE INSURANCE POLICY

Oh my, I beg you to leave this myth in the trash where it belongs, right next to low-rise jeans and thin eyebrows.

Do you need life insurance? *Yes.*

Do you need a million dollars' worth? Maybe; it *depends.*

I don't know what life insurance salespeople were doing back in the day, so I will only speak on the most recent batch flooding the social media platforms hoping to make a sucker out of a vulnerable person. Life insurance salespeople make bank by selling life insurance products. Their commissions are violently high and because of this will push you into a whole life insurance policy or IUL that you do not need.

Here me loud and clear: you need life insurance. Get life insurance. I repeat: get life insurance. I've stated it three times in hopes of keeping the trolls away that will undoubtedly still find themselves misquoting this chapter the minute they get their hands on it. Life insurance is a vital part of adulting and is an important part of your estate plan.

However, like your finances and estate plan, your needs will vary and will require updates as life progresses. Do not let anyone scare you into a policy that you don't need, can't afford, or don't fully understand. A million-dollar life insurance policy makes more sense for someone who is married or is part of a two-income household, has children, a six-figure mortgage, debt, etc. This person would need to leave more behind in their absence to support their current lifestyle and family members. In comparison, a million-dollar life insurance policy would make less sense for a twenty-one-year-old fresh out of college at the start of their career with no children, vehicle, or real estate. It is ever so clearly a different vibe.

Once you do decide on a policy that fits your needs, you'll be sure to add beneficiaries of your choosing.

MYTH FIVE: I DON'T HAVE ANYTHING TO LEAVE BEHIND

False! You have more to leave behind than you think.

In 2021, a close friend of mine passed away due to complications with COVID-19 and a preexisting kidney issue. He was a twenty-seven-year-old firecracker filled with so much love and light to share with the world. Our loss was devastating in every imaginable way. There are so many things about his absence that continue to break my heart in more ways than I could ever type on this screen.

Why am I sharing this right here right now? When we mourn young people who have passed on, there is an extra twinge of pain in our hearts when we think about all the life they will never get the chance to live. Twenty-seven years old is really young. Ridiculously, unequivocally young, especially when you take into consideration that the average male life expectancy in the US is seventy-seven years old.

No one expected to have to say goodbye to him when we did. It was unexpected and it was quick. When the dust seemingly settled, his mother and sisters were left to figure out how to access the parts of him that he didn't get the chance to plan for. Because in our minds we think we have time. We think what we have now is negligible and so we make a mental note to plan when we think there's something worth planning for.

Though it may be uncomfortable or bring forth feelings of uncertainty and sadness, your loved ones don't care if you only leave behind five cents, five dollars, or 500,000 dollars. They don't care if your password is "BladeRunner02" and you have a photo album dedicated to your favorite whiskeys. What they do care about is respecting your final wishes. No matter the size of your current estate, your loved ones deserve the peace and closure that comes with knowing for certain rather than the stresses and battles that come with not knowing for sure. Only you can provide that for them and the time to do that is now.

CHAPTER 10

DON'T MESS WITH THE IRS

I thought long and hard (well, honestly, probably about five minutes) about a witty pun to title this chapter, but then decided to go with something more direct. While the English major in me internally dies a little when clichés are used in writing, I'm willing to do so to make something abundantly clear. The only two things in life that are certain are death and taxes. I'm letting you know right now; you can eff around and find out a lot of things, but you do not mess with the IRS. If the IRS decides to pursue a case, tax fraud and tax evasion can carry steep jail time, ranging from one year for a misdemeanor, to three to twenty-five years for more serious offenses. And they know everything. So that person adding a child you've never met before in your life as a dependent on your tax return so you can get eight thousand dollars back is not only committing tax fraud, but they're also putting you front and center to audition for a role in federal prison. Something tells me an orange jumpsuit isn't quite your style.

WHY DO WE PAY TAXES?

I have to admit two things here:

1. I hate taxes.

2. I do not like doing things without a solid "why."

Oddly, I blame both confessions on the education system. I am fully aware that everything we never learned can't be blamed on the school system forever, but as someone who has worked for the NYC Department of Education for eleven years, they're going to have to take a collective L for this one. Of all the things that are not prioritized in the school curricula, taxes by far feel like the biggest slight toward financial development. This is a rather large claim to make given the state of educational censorship running rampant in the US right now, but I firmly stand behind it.

Though we have seen progress on a state-by-state basis, the lack of nationally mandated financial literacy in the classroom is a detriment to the financial progress of our modern society. When we further analyze the impact of financial illiteracy and the inequalities of our current tax codes on the poor and working-class populations, the stark disadvantages are more alarming than one may think.

A common saying that you may be familiar with is, "Ignorance of the law is no excuse." Basically you can't just break the law and say, "Oops, I didn't know I was committing a crime" as your defense because that custom orange jumpsuit will be ready and waiting for you in your size regardless of what you do or don't know. And yet, a 2019 NerdWallet study revealed that 48 percent of Americans do not know their tax bracket, and their 2017 study shows that 57 percent of Americans don't know what a W4 is.

For most of my adult life, the extent of my tax knowledge was basically limited to a general understanding of why we pay taxes and an understanding that every year I would have to file taxes. Nothing more, nothing less. I knew that we paid taxes basically because the government said so, and those taxes were used to support social programs. Needless to say, our taxes go way beyond that limited understanding.

Yes, taxes are used to fund the government's bills, but they also support the stability, growth, and functionality of our society. This includes things like education, healthcare, and infrastructure. Snarky parents never missed an opportunity to tell me that their taxes paid my salary, to which I always gently reminded them that I also paid taxes to keep public schools up and running as well. Taxes are a part of our civic duty and social contract with the government, like jury duty. Few people jump for joy to serve on a jury, and the only thing most people enjoy about filing taxes is the potential tax return.

We may not love it, we certainly don't have to understand every intricacy, but it's a necessity we cannot opt out of. If you exist in society, which, if you're reading this book, that's a clear-cut sign that you in fact do exist in society, you benefit from tax collection in some way, shape, or form. While the following is not an exhaustive list, here's a solid overview of how federal, state, and local taxes have supported your personal development or well-being.

FEDERAL TAXES

On a federal level, taxes help to mitigate the government's debts, improve defense, and upkeep the general welfare of society in the country. There are various types of federal and state taxes, but we are most familiar with income tax automatically deducted from our checks. Alongside federal tax, The Federal Insurance Contributions Act (a.k.a. FICA) established payroll deductions for Medicare and Social Security.

WHAT IS YOUR FEDERAL TAX USED FOR?

- Income security: (e.g., unemployment, nutrition assistance like SNAP, and military retirement)

- Highway maintenance

- Health insurance (e.g., Medicare, Medicaid, the Children's Health Insurance Program, and the Affordable Care Act)

- Economic security programs (e.g., earned income tax credit and the child tax credit)

- Benefits for federal retirees and veterans

- Interest on government debt

- Social Security

- National defense

STATE TAXES

The reasons we pay state taxes are quite similar to the reasons we pay federal taxes. The common differentiator is different states will have different processes and rules for collecting taxes. One state may collect sales tax and income tax while another may not. Anyone in NYC who grew up in the '90s and early '00s probably has a few fuzzy core memories surrounding travel to New Jersey to avoid sales tax on clothes, waiting for those annual "sales tax free" weekends in NYC to buy new clothes for school, and complaining about higher prices at Roosevelt Field Mall and Green Acres in Long Island because they got that extra extra tax. If you bought something at Queens Center Mall and had to exchange it in Long Island you would have to pull out a few extra dollars and be annoyed about it every single time! Ahh, memories!

Every state may have different policies surrounding income and sales tax, but all will have property, state, and local taxes. We all know New York has to be at the top of every list, and state tax is no different; with a whopping 14.1 percent tax burden, New York state-local tax exceeds the 2019 national average of 10.3 percent. Imagine my fleeting joy when I moved to Long Island and no longer had to pay city tax on my check but was hit with an even bigger property tax. Clearly, I need to move to Alaska, which currently does not have income or sales tax on its docket.

WHAT IS YOUR STATE TAX USED FOR?

On a day-to-day basis, your state taxes will likely be used for the following:

- Public schooling on the elementary and secondary level (this includes free 3-K and pre-K programs as well)

- Medicaid

- Community colleges

- Public health programs

- Corrections

- Transportation

- Public university systems

Local taxes fund similar programs as state taxes, with a focus on the maintenance of local infrastructure, sanitation (garbage removal and street cleaning), police and fire services, and K–12 public schools.

Raise your hand if you've benefitted from at least one of the programs or systems funded by our federal, local, or state tax contributions. So, you see, everyone must pay their share...or do they?

HOW DO TAXES ACTUALLY WORK?

In a stunning turn of events, as I gathered research in preparation to write this chapter and shit on the wealthy for not paying their fair share I stumbled into an interesting fact. A 2022 tax policy center analysis revealed that 72.5 million households (approximately 40 percent of the US population) will not pay federal income tax. Another shocking fact to me, 30 million households (16.5 percent of the population) will not be paying federal income taxes or payroll taxes. *Gasps!* How can this be? Well, as a thriving capitalist nation, there's always going to be an insurmountable wage gap. That's what thrusts capitalism forward. There must be a few people at the top, more semi-strugglers in the middle, and a large majority of overworked, overlooked, and underpaid at the bottom. Capitalism requires inequity and poverty to function.

The main reason that 40 percent of the population will not pay federal income taxes is that they barely earn a livable wage. Sixty percent of people who do not pay federal income tax earn less than $30,000 a year, while 28 percent make between $30,000–$60,000 annually. Under the IRS tax inflation adjustments for 2022, anyone making less than the federal standard deduction of $12,950 for single filers, $19,400 for heads of household, and $25,900 for married couples filing jointly would owe no federal income tax.

Here I was preparing to scream, "Eat the rich!" when the wealthy surprisingly are not afforded this tax benefit. Oh, don't get it twisted—it's still very much "eat the rich" around here all day, every day, because while they may not benefit from this tax provision, they substantially benefit from many others.

It is easy to misconstrue this progressive federal tax provision as a tax loophole to avoid civic and social duties, but the truth is this tax break is afforded to a vulnerable population that does not make much money in the first place. The majority of those who do not pay federal income taxes are the elderly living off of Social Security distributions, people with severe disabilities, and students. The second truth that needs to be screamed loudly to the rooftops: just because they are not paying federal income tax does not mean they are not paying taxes on the state and local level. Our tax codes and policies are rather complex, and the progressive nature of our federal tax codes is often undermined by the regressive nature of state and local taxes. This small grace is not a cop-out; it is one of the few that benefit and alleviate the economic challenges that lower-income earners face consistently.

Federal and state income taxes have historically worsened the financial inequities that marginalized groups often face at greater rates than their adulated counterparts. To understand how our tax systems and codes negatively impact people with lower incomes, we must first understand the basics of how taxes work.

Simply put, the taxes you are responsible for paying are based on your income, and the more you earn, the higher your taxes will be. However, that is where the simplicity comes to an end. There are several ways that taxpayers can reduce their taxable income using exemptions, credits, deductions, and exclusions. When the dust settles, your taxable income will be less than your gross income and will fall into a tax bracket.

Tax brackets help determine how much money you owe the IRS. Could the IRS simplify this and just tell us straight up how much we owe? Of course, they could, but where's the fun in that? Instead, you take your best educated guess and risk fees and or jail time if you get it wrong. How exciting!

This next fun fact is going to be a game-changer the next time you're at brunch or dinner with a finance expert who claims their bonus or raise is going to push them into the next tax bracket. Gracefully nod and smile right before you inform them, the tax bracket income levels are guided by a marginal tax rate system that prevents your income from being taxed at the same rate. Then order the tastiest dessert on the menu because you *deserve it*!

Just because you get a raise does not mean that your entire income is now going to be taxed at a higher rate. *False!* To understand how the marginal tax rate system works, let's look at the 2023 tax brackets and federal income tax rates for a single filer starting from 10 percent up to 37 percent for high-income earners. Though we're using the 2023 tax bracket specifically for single filers, remember that your specific filing status and taxable income will determine what bracket you're in.

2023 SINGLE FILER TAX BRACKETS

YOUR TAXABLE INCOME IS:	THE TAXES YOU OWE:
Not over $11,000	10 percent of taxable income
More than $11,000 but not over $44,725	$1,100 plus 12 percent of the excess over $11,000
More than $44,725 but not more than $95,375	$5,147 plus 22 percent of the excess over $44,725
More than $95,375 but not more than $182,100	$16,290 plus 24 percent of the excess over $95,375
More than $182,100 but not more than $231,250	$37,104 plus 32 percent of the excess over $182,100
More than $235,250 but not more than $578,125	$52,832 plus 35 percent of the excess over $231,250
More than $578,125	$174,238.25 plus 37 percent of the excess over $578,125

The taxable income and the tax obligation will vary for married couples filing separately, married couples filing jointly, and heads of household.

I am someone who does not like numbers to be thrown at them without some practicality attached. It helps me mentally process exactly what I need to understand. I hope I'm not the only one whose brain glitches out when numbers are spewed all over the place because I'm about to break down the tax bracket convo in a way that appeals to me!

Let's say your taxable income is $70,000 after all your deductions and exemptions are calculated. That $70,000 puts you in the 22 percent marginal tax bracket. However, you are not paying 22 percent on the entire $70,000.

- The first $11,000 is taxed at 10 percent: **$1,100**

- The next $33,725 (44,725–11,000) is taxed at 12 percent: **$4,047**

- The last $25,275 (70,000–44,725) is taxed at 22 percent: **$5,560.50**

- The total tax amount for your $70,000 taxable income is $10,707.50 (that's the $1,100 + $4047 + $5,560.50)

Another quicker way to gauge your tax obligation is to take 22 percent and apply it to anything you've made over $44,725. That means you will be paying 22 percent on $25,275 ($70,000 - $44,725 = $25,275). You'll take the $5,560.50 and add it to the $5,147 in the 22 percent marginal tax bracket (see previous chart), bringing your total tax obligation once again to $10,707.50. If you were to be taxed 22 percent on your entire taxable income of $70,000, you would have to pay $15,400 instead.

This is the basic structure of what happens every year when you file your taxes. So I know you're probably thinking, *okay, this seems straightforward and fair*. How could this or any type of tax obligation possibly be laced with inequity? It's just numbers!

EAT THE RICH: HOW TAXES PERPETUATE INEQUITY

REGRESSIVE TAXES

To fully understand how detrimental regressive taxes are, we must first understand what a regressive tax is. By sheer definition, as per Investopedia, "A regressive tax is a tax applied uniformly, taking a larger percentage of income from low-income earners than from middle- and high-income earners. With a regressive tax, the tax burden decreases as income rises." Examples of regressive taxes that we pay all the time are sales tax, property tax, and payroll tax.

Many regressive taxes still prevalent in the present day have a history deeply rooted in the Reconstruction era, the time period immediately following the end of the Civil War. I don't need to tell you, but I'm going to anyway. Many of these taxes were built as a resistance to wealth distribution that would lead to economic equality. So where we have progressive federal income taxes that force the wealthy to pay the highest marginal income tax rates, regressive taxes on a state-by-state level aren't designed to do the same.

Case in point, when you file your taxes annually, you have the option of choosing between a standard deduction and an itemized deduction. For the 2023 tax year, the standard deduction for a single filer is $13,850. This amount will be automatically deducted from your income if you forgo an itemized deduction. With an itemized deduction you claim certain expenses like donations, mortgage interest payments, and other forms of spending.

Most Americans choose the standard deduction because an itemized deduction only makes sense if you are claiming an amount greater than the standard deduction. Who benefits from itemized deductions the most? The wealthy. Why? Overall, most deductions benefit people with more money, particularly with SALT (state and local tax) deductions.

According to Americanprogress.org, 75 percent of Americans earning more than a million dollars or more claim the SALT deduction, in stark contrast to the less than 1 percent of taxpayers earning less than $30,000, who were expected to claim the same deduction in 2022. Just how much of an impact does the SALT deduction have on the wealthiest Americans? Nick Bufie, author of "5 Little-Known Facts About Taxes and Inequality in America," states, "Among the small share of taxpayers earning less than $50,000 who claim the SALT deduction, the average amount deducted is $4,686. But among those claiming the SALT deduction and earning $200,00 or more the average deduction is $9,735—close to the $10,000 maximum."

MORTGAGE INTEREST DEDUCTION

I have been able to itemize the interest I've paid on my mortgage over the last four years. While I personally benefit from this tax deduction, I am not daft enough to sit up here and lie about the tax inequity the deduction perpetuates. Mortgage interest is one of the few deductions that does not have a cap. As a homeowner with mortgage debt, I can deduct the full value of the interest I've paid in the year, while renters or homeowners with no debt are not afforded a similar deduction in any way, shape, or form. This deduction sits heavily within the racial wealth gap as homeownership rates in 2022 hover around 75 percent for white Americans, 45 percent for Black people, and 48 percent for Hispanic households. The usage of the mortgage interest deduction is greatly skewed with 70.5 percent of the people who claim it earning more than $100,000 a year. Only 5.2 percent of people who claim the mortgage interest deduction earn between $50,000–$100,000. To put these numbers into perspective, again I remind you don't be fooled by every "six-figure earner" on Instagram; only 18 percent of individuals and 34.4 percent of US households make $100,000 or more annually. To add further insult to injury, the wealthier you are, the more house you can afford, which means your mortgage is larger, thus leading to larger amounts of interest. Buffie continues, "Among those claiming the mortgage interest deduction, the average deduction is $10,864 for taxpayers earning less than $50,000 and $22,007 among those earning $500,000 or more." The disparity with this deduction is quite clear.

PAYROLL TAXES ARE A BITCH FOR LOWER EARNERS

The root of most tax inequalities lies within regressive taxes. Payroll taxes are highly regressive and may be in my humble opinion one of the worst offenders in this tax game. Federal payroll taxes are the second largest income stream for the federal government and are collected based on the income you earn from working. As a regressive tax everyone is starting off at the federal payroll tax level around 15.3 percent and if you have W2 employment, your employer typically covers half. It is possible that your state may also charge a payroll tax, and this is often unemployment insurance. Of course, the more you make, the less you are taxed, with the percentage drastically dropping to 2.9 percent on earnings between $147,000 and $200,000. What else happens when your income hits $147,001? You no longer have to pay into Social Security for the year. This contribution and benefit base changes annually and is set by the Social Security Administration. Overall, people with the lowest incomes in America are paying approximately 14.1 percent of their total income, while those making over six figures are paying about 9 percent of their total income. When you jump into seven-figure territory, millionaires are paying about 1.9 percent of their total income in payroll taxes. *Unreal!*

INFLATED PROPERTY TAXES

Redlining and reverse redlining have wreaked havoc on Black and brown communities' abilities to become homeowners for decades. Both redlining and reverse redlining have worked in tandem to target and center minorities in specific communities to then go and tax them twice as much as neighboring white rich communities. The Center for Municipal Finance analyzed twenty-six million residential homes sold between 2006 and 2016 to reveal that homes in neighborhoods with a Black population of 90 percent or more were taxed approximately 50 percent more than other neighborhoods in the same county. To quote one of my favorite lines from one of my favorite rappers, "Men lie, women lie, numbers don't."

HOW TO FILE TAXES

Hear ye, hear ye: Tax Day lands between April 15 and 18. If you've learned nothing from this chapter beyond this fact, you possess more knowledge than 56 percent of Americans. Since its inception in 1913, Tax Day has maintained the April 15 deadline with weekends and holidays as exceptions. In 2020 the government did extend the deadline to May 17 in response to the chaos of the pandemic.

I've never filed my own taxes, mostly due to ignorance and fear fueled by my ignorance. At the beginning of my income tax journey, I used common, run-of-the-mill tax preparation service and paid around thirty to one hundred dollars, dependent on the process. In the years when I used the tax preparation service that shall remain nameless, I was making less than $60,000 and I had no idea that I could:

1. Do it myself online for free.

or

2. Have it prepared by a professional for free! So here's what you need to know to get it done right.

GATHER ALL YOUR DOCUMENTS

I am not the most organized person in the world when it comes to taxes, and my accountant reminds me of this every year. You'll need the standard documents and a few extras, depending on your circumstances and lifestyle. The main documents you'll need to file your taxes are:

- W2. This is only if you are a W2 employee. If you are self-employed you'll need a 1099 instead.

- Any IRS, state notices, or official letters. This includes things like letters from your health insurance company declaring you were covered for the year or letters from your bank if you earned interest from savings.

- Charitable donation receipts as proof for your deduction.

- Property tax bill or mortgage interest statement.

- Copy of your previous year's return. This is usually if you see someone new to file your taxes. If you're a returning customer, they will likely have a digital copy of your return on file.

Of course, you'll need a government ID and will have to provide your social security number as well as the social security numbers of your children/other dependents.

DON'T OVERLOOK FREE OPTIONS

I'm not someone with many regrets, but not capitalizing on free tax preparation services may lowkey be one of them. The IRS Free File program is a public-private partnership between the IRS and tax preparation services. This also includes tax preparation software if you decide to file your taxes on your own. The guided tax preparation option of the program allows taxpayers whose adjusted gross income is $73,000 or less to have their federal tax return filed for free at an IRS partner site. A few of the IRS partners are companies like 1040NOW Corp, exTaxReturn.com, TaxAct, and TaxSlayer. For those whose AGI is more than $73,000, you can use free file fillable forms (equivalent to a 1040 form) but will require a bit more hands-on work to file your taxes yourself. Another free option is the IRS's Volunteer Income Tax Assistance (VITA) program and Tax Counseling for the Elder (TCE) program that offer free basic tax return prep for those who qualify. Those who qualify generally make less than $60,000 a year, people with disabilities, or taxpayers with limited English skills. You can find VITA and TCE sites near you by visiting irs.treasury.gov/freetaxprep. Outside of IRS programs, many states have their own free tax preparation services with similar requirements. For example, NYC Free Tax Prep is for NY residents that earned $56,000 or less as a single filer or a family that has made $80,000 or less. Check and exhaust all of the free tax options afforded to you, because paying $50–$200 for tax prep when there's a free option is ridiculous, trust me. I know first-hand!

TAX BENEFITS & ADVANTAGES

I use the term *benefits* and *advantages* loosely here, but the following deductions and tax credits listed below can be helpful to your financial circumstances when filing your taxes.

DEDUCTIONS

A tax deduction, a.k.a. a tax "write-off," lets you itemize certain expenses you've had during the year. These deductions reduce your taxable income, so you have a lower tax liability overall. Here are a few common deductions you can take when you file your taxes.

- Traditional retirement accounts (401K, 403B, 457, IRA)
- Charitable donations
- Property taxes and mortgage interest
- Student loan interest
- Health Savings Account (HSA) deductions

To claim a tax deduction, you have two options.

- **Standard Deduction:** This will be one flat rate that will be deducted from your adjusted gross income based on your filing status. In 2023 a person filing as single will receive the standard deduction of $13,850, whereas a married couple filing jointly will receive a standard deduction of $27,700.

- **Itemized Deduction:** This option is best used if your standard deduction is less than the sum of the items you are going to itemize. For example, my property tax and mortgage interest are more than the $13,950 standard deduction; therefore I itemize to "write off" more deductions. Itemizing does take more time and you do require proof for each deduction. Typically, the provider (your bank or other financial institution) will prepare the proof.

CREDITS

A tax credit is a reduction in your tax bill dollar for dollar. Some tax credits are also refundable (most are not) so you can receive a refund check for some credits. Tax credits usually reduce your tax liability on a greater scale than a tax deduction. A few common tax credits are:

- Earned income tax credit
- Household tax credit
- Child and dependent care credit
- Child tax credit
- College tuition tax credit

WHAT ABOUT THAT TAX REFUND THOUGH?

This is the "good part" or the part most people know about when they file their taxes annually. What you may not know is the reason you are getting a return is that there was some error that caused you to overpay during the year. I'm very much a win-is-a-win type of person, so I'm not here to rain on your parade. If you want to twerk it out together to celebrate your huge tax refund, I've got my Meg knees moisturized and ready to go! But I do want to keep you informed about what is going on with your money so you can make the best decisions for yourself.

In a perfect world, where the IRS told you exactly how much taxes you owe, you would not get a refund and you would not owe anything either. But we're in an endless guessing game filled with errors and penalties for those errors.

When you start a new job you are required to fill out a W4. When you fill out your information on the form, you also indicate what needs to be withheld from each check. I can't even tell you how shocked I was when my work mom explained the fundamentals of a W4. We constantly hear about claiming zero or 1, when the reality is you can claim anything; just be prepared to pay for that choice one way or another. Either you'll overpay or underpay in your checks, which will lead you to get a refund or owe money when you file your tax return.

I've always been encouraged to claim zero on my W4 so the most amount of taxes would be removed and I would lessen the possibility of owing. When I moved into my own home, I needed more money in my biweekly checks so I started claiming 1 instead of zero. This was a personal choice, and I understood the potential ramifications when tax season rolled around. When you file your taxes, that is the time to pay the piper, or in the case of a refund, the piper pays you.

Think of your tax refund as money you loaned the government interest-free because you overpaid during the year. Another scenario that makes a tax refund possible is those tax credits we spoke about a little earlier. Even if you've accurately filled out your W4, certain tax credits may qualify you for a tax refund. The largest tax credits that often lead to a refund are the child tax credit, earned income tax credit, American opportunity tax credit, and the premium tax credit.

And yes, it is possible to get a federal refund and owe money to the state, which is a scenario I have found myself in for the last three years. New York, get it together, please and thank you!

I understand the sudden rush of joy that occurs when that tax refund hits your account, but the best financial practice in this regard is to accurately fill out and update your W4 so the correct amount of money is removed from your checks.

DIFFERENT TYPES OF TAXES

I couldn't imagine leaving you high and dry without a tax breakdown to easily reference and mark up as you expand your tax knowledge even further. Here is a follow-up on the larger tax terms I've thrown around in this chapter so you can come back to them when you're trying to put a finance bro in their place.

TYPES OF TAXES	DEFINITION
Income Tax	A percentage of your income is withheld by the state or federal government to fund social programs and support government stability. (This will be the federal, state, and local taxes that come out of your checks.)
Payroll Tax	This tax also comes out of your check in the form of Social Security and Medicare. It is withheld from your pay and your employer pays it to the government on your behalf.
Corporate Tax	Corporate taxes are taken from a company's profits and used to fund federal programs.
Estate Tax	Estate taxes are tacked on to a person's estate at the time of death. Estate taxes are paid by the estate itself, but only if they exceed a specific threshold set by the state and federal governments. As of 2023 the federal estate tax exemption protects $12.92 million from taxes. However, you can face state estate taxes since their exemptions require a lower threshold. If you live in one of the twelve states and one district that collect estate taxes, you could have to pay taxes on estates as low as a million dollars. Those states include Hawaii, Illinois, Maine, Massachusetts, Maryland, New York, Oregon, Connecticut, Minnesota, Rhode Island, Vermont, Washington, and the District of Colombia.
Capital Gains Tax	Capital gains tax is levied when investors sell their assets. The amount of tax you pay will be based on the amount of time that the asset appreciated during the amount of time you held it. Surprising to me, but not to you because I got you—capital gains taxes also come into play when you sell your home! So it pays off to be a buy-and-hold investor as well as living in your home for more than one year to reap the benefit of a lower capital gains tax. For anything less than one year you will pay short-term capital gains, and that is substantially a higher tax rate for most. The long-term capital gains tax rate for 2023 is 0 percent, 15 percent, or 20 percent of the profit, dependent on your income (income brackets will be adjusted annually).

Sales Tax	This is the tax we pay for certain goods and services. The percentage you pay and what you pay sales tax on will vary from state to state.
Property Tax	Mentioned earlier in the homeownership chapter, property tax is based on the value of the land and property assets you own. It can go up or down depending on several external factors.

CHAPTER 11

RECLAIMING MY TIME: RETIRING AS A MILLIONAIRE

My good sis Maxine Waters is the most senior of the twelve Black women currently serving in Congress and is the second-most senior member of the California congressional delegation. As a member of the Democratic party, she is on her seventeenth term and chaired the Congressional Black Caucus from 1997–1999. In all her glory she still found the time to give us one of the most legendary memes of 2017 during a House Financial Services Committee hearing. After former US Secretary of the Treasury Steven Mnuchin made many blatant attempts to sidestep her question, she gave us one the most empowering catchphrases of all time: *Reclaiming my time!* You don't gotta tell me twice, auntie. *Heard you!*

For the last six years since the iconic phrase went viral, I have actively done everything in my power to not only reclaim my time right now but also reclaim my time in the future. I could go on record and say that everything I do is beneficial to my future self. However, the fourteen-hour hangover I had in Costa Rica a few months ago would strongly beg to differ. At that moment, I clearly wasn't trying to reclaim anything but my sobriety. I learned two lessons from that incredibly humbling experience that I am inclined to share with you. First, we're chasing progress, not perfection.

There are days when I am 100 percent tapped into my reclaiming time for my future self. Those are the days when I adult the best and take all the responsible steps to reach the goals I have outlined for myself. At those moments, you cannot tell me shit. It's just me and my color-coded twenty-step to-do list organized by time and location. Then there are the days when my biggest accomplishment is eating one meal and walking my dog. I am who I am, and I make no excuses about it. The trick here is to have more responsible days than accidental fasting days.

Oh, what was the second lesson I learned when I was fighting for my life? I am not twenty-two years old anymore, and tequila shots on an empty stomach will always be a bad idea.

TEN WAYS TO RECLAIM YOUR TIME

Though I don't successfully reclaim my time every single day, the ten steps outlined below are an active part of the larger picture. These routines are not only helping me reclaim my time, but they are also helping me capitalize and monetize my time in a way that is truly life-changing. I'm talking millionaire vibes on yachts in Dubai eating caviar life-changing. Okay, let me pull it back two steps. Y'all already know millionaire status is not an *if* but a *when* over here, but I have no interest in yachts or caviar since I get wicked motion sickness and don't eat anything from the sea. *Gasps!* I know my Black folks are shocked by that one, but let's not linger on my seafood-free diet too long—we got work to do!

My relationship with money has positively shifted over the last few years, and I'd like to think that these ten steps have been a huge reason why. I do want to reach millionaire status, but it's not to spend money on things that may make me "look" like I have money. Honestly, and I mean this from the bottom of my heart, chaotic chic Target shopper is my favorite aesthetic. Having a million-dollar net worth isn't for looks; it's for security and freedom. Another super honest moment for you: 90 percent of the world's millionaires are men, 76 percent of millionaires are white, and only 8 percent of US millionaires are Black. Those numbers don't sit right with me, and they shouldn't sit right with you either. Let's change them.

ONE: BUILD AN FU FUND

Yeah, you read that right, and that FU stands for exactly what you think. Though I wish I could take credit for the remarkably explicit and fiscally responsible term, I unfortunately did not make this concept up. I did, however, adopt it into my financial routine as soon as I monetarily could. An FU fund gives you freedom, and freedom gives you choice. Like the remarkable Louanne Johnson, portrayed by the impeccable Michelle Pfeifer in *Dangerous Minds*, once said, "I will not carry myself down to die when I go to my grave my head will be high." Well, technically it was Bob Dylan's line first, but you see my point here. The freedom of choice is one of the most powerful tools you can have in your arsenal along with the freedom of time. Your FU fund will give you both.

Unlike an emergency savings, which is used for life's unexpected occurrences, your FU fund gives you the power to walk away from anything negatively impacting your mental and physical well-being. Your emergency savings fund would be used for basic expenses like your housing, loan payments, and utilities. Your FU fund is used to fill in the gaps during a career break or transitionary period. Instead of feeling pressure to stay at a job or work in a toxic environment, your FU fund lets you politely (as politely as you choose) stick the middle finger up as you walk out the door.

Your FU fund does not have to be used for an emergency, but some overlap may occur if you experience sudden job loss. The first thing to consider when funding your FU account is a timeline. Just like with an emergency savings fund, you'd theoretically have three to six months' worth of expenses set aside, your FU fund will also have a timeline. So if you know you want to travel for a month, your FU fund would be able to sustain that month of travel even if you have no new source of income.

HOW DO I GET STARTED SAVING MY FU FUND?

- **Budget first:** I've added my FU fund as a byline in my budget. I like to have a thicker emergency savings fund because as a homeowner, there's an emergency every five seconds. Once I fully funded my emergency savings, I split the amount being funneled in for emergencies into extra investment money (we'll get to that in step three) and my FU fund. This is why monthly budgeting is so crucial in my financial routines because each month is different.

- **Decide on your why:** Once you've figured out how much you can afford to direct into your FU fund, figure out a cadence and what you want to do with that money. My FU fund is currently allotted for monthly. If and when an emergency arrives, and I have to tap into my emergency fund, then I will shift my funds back into replenishing my emergency savings. Do we see why personal finance is so personal? This isn't the only way to build an FU fund, but it's the way that works best for me and my budget. Once I found my rhythm, I had to decide what this fund would be used for. Would it be to give me the freedom to go back to school? Take two months off to travel? Learn a new skill? Each reason would require a different amount of money, so it's best to choose one to two things that you would like to use your FU fund for.

- **Set a goal and a timeline:** Eventually I decided that my FU fund would be used for time off just in case I am laid off. With the economic climate and current job market I am aware that I no longer have the security of being a classroom teacher, and tech layoffs are running rampant. Since I am not in a toxic work environment and don't hate my job, my FU fund is in just-in-case mode. It is being funded with the idea that I could be laid off at any time and will use the FU fund for taking time with myself to create and grow my brand instead of rushing to find another role. To achieve this I've set **my goal** of three to six months of FU money without a steady nine-to-five paycheck. **My timeline** to reach this was six to eight months. And at the end of this month (eight months after I set my timeline) I have just about reached my goal! Take that, corporate America!

TWO: INVEST EARLY & OFTEN

Though I picked up this specific phrase from Jeremy Schneider of "The Personal Finance Club," it's a concept I was already fully aligned with. I will never stop talking about the magic of compound interest. And if you want to unlock the real secret sauce of investing, you'll need two ingredients: compound interest and time. You can't have one without the other. They rely on each other to successfully buy back your time. One of my favorite ways to spend my time is calculating the amount of compound interest my investments will earn after a certain amount of time.

Is that an incredibly nerdy way to spend a Sunday afternoon? Probably. It's also motivating AF. Don't believe me?

After eleven years of investing, I currently have about $130,000 in the market across five accounts. Let's pull out my favorite compound interest calculator (because let's be honest, there's no way I'm doing the math by hand; me and basic arithmetic do not get along). I use the digital compound interest calculator on investor.gov because it's simple, straightforward, and free.

This is how we'll fill out the numbers:

STEP 1: INITIAL INVESTMENT

INITIAL INVESTMENT*
Amount of money that you have available to invest initially.

$130,000

STEP 2: CONTRIBUTE

MONTHLY CONTRIBUTION
Amount you plan to add to the principal every month, or a negative number for the amount that you plan to withdraw every month.

$0

LENGTH OF TIME IN YEARS*
Length of time, in years, that you plan to save.

30

STEP 3: INTEREST RATE

ESTIMATED INTEREST RATE*
Your estimated annual interest rate.

8

INTEREST RATE VARIANCE RANGE
Range of interest rates (above and below the rate set above) that you desire to see results for.

1

STEP 4: COMPOUND FREQUENCY

COMPOUND FREQUENCY
Times per year that interest will be compounded.

Annually

We've got my $130,000 initial investment currently in my accounts, with $0 monthly contributions, an 8 percent interest rate, and a 1 percent interest rate variance. Although the S&P500 has returned 10 percent on average since its inception in 1957, I use 8 percent with a 1 percent variance for safe measure. This means if I stopped investing today and left my invested money to compound for thirty years, at sixty-five, around the typical retirement age, I'd have $1.3 million. At 9 percent interest, I'd have $1.7 million, and if the market took a bit of a dip and returned only 7 percent, I'd have $989,000.

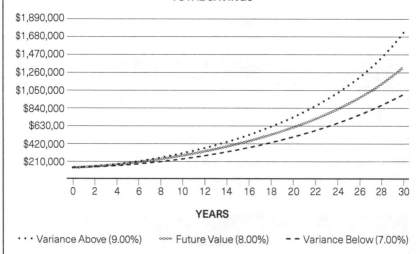

THE RESULTS ARE IN

IN 30 YEARS, YOU WILL HAVE $1,308,145.40

The chart below shows an estimate of how much your initial savings will grow over time, according to the interest rate and compounding schedule you specified.

Please remember that slight adjustments in any of those variables can affect the outcome. Reset the calculator and provide different figures to show different scenarios.

TOTAL SAVINGS

$1,890,000
$1,680,000
$1,470,000
$1,260,000
$1,050,000
$840,000
$630,00
$420,000
$210,000

0 2 4 6 8 10 12 14 16 18 20 22 24 26 28 30

YEARS

· · · Variance Above (9.00%)   ∞∞ Future Value (8.00%)   − − Variance Below (7.00%)

Not too shabby for $130,000 compounded over time. Of course I don't plan on stopping my investments—because:

1. Hello, the name of this tip is to invest early *and* often!

2. I'm reclaiming my time! I don't want to retire at sixty-five. The longer you wait to get started, the more money you will have to invest to reclaim more of your time.

I sat down with published author Naseema McElroy, a labor and delivery nurse and the founder of Financially Intentional, to discuss her amazing financial journey. Naseema took control of her finances and overcame bankruptcy and divorce all while breaking the cycle of living paycheck to paycheck. By shifting her mindset around money, she has paid off one million dollars in debt and grew her net worth to six figures in three years without living in deprivation. Besides creating healthy financial routines for herself, Naseema is also a huge proponent of investing for her two young children. Prior to investing for her children, I asked Naseema to explain the "why" behind her debt-payoff journey. Naseema went on to explain, "I was a single mom with a one-year-old daughter making $230,000 a year but living check to check. I was scared that if something were to happen to me there would be nothing for my daughter. I got to that sick and tired of being sick and tired place and knew I needed to take action."

After taking actions such as: immersing herself into the world of personal finance through podcasts and audiobooks, creating a thousand-dollar emergency fund, and adopting the debt snowball method, Naseema set a goal to be debt free by her thirty-sixth birthday. That would involve paying down $6,000 a month to meet her debt-payoff goal. Even when several hardships surfaced like the $30,000 IRS bill, and $15,000 divorce settlement, Naseema stayed the course and updated the timeline as necessary. When that debt-free moment finally happened, she set her sights on investing early and often for her children. I asked Naseema to expand on how she has begun building generational wealth for her children while teaching them about the steps she is taking. She stated, "My kids are young at three and eight. They have been around me in growing my personal finance business for the last few years so talking about money is normalized in our household. There is no shortage of consumer messaging aimed at my kids. They have plenty of toys, electronics, and clothes so I turn the things that they like into lessons for them to be owners. Outside of their 529s and Roth IRAs where I invest in index funds, they each have brokerage accounts where I let them buy individual stocks of the companies they love. They get a hundred dollars each month to invest in the stocks they want to invest in and compete for returns (the baby is winning)."

Naseema has also started to introduce financial concepts and investing terminology as well. "They love when the market is down (when the stocks are red) because they know things are on sale and they can buy more with their hundred dollars. Instead of toys and the normal gifts for birthdays and holidays, I share my kids' stock wish list via Stockpile (their brokerage). My kids also know they are a part of Financially Intentional, they know their pay goes into their Roth IRA, $1,500 a year each currently. They also help me with my brand campaigns, and I take them to conferences like FinCon to expose them to finance even further."

I certainly did not have a Roth IRA at eight years old and knew nothing about the market being down at three. In fact, let's continue to use my investing timeline as our primary example. I started investing at twenty-two years old in my 403B, which means if I retire at sixty-five, I will have had forty-three years of compound interest on my side. If I had started four years prior at eighteen years old by maxing out a Roth IRA, I would have had an extra $18,000 in contributions compounding for forty-seven years. What does that look like? A whopping $670,176. What does $18,000 look like compounded for forty-three years? We're down to $492,599. And just for shits and giggles what would that $18,000 amount to if I invested it right now at thirty-five and watched it compound for thirty years? Well, future millionaires, we've lost quite a bit more and landed at $181,127. At eighteen, I had more time and needed less money. At thirty-five, I must do more to reclaim my time.

But a million dollars ain't a million dollars anymore. Yes, that is correct. Due to inflation, a million dollars today does not go as far as it used to. But here are three things to think about when this line of conversation comes up.

- **Have you heard this all-too-commonly-used phrase before?:** "Real quick, let me hold a million dollars!" No? That's probably because a million dollars is still very much a large life-changing amount of money. People don't just have an extra million dollars lying around to lend to someone. While a million dollars today may not be the million dollars of yesteryear, we can collectively agree that a million dollars is still a lot of money. What we're not going to do is turn our noses up at the idea of having a million dollars, because if someone walked up to you today, in ten years, or in thirty years and offered you a milli, you'd take it.

- **Calculate your numbers:** If the thought of having a million-dollar net worth fills you with anxiety and dissatisfaction, what number would make you feel safe? Reclaiming your time is all about casting that safety net that gives you back the power of time. That may not be a million dollars; your lifestyle may demand more. Is it two million? Three million? A million dollars doesn't have to be your target, but you need one to plan backward, work toward your goal, and proceed to the following tip.

- **Factor in inflation and taxes:** Don't worry, I'm keeping my promise to you from Chapter 1. You do not have to do this math by hand. There are tons of digital calculators available online (mine is listed in the resources at the back of the book) that will help you factor in inflation and taxes when you are preparing to withdraw your money. These calculators use the inflation-adjusted return, which is "a measure of return that takes into account the time period's inflation rate...to reveal the return on an investment after removing the effects of inflation." This will let you calculate how long a million dollars will last for your specific lifestyle needs.

Besides these three conversation starters, it is also important to bring in the 4 percent rule, made popular by William Bengen. His 1994 findings state that if at least half of your retirement money is invested in stocks and the other half is invested in bonds, you are likely going to be able to annually withdraw an inflation-adjusted 4 percent for thirty years. So if you retired between sixty to sixty-five years old, your investments would last until you reach ninety to ninety-five years old.

Even with our current economic environment giving the 4 percent a run for its money, using dynamic withdrawal strategies based on the returns of your investment that year is still effective in giving you a lasting amount of wealth in your golden years. And to be frank, in 2022, people between the ages of sixty-five to sixty-nine were retiring with an average of $206,819. I'd rather have the million and I'd rather you have it too!

So, if the investing chapter itself wasn't a sign, let this teeny tiny paragraph do it for you. Don't get hung up on the fact that you didn't start investing at three years old. Don't trip over the numbers when you think about what "could have been." Instead, just start. Open that brokerage account and throw ten dollars into that IRA because you can't invest in yesterday. You can only invest in today to reclaim your time tomorrow.

THREE: PRIORITIZE VALUE SPENDING

Believe it or not, I wouldn't consider myself to be a penny pincher. I would call myself frugal in most scenarios, but I am not against spending money, and strangely enough, I don't think every dollar needs to be saved or invested. I do, however, wholeheartedly believe in prioritizing value whenever I spend my money. Value spending requires you, the consumer, to think about what your purchase actually costs. That means looking beyond the ticket price and thinking about what this expense adds to the overall picture. As a value spender you make mindful decisions in your budget that help keep you aligned with your goals and what matters to you the most. I find that when I take the time to think about what this purchase means to me outside of a quick dose of fleeting serotonin, I spend with intention. Instead of bolstering overconsumption I spend only on what I want instead of what I'm told I should want, which as a citizen in the thick of a social-media-blitzed nation built on capitalism is no simple party trick.

The defluencer trend on TikTok wouldn't be a thing if more of us leaned into value spending. The Dyson hair dryer isn't a miracle product; the Loreal mascara isn't life-changing; and spending fifty dollars on the Stanley Cup reusable water bottle isn't going to magically make you more hydrated. We are constantly inundated with content that does one of two things: promotes overconsumption one link in bio at a time, or content that shames you for buying the same things they were just promoting two videos prior. Value spending gets rid of the noise and focuses on implementing purchases that are worth your time.

In the spirit of maximizing and reclaiming our time, here are three quick ways to implement value spending into your day-to-day financial routines by tomorrow:

- **Calculate your time into your purchases:** When you think about value-based spending you always need to consider how much of your time is being put into the purchase of the item you want. This example is for my sneakerheads, because as a former sneakerhead myself, I know we get a lot of shit for buying the latest drop. Don't even argue with the naysayers; simply tell them to pick up a copy of this book, head to Chapter 11, and skip to step ten. Now if you are someone who truly finds joy in sneaker culture and you want to add a byline into your budget for your sneaker passion, you'll also want to use the value-based spending formula. You take the purchase price of the item and divide it by your hourly wage. When you see the amount of time it will take you to earn the money to make the purchase, ask yourself, "Is this purchase worth this amount of my time?" When I was in high school and college the answer for me was always: yes. At that time eight to nine hours of my time for the latest pair of Jordans was 100 percent worth it to me because it was something that I valued. I did not feel ashamed or embarrassed. As I got older and my values shifted, so did my value spending. All that to say, if the J's mean that much to you, buy the J's. If you see how much of your time it will take to cover a purchase and you don't feel comfortable, that means it is not quite something you hold in high priority and you can either:

  a. Decide not to make the purchase at all.

  or

  b. Save the purchase for a later time.

- **Set expense parameters for yourself:** While the first tip feels empowering and freeing, the second tip will bring in more reality. Value spending still needs to be a part of your budget so you can continue to meet all of your financial goals. Traveling is high on my value spend list and traveling also can be an expensive spend. That means I can't travel all day every day because I have a mortgage to pay and a dog to provide for. Do I want to grab any and every travel deal that pops up on Scott's Cheap Flights? Yes. Do I jump at every chance to take a flight? No. I wish I could, and without value spend parameters and a budget I likely wouldn't be able to travel as much as I do now. Intentionally create parameters for your value-based spending that consider the average expense and your budget. I set aside a specific amount per year for travel and travel alone. That is my value-based parameter, and when the travel fund runs out, so do the travels!

• **Place yourself in your budget:** I said it before in Chapter 1, and I'm gonna say it again! Your budget needs to have a byline specifically for expenses that you enjoy. It doesn't have to start off big but creating a functional budget that implements your wants and needs is crucial. I call that byline my self-care fund, and it gives me the freedom to spend on things I love and value without disrupting my financial success. When I first started managing my finances, I had to train myself to spend money on myself. It felt like a waste or a detriment to my financial progress, but the reality was the first few years where I only focused on paying down my student loans, I was miserable. I didn't enjoy many aspects of life because I felt the need to punish myself for taking student loans in the first place. That was a detriment to my mental health and made my relationships with my friends and family uncomfortable. You deserve to spend money on things you love. You deserve to spend money on yourself.

FOUR: HIRE PROFESSIONALS

I've carried the DIY instinct with me through my adolescence and most of my adulthood. I'm not sure if it was a trauma response or the first gen/eldest daughter mentality whooping my ass, but it cost me way too much time, energy, and money. In 2021 I read three books that changed my outlook and perspective on time and money. *The 4-Hour Work Week* by Timothy Ferriss, *We Should All Be Millionaires* by Rachel Rodgers, and *The Big Leap* by Gay Hendricks. Each book said it in their own way but reaffirmed that the best zone of function you should be operating in is your zone of genius. Initially coined by

Gay Hendricks, the zone of genius is where we capitalize on our innate abilities as opposed to leaning in to learned skills and behaviors.

Unfortunately for many of us we teeter between our zone of competence and zone of excellence. These two zones allow us to operate between doing things we are efficient at and things we are tremendously skilled at. Operating efficiently in your zone of competence gives you an overwhelming feeling of safety because it doesn't force you to push beyond what you can easily manage and get done on a day-to-day basis. Your zone of competence is not unique to you, because anyone can perform the same routine on any given day. Think of your zone of competence as the equivalent of being a sales rep on a call following a script. It's easy, you can get it done, but you don't have to put much thought, effort, or creativity into it to be successful.

As a teacher, I wholeheartedly functioned in my zone of excellence. Hendricks sat down with Forbes to explain, "Most successful people are operating in their zone of excellence, in which they are doing things at which they are highly skilled. This zone is ultimately unsatisfying, though, because it does not engage the innate genius of the individual." I was a good teacher, dare I say a great teacher, but after the first few years I was on autopilot. My lessons and units were strong and creative enough to rinse and repeat with minor adjustments year after year.

Though it may seem that I have gone on an immense tangent from where we began, let me connect the dots for you and bring it all together. To successfully get to my zone of genius and unlock my full potential, I had to push through every previous step, including zone one: the zone of incompetence. My incessant need to DIY every single aspect of my life kept me in my zone of incompetence far longer than necessary. I felt like I was doing myself a favor by trying to save time and money, but I was doing just the opposite.

Your zone of incompetence is going to feel overwhelmingly frustrating because you are engaging with a task that you not only don't understand but you also don't have the skill set to handle. I am not medically inclined, so when I get sick, I go to the doctor. I know nothing about cars, plumbing, or taxes, so I hire mechanics, plumbers, and accountants. I do not know how to code, build websites, or make apps, so I hire web developers and web designers to bring my ideas to life. It took me a long time to understand that if I truly wanted to work in my zone of genius, I had to let go of trying to do things I just didn't know how to do well and would take me too much time to learn how to do amateurly.

This, of course, is not to say that you shouldn't learn new skills and implement them into your zone of genius functionality. It also isn't brushing off the fact that hiring professionals takes capital and if you do not have the money available, DIY problem-solving may be your only option at this present moment. I get that 100 percent. What this is saying is when you can successfully loosen the reins, do it, because holding on to tasks and processes that prevent you from doing what is most effortless to you, that is a disservice. We all want to be superman and superwoman, but the smartest and most successful superheroes know when to tap into the fight themselves and when to send in their team! Beyoncé is not a one-woman show—her success is very much dependent on the conglomeration of her team. Though we don't got Beyoncé bucks just yet, outsourcing as much as you can when you have the ability to do so is a game-changer for your time and your earning potential.

FIVE: BUILD PASSIVE INCOME STREAMS

I know we spent a great deal of time talking about passive income in Chapter 7, so I won't belabor the point too much further. You do not want to rely on one stream of income. Life is beautiful, and exciting, and inspiring. But let's not forget that life can also be hella hella hella unpredictable and humbling. Give yourself the opportunity to walk away from things that no longer serve you, as well as buy back your time. The more passive income streams you have, the more you can invest, the quicker you can fund your FU account, and the earlier you can retire. I won't be doing my little dancey dance on TikTok forever, and I definitely won't be setting up my ring light to film weekly YouTube videos for the next twenty years. And if there's one thing I know beyond a shadow of a doubt, I certainly won't be working anyone's nine-to-five for the next thirty years. With this sense of self-reconnaissance, I know that my time earning certain streams of income will eventually come to an end, but my taste for the finer things in life (housing, health insurance, and pizza) will still require that cash money. Build multiple streams of passive income to allow for multiple choices in your future. Nobody backs baby into a corner or whatever Patrick

Swayze said, and nobody is backing you into one income stream. Your current talents and skillset are enough to have at least two streams right now, and if not, see tip eight.

SIX: AUTOMATE AS MANY THINGS AS YOU CAN

The older I get, the less I remember. My brain isn't functioning at the same capacity it used to, and I'm too tired to fight father time. Automate as many processes as you can to free up more of your personal time. By taking steps to automate the manual processes in your monthly financial routine you not only take back your time, but you also easily save and invest while making it more difficult to miss payments. I have enough to think about and certain things in life just can't be automated, but wherever I can, I do. That means tasks like saving, investing, and bill payment are all set up to auto-transfer payments, so I don't have to. The trick to successful automation requires an initial bout of organization and monthly check-ins.

Most of my financial automations occur on the fifteenth of the month. This date has no great significance; it was the date that I used to get paid when I was in the classroom. You can pick any day, but it's ideal to choose a date that is complimentary to payday. The payments that couldn't be moved to the fifteenth I made a note of those dates in my calendar and turned on notifications so I could be cognizant of pending payments being deducted. This helped ensure that I always had money available in my account to cover the transactions.

The last piece of organization needed for successful automation is a check-in. I do this check-in during my monthly money dates. Check-ins consist of looking at my monthly expenses to identify any bills that have increased since last month. This helps me keep an eye on my monthly expenses because I am the queen of ignoring a branded email and would likely miss a price increase announcement if it landed in my inbox. This is how I caught the increase in my Wi-Fi and mobile phone bill and new steaming service pay structures. It's better to catch these increases as they first occur so you can adjust your budget to cover additional costs or cancel the subscription/service. #StayWoke because those overdraft fees are still a thing though many banks have allegedly walked away from them.

If you can automate a process, *do it*, but don't do it blindly. Keep an eye on any transactions and enjoy the fact that you can use your brain power to remember music lyrics better than you could ever remember your schoolwork. A fact that effortlessly ticked off my mother every time my brother rapped a Jay Z song while struggling to correctly spell important on his English homework.

SEVEN: ASSESS & REASSESS YOUR NUMBERS

Whatever financial plans or long-term goals you have for yourself will be challenged. You know the saying, "You make plans and God laughs"? Well, sky daddy gets a huge chuckle whenever we set financial goals that we think will go unchallenged. The birth of a new child, a promotion at work, an unforeseen layoff—life isn't linear, and your personal finance journey will *not* be linear either. There will be big and small challenges that present themselves along the way and the only way to be successful is to pivot and persist. Be open-minded to making changes so do not stand in the way of your progress. Started making an extra hundred dollars a month? Great, update your saving or investing goals. Experienced a divorce and no longer operate in a two-income household? Update your debt-payoff schedule so your timeline reflects this change. Moved to a new city with a higher cost of living? Update your savings goals on your next money date so you can continue to budget effectively.

Assess and reassess your numbers whenever life demands it.

EIGHT: CONTINUE TO LEARN & UPSKILL

One of my favorite things about being a teacher was seeing that little light bulb pop up overhead when a student learned something new or figured out something they were struggling with. As adults we don't take the time to play, grow, and learn how we did as children. Reasonably so, as an adult I can firmly admit, the level of responsibilities required of me at this end of the lifecycle has taken me by surprise more times than I care to admit. I don't know what I was prepared for exactly, but it wasn't all of this.

So believe me when I tell you, after dodging constant adulthood right hooks, I don't always feel like running around learning new things the way I did at six. But every time I feel too tired to try something I've wanted to try, or start to complacently rest on my laurels, I'm reminded that every single new skill I've adopted as an adult is the reason you have this book in your hand right now. By continuing to learn and upskill in a way that felt authentic to me, I unintentionally built the life of my dreams. At twenty-five years old I launched my first blog, at twenty-seven I became an entrepreneur, at twenty-eight I wrote and produced an award-winning web series, at thirty-three I successfully transitioned from teacher to tech, and at thirty-four I invested $50,000 in the stock market.

I taught myself to invest, practiced screenplay formatting, learned how to run a monetized blog, spent hours learning about graphic design, read article after article about digital photography and videography, and took risks with editing tricks I learned on YouTube. I wanted to give myself the opportunity to play so I took classes about random things like typography and color theory because Steve Jobs, an oddly strong motivator of my day to day, inspired me to learn what I want without trying to rationalize its relevance or importance. Little did I know that my random knowledge of typography and color theory, matched with my newly acquired graphic design skills, would directly lead to attracting over 100,000 followers on Pinterest, resulting in 200,000 monthly page views on my little WordPress blog.

Every new thing I've learned has strengthened or created a new stream of income in my life. However, I don't think every skill or hobby you adopt needs to be monetized. That is the perk, but there is nothing wasted when it comes to self-improvement, whether it makes you money or not. I never thought that a typography class would amplify my graphic design skills, which would then lead to content creation. I took a typography class because it sounded cool and felt like a fun fact I could use at a dinner table. I had no monetization strategy when I walked into my color theory class; I wanted to learn how color impacts human behavior. It sounded hella cool and would be another great hat trick to pull out at brunch. I take my reputation as the human version of Google *very* seriously!

Continue to learn and upskill authentically, and I promise you it will lead to one of two things. You'll either build a skill into your arsenal that you can monetize into a new stream of income, or you will have a new skill that improves your mental health and encourages personal development. And maybe, just maybe, you'll get both. A win on every accord.

NINE: CAREER DEVELOPMENT & JOB HOPPING

As always, I like to start with the facts and then proceed to share my snarky opinions about them. The pandemic caused many traditional practices to shift as the economy and labor market tried to retain some form of normalcy in an anything-but-normal time. Traditionally employees would see annual raises between 1–4 percent as a means of keeping up with inflation. Though 2022 has seen a much larger increase at an average of 7.6 percent, wage growth for those who remain at their job averages closer to 5.8 percent. That does not come close to the average 14.8 percent salary increase people saw by changing jobs. One thing we can't gloss over is while writing this book, inflation has hovered around 6–9 percent. Wages are doing better, but they are still not keeping up with inflation despite their many attempts.

Gone are the days when we stay at a job for a decade because it's the right thing to do. We're not giving out blind loyalty to companies the way we used to, and I for one am thrilled about that. A 2014 Forbes report states that staying employed at the same company for over two years on average leads to a 50 percent decrease in lifetime earnings. The Bureau of Labor Statistics reports that overall workers change jobs on average every 4.2 years, but the median time spent at a company for workers aged twenty-five to thirty-four is 2.8 years. Shout out to my millennials, who always seem to know the vibes.

Do not be afraid to job hop with intention, especially when an employer is a detriment to your mental and emotional health. As James Baldwin dropped nothing but truths when asked about the mythology of the American Dream, "I have no dream job, I do not dream of labor." Uhh, *hello*, I couldn't have said it any better myself. You may be doing work that you love, you may enjoy your employer and colleagues, but baby, if it comes between you and that job, I'm choosing you and you have to choose yourself too. Companies don't owe you anything; never stop developing your skills and documenting your growth. In the spirit of staying ready so you never have to get ready, take these three small steps to help you reclaim your time at your job.

- **Create a humble brag folder:** Documents all of your achievements, no matter how big or small. I save mine on a hard drive and it's filled with copies of emails, awards, metrics, comments, feedback, and annual reviews. I've been keeping this humble brag folder since my third year in teaching when I won the Top 40 under 40 at twenty-five years old. I've since added copies of my observation reports from my administrators, screenshots of emails and Slack messages from my manager and CMO, and last but not least any testimonials I've received for webinars and product launches for the *Millennial in Debt* brand. Even if I don't use the folder to land a new role, it is also a nice reminder of how people have interacted and engaged with my work ethic.

- **Update your résumé:** Before I transitioned out of teaching, I hadn't updated my résumé in eleven years. I didn't feel the need to, because I was a teacher and thought I'd always be a teacher. When I looked at my résumé for the first time in 2021, I had no idea where to start. The job market was definitely not the market it was a decade prior, and even if it was, I was rusty. It took me way longer than I intended to create a résumé that took my application from automatic rejection to one to three interviews a week.

- **Soft search new roles:** If you do not want out of your job immediately, I still suggest a soft search for roles that you may be interested in, roles that align with your current skill set, or roles that would be a lateral move from your current job. The difference between a soft search and a more focused hard search is timing. For people actively seeking to leave their current job in the next three to six months, you will need to search a little more aggressively so you can apply to forty to fifty open roles a week. The purpose of the soft search, however, is so you can remain in the know without necessarily applying unless the role feels 100 percent right. You're keeping your finger on the pulse of the job market so that if and when you decide to fully jump into a new job search, the results aren't jarring. It was a huge culture shock when I started to apply for roles outside of education. It added another layer of stress to an already stressful job search. Stay cognizant of what roles exist in your industry or transitional industries so you can take note of your transferable skills and prioritize career development.

TEN: MIND THE BUSINESS THAT PAYS YOU

This is by far my favorite way to reclaim my time and I have a sneaking suspicion that it will be your favorite too. When you stay out of business that doesn't concern you, you'll find it is a lot easier to stay focused on the business that pays you. You won't feel the need to keep up with the Joneses because you won't know what the f—k they're up to. FOMO has cost people many unnecessary dollars they had no business spending. You don't need to be in the club *every* weekend because it looks lit on Instagram. You don't need to purchase a new outfit for *every* dinner or brunch you attend. You have bomb fits in your closet already and you do laundry. Throw that dress back on—you *know* which one I'm referring to—and smile proudly in those pics. And you most certainly don't need to catch every Jordan or Ivy Park drop. You know Bey is minding her beautiful Black business all the way to the billionaire's table. You can, however, sell feet pics if you must to cop them tour tickets because seeing Bey live is a life-changing experience everyone should enjoy at least once. See tips three and five as healthy reminders.

In every decision you make, whether it's financial or personal, always seek to prioritize the value it brings to you and *only* you. If you cannot quantify the value of something in your life, chances are it is detracting from your progress, and that is too high of a price to pay. Your money, energy, and most importantly, your time are invaluable resources that should be protected and disseminated wisely. Everything and everyone do not deserve access and don't be scared to revoke access when the situation no longer serves you.

CHAPTER 12

FIRST COMES LOVE, THEN COMES THE PRENUP

A few weeks ago, while browsing the wild streets of Twitter, I ran into an oddly profound quote. And if you've ever spent five minutes on Twitter, you know all too well what a rarity that is. The quote said something along the lines of, if you choose not to get a prenup you are actively choosing to let the government decide on the outcome of your life if your marriage does not go as originally planned. Throughout my entire adult life, I have always been a fan of the prenuptial agreement, and that glaring moment of insight on Twitter perfectly summed up why.

As a thirty-four-year-old unwed, sometimes single-*ish*, self-proclaimed old maid, I may not seem like the right person to be giving advice about prenuptial agreements. What if I told you I'm just the right type of person you need to hear from? I'm the impartial, unbiased bestie rooting for you and helping you set your plans in motion to live your best financial life. So that's exactly what I'm going to do!

Just like your budget, savings plan, and estate plan, a prenuptial agreement is a tool used to preemptively protect you from the unknown. It gets a bad rap because people think that if you obtain a prenup, then you are betting against your marriage. I, on the other hand, would like to argue that a prenup is nothing more than an additional means of support in your relationship. Newsflash: No one ties the knot thinking their marriage is going to fail, but the 600,000 Americans divorced every year pay an average of $15,000–$20,000. Divorce costs sustain an eleven-billion-dollar legal industry annually. These costs are a glaring reminder that falling in love does not cost a thing but falling out of love sure does.

People's needs and desires change all the time; it is a common shared experience we as evolutionary humans all have. If you ask a five-year-old what they want to be when they grow up, chances are, you'll get a much different answer from them when they turn fifteen. Ask them again at thirty and that answer is likely to have changed again. What I needed from my junior high school boyfriend at thirteen is nowhere near what I needed from my college boyfriend at twenty and doesn't come close to what I need currently need from my significant other at thirty-four.

We as a collective species grow and evolve constantly, and sometimes your partner is unable to withstand those changes. It doesn't mean they don't want to; it doesn't mean they haven't tried; it means they no longer are the right fit. That realization is difficult to understand, let alone accept, and to then have to figure out how to equitably separate your entire existence together is the opposite of choosing to protect your peace. And I very much want you to always protect your peace to the best of your ability.

I am an unbelievably private person, which is hard for my audience to believe because I share so much of my life with the masses. However, there's one major topic of my life that I skirt around consistently on the interwebs: my love life. And while I mostly plan to skirt around it in this chapter as well, I am going to give you a small glimpse behind the curtain as we dive into the awkwardness that must be overcome when discussing money with your partner.

My significant other and I have known each other since the fourth grade. He is absolutely one of my best friends, and there is no doubt in my mind that fifty years from, now we'll still be sitting on our couch watching random movies 'til 3:00 a.m. as I eat special brownies and he slowly sips on the cognac he keeps asking me to try. He is my person.

I am aware that our life together absurdly fits the plotline of a Disney fairytale or Netflix romantic comedy. We've got Cory and Topanga vibes written all over our story. As cuddly and sweet as all of that sounds, when we decide to get married, we are 100 percent getting a prenuptial agreement. That doesn't mean we don't believe in the permanence of our marriage, nor does it take away from how much we love each other; on the contrary, it enhances it. If the thought of me obtaining a prenuptial agreement in a happy and secure relationship feels unidentifiably jarring or strange to you, we've got some unlearning to do in this chapter.

It is not surprising that people choose to fall in love with the Diet Coke version of what love looks and feels like instead of falling in love with what love actually is. We are constantly inundated with TV shows and movies that present this idea of a perfect couple madly in love for audiences to pine after and root for. They have their ups, they have their downs, and they dabble in toxic behavior every now and then to keep things spicy. Carrie and Mr. Big ring a bell?

At the end of the day, we as the audience consume the same repackaged formula, label them #GOALS, and make a mental note that one day we will find the Jim to our Pam or the Zack to our Kelly. Those couples don't have prenups; they don't need them because their love is so strong; they will absolutely be together forever. Just once I would love to see a rom-com with two characters who awkwardly bump into each other, fall madly in love and after their over-the-top engagement, the scene cuts to them scheduling a meeting with their lawyer to draw up their prenup contract. Not sexy? Perhaps. But neither were 401Ks until I glammed up their benefits to you earlier in the book. Sexy is relative; financial protection is imperative.

There's a Dr. Strange infinite amount of relationship dynamics that express and receive healthy romantic love differently. There is no one way to love. However, what I will say is that solid, healthy love, no matter how it is expressed in your relationship, should be protected. A prenup is a layer of protection, and I don't care how unhinged you think I am for comparing a prenup to a condom—yep, that's what I just said—that is essentially how you can think of it moving forward. Both you and your partner are protected while you make life-changing adult moves. However, you want to interpret *adult* in that last sentence is completely fair game. I meant it *exactly* how you think I did.

FIVE REASONS YOU NEED A PRENUP

Like estate planning, prenuptial agreements are often considered to be a thing that only wealthy people do. And just like in the estate planning chapter, I'm here to tell you that's incorrect. I don't like speaking superlatively so I try to do it rarely as possible. I'm going to do it right now, so you know how serious I am: I think that *every* married couple should have a prenuptial agreement. Do I think people who don't have one are doomed? No! Unprotected? Absolutely.

When you marry someone, at least in my mind, your lives often become an amalgamation. You experience a period of transition that often involves figuring out how to bring pieces of your life together with pieces of their life to form one new puzzle. Even if you have lived together as a couple, you are now evolving into a married couple. It may look similar, but it is not congruent. You'll possibly have children together, buy property together, share financial accounts, list each other as beneficiaries, etc. You get the point.

Truth moment: Sometimes I need more convincing to do things, even when I know I should. If you're anything like me you may be hearing me but aren't really on board with the whole prenup thing just yet. You're not diametrically opposed (yes, another *Hamilton* reference sprinkled in with ease), but you aren't convinced a prenup is an absolute necessity. As a millennial who has shamefully spent way more time on Buzzfeed than she cares to admit publicly, you can convince me to believe a lot more things with a solid listicle. With that in mind, I'll use the same magic here as I provide you with five more reasons you should strongly consider entering a prenuptial agreement with your soon-to-be spouse.

1. **You want to protect your privacy now and in the future.** My partner and I are a relatively private couple and try hard to properly protect each other's privacy. But let's be all the way honest here: I'm the owner and face of a company that currently has an audience of over 300,000 people. Due to the nature of my work, the type and level of privacy I have isn't the same as his. And nothing solidified that more for both of us than when we ran into a group of my followers in Mexico during Baecation. Prenups create a layer of protection for both parties' right to privacy. That means no tell-all books, messy podcasts,

social media exposés, or other types of publications allowed. This prevents any private personal matters from being publicly disclosed. This is a benefit for both of us because I'm not saying my followers are comparable to the #BeyHive, but if I say we ride at dawn, they are locked, loaded, and ready to go. I love that for me!

2. **You or your partner are business owners:** As a business owner, I am immensely passionate about making smart financial decisions to increase revenue and profit. This was one of the larger deciding factors in our conversations about obtaining a prenup. Why? Because *Millennial In Debt* was formed prior to our nuptials. I have worked extremely hard to build the business independently from the ground up, and we do not want it to be negatively impacted in the case of divorce. My business is also structured as an LLC partnership, which means that the decisions I make about *Millennial In Debt* impact not only me but my business partner as well.

   Obtaining a prenup to protect your business does not mean that you are keeping that part of your life separate from your significant other. In fact a properly structured prenuptial agreement will outline what percentage of the business, if any, your spouse is entitled to now and in the future.

3. **Got debt...no? Now you do:** I would like to propose an amendment to the traditional wedding vows we've come to know and expect in 96 percent of romcoms. You know the spiel, "for richer or poorer, in sickness and in health, 'til death do us part." You may now kiss the bride, wham, bam, cocktail hour begins! Aht aht aht...not so fast. Before you hit that "I do" I would like to add "for richer or poorer, *new debt and some old*..." you know how the rest goes.

   Premarital debt, for the most part, will stick with the original borrower regardless of whether they are married or not. Notice I said *for the most part*, because just like with the English language, there is always an overly complicated exception to any rule. Where there's a will there's a way and creditors will find ways to tap into your joint assets even for premarital debt. What about debt that is taken on during your union? Any debt that occurs while you're married is a whole different story. The spouse that did not incur the debt or is debt-free is now at a disadvantage without a prenup.

A prenuptial agreement will solidify that all premarital debt will be paid by the spouse that signed the promissory note on said debt. A secondary stipulation a prenup can enforce is that any debt incurred during the marriage will not be paid with joint funds or assets.

4. **One or both of you have a child:** This is about to date me a bit, but roll with me through memory lane. During the earlier seasons of the VH1 reality show *Love and Hip Hop* we saw Yandy Smith and Mendeecees Harris tie the knot in an overly extravagant wedding special in 2015. A year after the episode aired, it was revealed that although Yandy and Mendeecees were married in the eyes of reality TV, they were never officially married in the eyes of the law. Why? Because of Mendeecees's troubles with child support. If their marriage were to be legalized, their assets would have merged, and Yandy would be liable for the child support that was due.

   I'm no ShadeRoom, and I certainly do not know these people so to speak beyond what was clearly expressed by both parties would be messy AF in a personal finance book. What I will say is Yandy had every right to protect her assets in a way that made the most sense for the couple at the time. There is another way—a prenup.

   When children are involved in your matrimonial merger, a prenuptial agreement not only ensures that your assets remain separate property, but it also allows for the spouse with children to create a living trust. A prenup helps you avoid the messiness that can arise in complicated family dynamics where multiple people, especially children, are being provided for financially.

5. **One or both of you have been married before:** If you've walked that walk and talked that talk before, especially if you've gone through a harrowing divorce, it is definitely wise to create a layer of protection for yourself and your future spouse. Besides learning from past mistakes (fool me once, you can't fool me again, or whatever George W. said), you also want to ensure that your previous divorce does not find itself financially entangled in your current marriage.

SIX THINGS YOU NEED TO KNOW ABOUT PRENUPS

Okay, the listicle and the condom comparison convinced you; you're on board! Here's what you need to know to take your first steps.

ONE: HOW TO FILE ONE

You know how HGTV got us to believe that we could DIY anything? I promise you: you cannot DIY this one. You better get somebody else to do it, and by somebody else I very much mean an attorney. Once you and your future spouse agree to get a prenup, you will find an attorney that meets your needs and price point. Once the ball is rolling with your attorney, you can expect the process to play out in the following manner (give or take variations for specific or unique circumstances).

- Your attorney will ask that each of you gather your financial information in one space. Like your estate planning folder, you'll need to include your assets and liabilities.

- With the help of your attorney, you will then outline your financial and marital goals. This will be the time to ensure that your goals, both short- and long-term, are in alignment.

- A draft of the agreement will be written up. This is the time negotiations ensue. Many believe (I am one of the many) it is a wise decision for each person in the relationship to have their own attorney in the process, specifically for negotiations at this stage of the process.

- Review stage: Both parties will have the opportunity to look at the details of the agreement post-negotiations. If everything checks out and no updates are needed, you then move into the final step of the process.

- Execution: This is when your prenuptial agreement will be solidified, and you have just completed a major adult move! High-five your partner, grab a glass of champagne (or sparkling cider), and toast to protecting your love!

TWO: WHAT A PRENUPTIAL AGREEMENT PROTECTS

Prenups are typically focused on protecting your finances. Without one the government will usually step in and make decisions on your behalf based on the city and state you live in. So if you live in a community property state, your marital assets *and* debt will be split 50/50. This 50/50 split will include income, retirement accounts, inheritance, real estate, bank accounts, investments, and more. In an equitable distribution state, the government would once again step in to split your marital assets and debts "fairly," which may not be a 50/50 split. Either way that is leaving far too much up to chance.

Here's a non-exhaustive list of the typical items included and protected in a prenup:

- **Debt:** How will debt be divided in the case of a divorce? This will include clarification regarding premarital assets and debt as well as assets and debt acquired in the marriage.

- **Business owners:** How will the profits in one or multiple businesses be split? If family businesses are also involved, a prenup will outline specific provisions that will keep the family business solely with the family.

- **Property distribution:** Basically, this line item specifies who gets the house, or if you have multiple properties, who owns which house? Will you be splitting the financial responsibilities, or will one person be responsible for the entire property on their own?

- **Estate plans:** Will adjustments be made to the estate plan once a divorce has been finalized? Or will I remain on the estate plan as initially outlined?

- **Children:** A detailed outline of assets and inheritance distribution will need to be outlined if there are children involved, especially if they are children from previous relationships.

- **Inheritance:** Will your former spouse have access to or a claim to part of your inheritance when you receive the total amount?

THREE: WHAT A PRENUPTIAL AGREEMENT *DOESN'T* PROTECT

Though it seems that prenups cover every aspect of your personal finances they do not protect everything.

- **Child support and child custody matters** aren't permissible in a prenuptial agreement. Those concerns would need to be brought to court.

- **Personal matters:** You can't add a laundry list of how the responsibilities of the household will play out. So if you want your spouse to take out the garbage or clean the bathroom weekly that's a convo you're going to have to take to the streets. The only *loophole* when it comes to personal matters in a prenup is if these matters are related to finance. For example if you are outlining certain financial expectations from your partner once you get married such as who will pay certain bills, how tax returns will be filed, and how your investments will be handled. But if you want to ensure your spouse cooks three times a week or always puts the toilet seat down, *to the streets* you go!

- This should go without saying, but I'm going to say it anyway to cover all our bases. Any illegal things—*assets, businesses, etc.*—will not be covered or protected.

FOUR: THE COST OF AN AVERAGE PRENUP

When it comes down to it, a lot of the things we know we should do we don't do because cost is a barrier. A properly structured prenup has a wide range similar to the price range for estate planning quoted in Chapter 9. You may have a simple prenup that doesn't require any bells and whistles, or you could have a contingency-filled prenup that requires more time, attention, and paperwork. Due to the wide variety of needs, circumstances, and your location, a prenup could cost a couple anywhere from $500 to $10,000. The average national cost of a prenup for most Americans hovers around the $650 mark.

Let's crunch some numbers, shall we? According to the Wedding Report, the average cost of a wedding in 2022 was $27,000. With a quick pivot into divorce stats, at a 40–50 percent divorce rate the average 2023 divorce in the US costs $15,000–$20,000. An uncontested DIY divorce can cost as low as $200 while an uncontested divorce with legal support averages closer to $2,000.

What's the likelihood that you'll have an uncontested divorce? Really high if you have a prenup. I like the sound of having to pay $200–$2,000 way better than potentially paying $15,000–$20,000 because I didn't take the necessary precautions. Your peace and your pocket will be forever thankful.

FIVE: WHAT IF I'M ALREADY MARRIED?

All hope is not lost! In fact, no hope is lost. You can still protect yourself, your spouse, and your finances by signing a postnuptial agreement. A postnup and prenup are similar except for two major differences.

- The first difference is easy to spot just with the mention of the name itself. A postnup happens after you have already tied the knot.

- Not every state recognizes or allows a postnup, so it is important to clarify whether this will be something you're capable of doing.

If you do have a prenup and face a large lifestyle change, you can still initiate a postnup to amend your prenuptial agreement as it stands.

SIX: IT ALL STARTS WITH A CONVERSATION

According to a 2019 TD Bank survey, 43 percent of those keeping a financial secret from their partner are hiding their credit card debt. What else isn't being discussed? Unpaid student loans, gambling, and secret bank accounts. I understand there is a level of discomfort that fills the air when it comes time to discuss finances with a romantic partner. Even though I reveal every nook and cranny of my finances on Beyoncé's internet, I still get a little anxious about being financially naked with my significant other. It hits differently.

However, those conversations, no matter how uncomfortable, are necessary to sustain a healthy, honest relationship. The same "Love and Money" TD Bank survey also revealed that "nearly 40 percent of those ages twenty-three to thirty-eight admit to fighting about finances at least once a week." I don't know about you, but I can think of a hundred other things I'd rather do on a weekly basis with my partner that do not involve arguing about money. Money is interwoven into a substantial amount of your day to day; you have to talk about it. The initial money conversations when your relationship transitions from puppy love to full-grown, bill-splitting adult relations will help both parties understand their financial compatibility.

- Is there someone in the relationship who spends more or struggles to save?

- Does your other partner have strong money management skills?

- Do you both share similar long-term financial goals?

- How do you want to split the major bills in your household?

You will never truly know without that first conversation leading the way for future conversations. Becoming emotionally vulnerable with one another took some work, didn't it? You didn't just wake up one day madly in love with a full understanding of each other's emotional needs. It will be the same process when you begin to embrace financial vulnerability with one another as well.

As you consistently take your partner on money dates, you will become more comfortable. Do you remember how uncomfortable your first money date with yourself was eleven chapters ago? Because I do! Give it some time to simmer! The most important thing to remember, whether you're creating your first dual household budget, opening a savings account together, or broaching the topic of a prenuptial agreement, approach it with kindness, understanding, and respect.

Your conversations won't always be roses and butterflies. Some will be harder than others, and even after years of discussing money together you may find some topics still create a wave of discomfort between the two of you. That's okay; it is completely normal. Remind yourself that this isn't an MMA fight.

You're not in the WWE, so your conversations should not lead to someone emotionally or physically body-slamming you to the ground. You are both on the same team, working to be on the same page when it comes to your finances.

You know your partner best. You know their habits, what makes them laugh, what foods they love, their hopes, and their fears. Conversely you also know yourself better than anyone else ever will. Use both of those facts to your benefit when approaching conversations about money and a prenuptial agreement.

CONCLUSION

My dearest future millionaires, our time together is coming to a temporary end. So where do we go from here? I don't know about you, but I'm having a hard time letting go of what we've got going on here. I mean, after about 80,000 words of affirmation, I'm invested. We've shared some laughs, perhaps shared some tears (I know I most certainly have), and most importantly, we've shared a financial safe space. We openly discussed money with zero shame or judgement, and I love that for us.

I can't just spill my deepest money secrets with you and walk away, but I also know as a future millionaire armed with a new wealth of knowledge, I've got to let you fly on your own. So for now, I will leave you with my final words of wisdom to properly send you on your way.

There's always going to be someone somewhere who doesn't think you're doing the "right things" with your money. They're going to try to point you in a million and one directions and be the first to point out your mistakes. "You aren't saving enough," "You're investing the wrong way," "You're just bad with money." That's just noise. And what we're not going to do is allow that noise any rent-free space in our heads—surely not with these rent prices as high as they are!

Improving your relationship with money is a transitional experience that takes discipline and time. It can be uncomfortable, difficult, and at times, the small changes you've made can feel pointless. But when you look back at where you started and see the distance you've covered, there's no denying your progress. Your success is inevitable.

And if you're skimming through this book at Costco and somehow landed on this page...go try the pizza bagel samples near the freezer section in the back. They do not disappoint!

MILLENNIAL IN DEBT'S FAVE FINANCIAL RESOURCES

For Digitally Tracking Your Net Worth:	Empower (formerly known as Personal Capital)
Investing Brokerages:	Vanguard, E*Trade, Fidelity
Beginner-Friendly Brokerages:	Acorns, Betterment (Robo Advisor), Wealthfront (Robo Advisor)
Site for Calculating Compound Interest:	Investor.gov
Budgeting App:	UseMuch
High-Yield Savings Accounts:	Capital One 360, Ally, American Express, Marcus by Goldman Sachs
Investment Inflation Calculator:	bankrate.com/retirement/roi-calculator/
Where I Get Credible Money News:	Investopedia.com, Finance.Yahoo.com, Nerdwallet.com, Bankrate.com

ACKNOWLEDGMENTS

First, I want to thank Sky Daddy for giving me the ability to transition the chaos in my head to thoughts on paper. To my friends and family, your support of this book at every stage of the process has been paramount. I am eternally grateful, and I promise to stop sending three-minute voice notes to the #ShadeRoom group chat.

Thank you to the amazing personal finance creators who took the time to share their stories and words of wisdom with us all. These chapters just wouldn't hit the same without you in them.

A Boogie with the Booty, you are the first pre-order for my first book. You've read and listened to so many iterations of these chapters while simultaneously being a dope ass mother of two. Thank you for being this book's biggest cheerleader.

My love, your encouragement and incessant need to make sure I eat at the end of every eight-hour writing day helped me power through every moment I wanted to say, "*Eff* this book." Thank you for navigating the stresses of this process with such grace and patience...and pizza! You and me, always.

My team at Mango, thank you for listening and standing so firmly behind my vision for this book. We have done immeasurably valuable work together. I could not have asked for a better experience as a first-time author.

To Shakira, my business partner, my best friend, my soulmate. You came to me ten years ago with an idea to start a little blog about hair. That blog changed the trajectory of my life. This book exists because of you. My lifelong dream has become my reality because you challenged me to be brave. Infinite gratitude could never be enough.

ABOUT THE AUTHOR

Melissa Jean-Baptiste is a first-generation Haitian American who has built a platform dedicated to helping Millennials and Gen Z restructure their relationships with money, obtain financial freedom, and build generational wealth. As the eldest daughter of immigrant parents, she had to lead by example and was determined to achieve the elusive American Dream. As her first party trick, after four years at Adelphi University, she graduated cum laude with a BA in English Literature and an MA in Adolescent Education. During her eleven-year tenure as a New York City high school English teacher and adjunct professor, Melissa implemented valuable shifts to her instructional design to provide her students with a modern curriculum that would be pivotal to their personal growth outside of the classroom. She would later become the lead instructional designer and curriculum developer for the English department and CollegeBoard Advanced Placement courses.

Melissa went on to write and produce the award-winning web series *Millennial in Debt*, which highlighted the overwhelming nature of navigating adulthood due to a lack of accessible financial education. As Melissa navigated her own personal finance journey, she documented her money mistakes and lessons publicly to teach others how she paid off $102,000 in student loan debt and bought her first home on a teacher salary. As a personal finance and career development coach, Melissa's ultimate goal is to teach her audience how to be future millionaires.

With an audience of over 300,000, Melissa continues to be a financial thought leader and teacher, providing fundamental financial lessons while leading crucial money conversations in a creative manner. Melissa is always one swipe away on all social platforms by following: @Millennialindebt.

INVESTING GLOSSARY

On the following pages, you'll find an investing glossary with thirty common (and sometimes confusing) investing terms. Here's the best way to implement them into your day-to-day:

- Choose one to two terms you're unfamiliar with (you can choose more if you'd like) and explain them in your own words.

- Once you've explained them in your own words, use these terms at some point in the next few days. Use them at work, on your social platforms, at the dinner table, in your journal—wherever you feel comfortable. Why? Because once you can explain them and use them in the real world, you're committing them to memory. You're strengthening your investing muscle.

- Then...repeat! Once you've used your first one to two terms successfully and you feel like you have a complete understanding, choose another one to two terms and do the same thing all over again.

INVESTMENT TERM	DEFINITION	EXPLAIN IT IN YOUR OWN WORDS:	PUT THIS TERM INTO PRACTICE:
1. 401K Plan	An employer-sponsored retirement savings plan that gives employees a choice of investment options. Employers in a traditional 401(k) plan will often match a percentage of your contributions.		
2. 529 Plan	A tax-advantaged savings plan designed to encourage saving for educational costs. 529 plans, legally known as "qualified tuition plans," are sponsored by states or state agencies.		
3. Asset	Any tangible or intangible item that has value. A bank account, a home, or shares of stock are all examples of assets.		

4. Asset Allocation	A process that involves dividing your investments among different categories, such as stocks, bonds, and cash.		
5. Asset Classes	Investments that have similar characteristics. The three main asset classes are stocks, bonds, and cash.		
6. Bear Market	A time when stock prices are declining and market sentiment is pessimistic. Generally, a bear market occurs when a broad market index falls by 20% or more over at least a two-month period.		
7. Bid Price	The highest price a buyer will pay to buy a specified number of shares of a stock at any given time.		

8. Bonds	A debt security, similar to an IOU. Borrowers issue bonds to raise money from investors willing to lend them money for a certain amount of time. When you buy a bond, you are lending to...		
9. Brokerage Account	A company that buys or sells goods or assets for clients.		
10. Bull Market	A time when stock prices are rising and market sentiment is optimistic. Generally, a bull market occurs when there is a rise of 20% or more in a broad market index over at least a two-month period.		
11. Capital Gain	The profit that comes when an investment is sold for more than the price the investor paid for it.		
12. Certificate of Deposit (CD)	A savings account that holds a fixed amount of money for a fixed period of time.		

13. Commissions	When you buy or sell a stock through a financial professional, the commission compensates the financial professional and their firm.		
14. Compound Interest	Interest paid on principal and on paccumulated interest.		
15. Day Trading	The purchase and sale, or the sale and purchase, of the same security on the same day in a margin account.		
16. Defined Benefit Plan	Also are known as pension plans, employers sponsor these plans and promise the plan's investments will provide you with a specified monthly benefit at retirement.		
17. Dividend	A portion of a company's profit paid to shareholders. Public companies that pay dividends usually do so on a fixed schedule.		

18. Dollar-Cost Averaging	The process of investing your money on a schedule, regardless of whether the market is up or down. This is a great strategy for people with low risk tolerance because it decreases the impact of market volatility on your investments.		
19. ESG Investing	**E**nvironmental, **S**ocial, and **G**overnance investing is a way of investing in companies based on their commitment to one or more ESG factors. It is often also called sustainable investing.		
20. Exchange Traded Fund (ETF)	A type of investment fund that trades like a stock. Investors buy and sell ETFs on the same exchanges as shares of stock.		

21. Expense Ratio	The fund's total annual operating expenses, including management fees, distribution fees, and other expenses, expressed as a percentage of average net assets.		
22. Foreign Currency Exchange (FOREX)	A price that represents how much it costs to buy the currency of one country using the currency of another country.		
23. Initial Public Offering (IPO)	Generally refers to when a company first sells its shares to the public.		
24. Market Capitalization	The value of a corporation determined by multiplying the current public market price of one share of the corporation by the number of total outstanding shares.		
25. Mutual Fund	A managed professional portfolio that purchases securities with money pooled from individual investors.		

26. Price Earnings Ratio (P/E Ratio)	A way of gauging whether the company's stock price is high or low compared to the past or to other companies.		
27. Real Estate Investment Trust (REIT)	A REIT is a company that owns and typically operates income-producing real estate. They make it possible for people to invest in and earn dividends from real estate without having to buy the property themselves.		
28. Robo Advisor	Generally refers to an automated digital investment advisory program. In most cases, the robo-adviser collects information regarding your financial goals to set up your portfolio.		

29. Stock Split	An increase in the number of shares of a corporation's stock without a change in the shareholders' equity. Companies often split shares of their stock to make them more affordable to investors.		
30. Target Date Fund	A diversified mutual fund that automatically shifts toward a more conservative mix of investments as it approaches a particular year in the future, known as its "target date."		

Mango Publishing, established in 2014, publishes an eclectic list of books by diverse authors—both new and established voices—on topics ranging from business, personal growth, women's empowerment, LGBTQ+ studies, health, and spirituality to history, popular culture, time management, decluttering, lifestyle, mental wellness, aging, and sustainable living. We were named 2019 *and* 2020's #1 fastest-growing independent publisher by *Publishers Weekly*. Our success is driven by our main goal, which is to publish high-quality books that will entertain readers as well as make a positive difference in their lives.

Our readers are our most important resource; we value your input, suggestions, and ideas. We'd love to hear from you—after all, we are publishing books for you!

Please stay in touch with us and follow us at:
Facebook: Mango Publishing
Twitter: @MangoPublishing
Instagram: @MangoPublishing
LinkedIn: Mango Publishing
Pinterest: Mango Publishing
Newsletter: mangopublishinggroup.com/newsletter

Join us on Mango's journey to reinvent publishing, one book at a time.

CPSIA information can be obtained
at www.ICGtesting.com
Printed in the USA
JSHW021211280423
41000JS00002B/2

9 781684 811830